W9-CME-765

EPOCHS IN THE LIFE OF THE APOSTLE JOHN

This Book

has been presented to the

CHURCH LIBRARY

of Birdville Baptist Church

by: Adult 3 Men's Class

IN MEMORY OF

R.A. Fetter, Sr.

EPOCHS IN THE LIFE

OF THE

APOSTLE JOHN

A. T. ROBERTSON, A.M., D.D., LL.D., Litt.D.

BIRDVILLE
BAPTIST CHURCH
LIBRARY

BROADMAN PRESS
NASHVILLE, TENNESSEE

Paperback edition issued by
Baker Book House
First printing, September 1974

Complete Set
4214-51
ISBN: 0-8054-1351-0
This volume
4213-49
ISBN: 0-8054-1349-9

To

JOHN ALLEN EASLEY

A Loving and Beloved Disciple

PREFACE

One greatly dares to-day who writes a book on the Apostle John, for one is challenged at every turn by this scholar or that. Yet each man must speak for himself and tell the truth as he sees it. "We know very little about the Apostle John," says Dr. D. A. Hayes (*John and His Writings*, p. 15). But Dr. James Stalker (*The Two St. Johns of the New Testament*, p. 14f.) sees more clearly: "Although the materials for writing the life of St. John are meagre, yet no other figure of the New Testament—not even St. Paul or St. Peter—makes such a distinct impression on the mind of every reader. This is due to his marvellous originality."

Such a vivid picture of the Beloved Disciple is possible only if one identifies the Beloved Disciple of the Fourth Gospel with the Elder of the Epistles and the John of the Apocalypse. But Canon B. H. Streeter (*The Four Gospels*, p. 432) thinks that "it is a mistaken identification" when the elders of Ephesus assert (John 21:24) that the Beloved Disciple (the Apostle John) is the author of the Fourth Gospel. The rather Streeter holds that the author distinguishes between himself and the Apostle John, whom he idealizes as the Beloved Disciple who understood Christ best of all.

However, after a lifetime of study of the Johannine problem as presented by Bretschneider, Baur, Bacon, Moffatt and all the rest, my own mind finds fewer unsolved difficulties in the single great figure who wrote the Johannine literature and became the eagle who soared above the clouds into the clear sky of eternal truth in Christ. So then this volume completes the *Epochs* series (Jesus, Paul, Peter, John), though the volumes on the Baptist (*John the Loyal*) and *Luke the Historian* could well be included.

Louisville, Ky.

A. T. R.

CONTENTS

I

A LONG LIFE IN THE GREATEST ERA

1. *A gracious, though retiring, personality.* "The starting-point for any profitable study of the Fourth Gospel is the recognition of the author as a mystic—perhaps the greatest of all mystics," contends Streeter (*The Four Gospels*, p. 366). In this view lies the truth. This mystic is the Apostle John, according to the Irenaeus tradition (which has the well-nigh unanimous support of early writers), and the internal evidence does not overthrow it. Stalker is right in finding the impression made by John clear and distinct, and yet Hayes is correct, also, in observing how few are the details that give us this vivid picture.

In the Gospel of Matthew John is mentioned by name only four times—three times as the brother of James (4:21; 10:2; 17:1), once as one of the sons of Zebedee (26:37). In Mark's Gospel he is named ten times, seven times in Luke, but in the Fourth Gospel his name does not occur at all, though the sons of Zebedee are named once (21:2). The name of James, his brother, is likewise absent from John's Gospel. In the Acts, John is mentioned nine times. "It would be safe to say that the New Testament tells us five times as much about Peter as it does about John" (Hayes, *John and His Writings*, p. 20). It seems clear that the young brother of James was not any too prominent in the apostolic circle and, along with James, may have been the object of some jealousy—partly because of the ambition of the mother of James and John to win first places for them in the political kingdom of the Messiah that they were expecting. In his own Gospel John keeps himself out of

sight save in the "we" passage in 1:14 ("we beheld his
glory") like that in I John 1:1-3 where the same word ("we
beheld," *etheasametha*) occurs, in the "I" passage in 21:25,
in the five passages where he is called "the disciple whom
Jesus loved" (13:23; 19:26; 20:2; 21:20-24), and in some
other indirect allusions like "another disciple" (18:15f.),
"that one" (19:35), "the other disciple" (20:2-8).

It is certain that there was something fine and winsome
in the Beloved Disciple to win the affection of Jesus in so
marked a degree. He had the post of honour on the couch
in front of Jesus at the last passover meal and was proud
of the dignity of having reclined his head on the bosom of
Jesus: he mentions it three times (Jo. 13:23 *kolpos*, 25
stethos and 21:20). He was sometimes termed *ho Episte-
thios* (the one who reclined on the Lord's bosom). It is not
necessary to attribute undue pride to John in thus concealing his name under the title that revealed the Master's
special love for him. If "Peter was garrulous to the limit,
John was reticent to a fault" (Hayes, *ibid.*, p. 17). But we
must take John as he is, if we can do so. He was not concerned to show himself, but only Jesus. "In the Fourth
Gospel John himself never is visible and Jesus never is in-
visible."

It was given to John to see more than others did in the
person and work of the Master, and to draw the greatest
portrait of Christ that the world has ever had. He was a
mystic in the highest sense, a seer with a prophet's vision,
a historian with an eye for the essential facts, and an artist
with dramatic skill able to reproduce Jesus as the Incarnate
Son of God, made flesh and moving among men whom he
came to save. Let us gather together the known items about
his family life. His own name John was common enough,
as is shown by its being given to the Baptist and to the
father of Simon Peter. It is the Greek form of Jehochanan
(Jochanan) and means "gift of Jehovah" or "Jehovah is
gracious." He illustrated the graciousness of the Lord in
his life.

2. *John's father*. His name was Zebedee, meaning "my gift" (I Chron. 27:27). He was a fisherman of Galilee by trade. He was present by the Sea of Galilee when Jesus called James and John, Andrew and Simon, to leave all and follow him (Mk. 1:19f.; Matt. 21f.; Lu. 5:10). John and James then left their father, as well as the boat. Zebedee is left with the hired servants, to dispose of the catch of fish and the business of the company. He appears no more in the Gospels save as the father of James and John. The mention of the mother as present with James and John (Matt. 20:20) may imply that he was no longer living, though that is by no means certain. At any rate he did not, himself, travel around with Jesus, as the mother did. Apparently he was a man of substance, since he employed hired servants in his fishing business.

3. *John's mother*. It is often supposed that she is Salome, since Mark (15:40) names "Mary Magdalene, and Mary the mother of James the less and Joses, and Salome" as the women beholding from afar the death of Jesus on the Cross, while Matthew (27:56) mentions "Mary Magdalene, and Mary the mother of James and Joses, and the mother of the sons of Zebedee." It is possible that the third woman is the same in both lists. If so, Salome is the same as the mother of the sons of Zebedee. Salome is a Hebrew word that means "peaceful" (though it was the name of the notorious sister of Herod the Great who was anything but peaceful). John (19:25) gives a list of women by the Cross, including the mother of Jesus: "His mother, and his mother's sister, Mary the wife of Cleopas, and Mary Magdalene." Leaving aside the mother of Jesus and Mary Magdalene it is not clear whether "his mother's sister" and "Mary the wife of Cleopas" are two women or one and the same. There is no "and" before "Mary the wife of Cleopas." If only one person is meant, then the sister of the mother of Jesus is Mary the wife of Cleopas. If two persons are meant, then the sister of the mother of Jesus may be Salome (Mk. 15:40) and the mother of the sons of

Zebedee (Matt. 27:56). If Salome is the sister of Mary, the mother of Jesus, and the mother of the sons of Zebedee, James and John are cousins of Jesus.

This is entirely possible, but not quite certain. There seems no way to reach a definite conclusion in the light of our knowledge to-day. If they are cousins, some light is thrown on various matters, such as the inclusion of James and John with Peter in the inner circle of three and the daring of the mother of James and John (Matt. 20:20) in claiming the two chief places for her sons. But the special love of Jesus for John rested on something more than such a merely personal tie. The young John had in him the finest kind of stuff that appealed to the heart of Jesus and made possible the highest and holiest friendship that earth has known. Salome, at any rate, was earnest and zealous in her work for Jesus, being one of the women that followed Him from Galilee (Matt. 27:55), ministered of their substance (Lu. 8:3), watched the Cross from afar (Mk. 15:40), and prepared spices for the tomb (Mk. 16:1). If John is the most feminine of the Apostles in his intuitive insight, we can discern the influence of his mother's fine nature in the son.

4. *His brother James.* The Greek is Jacob *(Jakōbos)* and in the Old Testament the name is used to designate the patriarch only. In the New Testament, however, it is used to mean: the father of Joseph, the husband of Mary (Matt. 1:16); the father of "Judas not Iscariot" (Lu. 6:16; Jo. 14:22); James the son of Alphaeus (Mk. 3:18); James the Less (Mk. 15:40); James the Lord's brother (Mk. 6:3), and this brother of John. James, "the brother of John," as Luke terms him in Acts (12:2), is sometimes called James the Greater, in contrast with James the Less (Mk. 15:40). He was probably older than John, since he is always mentioned before John except by Luke—twice in the Gospel (8:51; 9:28) and twice in Acts (1:13; 12:2).

Sometimes we have simply "James and John" (Lu. 5:10; Mk. 1:29; Lu. 6:14; Mk. 9:2; Lu. 9:54; Mk. 10:35; 41:

13:3), or "James and John his brother" or "James and John
the brother of James" (Mk. 1:19; Matt. 4:21; Mk. 3:17;
5:37; Matt. 10:2; 17:1). Sometimes the item is added
without their names being given, that they are sons of
Zebedee (Mk. 1:19; 3:17; Matt. 10:2; Mk. 10:35; Matt.
20:20). They are both fishermen, like their father, and
partners with Andrew and Peter (Lu. 5:7, 10) when all
four are called to follow Jesus. Apparently James was
brought to Christ by John—if we so understand the word
"first" used of Andrew in John 1:41. He is not mentioned
apart from John and, like John, was one of the inner circle
of three (Peter, James, John) who were chosen by Jesus to
be with Him in the house of Jairus, on the Mount of Transfiguration, and in the Garden of Gethsemane. He is named
as being with John in the house of Simon and Andrew when
Simon's mother-in-law was healed (Mk. 1:29). He was one
of the four (Peter, James, John, Andrew) who questioned
Jesus on the Mount of Olives about his words concerning
the destruction of the temple (Mk. 13:3). He joined with
John in suggesting the destruction of the Samaritan village
(Lu. 9:54). He joined with John and their mother in asking for the two chief places in Christ's Kingdom and thereby
incurred the indignation of the other ten apostles (Mk.
10:35, 41; Matt. 20:20, 24). He was the first martyr
among the twelve apostles and received literally the fulfilment of his boast that he was able to drink the cup that
Christ would drink and to be baptized with the baptism of
blood.

It is not clear why it was James instead of John who was
the victim of the wrath of Herod Agrippa I, in A.D. 44,
unless because James was an aggressive and outstanding
leader of the Jerusalem Christians (Acts 12:1f.). There is a
story from Clement of Alexandria told by Eusebius (He. ii.9)
to the effect that in the trial of James by Herod the accuser
was so moved by the heroic constancy of James that he became a Christian and died with James. There is no confirmation of the story but clearly James, as well as John,

won the special love of Jesus and was trusted by the Master.
He was worthy of his great brother, though probably not
his equal in intellectual power and spiritual insight.

5. *His early home and education.* It is not clear where
John was born. We know that Philip and Andrew and
Peter were from Bethsaida in Galilee (Jo. 1:43) and that
Zebedee and James and John were partners with Andrew
and Peter in the fishing business on the Sea of Galilee (Lu.
5:7, 10), on the western shore (Mk. 6:45) near the entrance of the River Jordan. Dr. Thomson identifies this
Bethsaida with *Abu Zany;* Major Wilson with *Khan
Minyeh.* But some scholars, like Bernard, in spite of the
plain meaning of Mark 6:45, see only one Bethsaida—
Bethsaida Julias on the eastern side of the lake (Lu. 9:10).
The western Bethsaida was not far from Capernaum. That
fact makes it easy to see why Capernaum soon became the
home of Simon Peter and Andrew (Mk. 1:21, 29)—perhaps
after the marriage of Peter who then lived in Capernaum
with his mother-in-law. It may well be that Bethsaida was
the birthplace of John and that Capernaum was the home
of his family after he went into business partnership with
Andrew and Simon. "If so (i.e. Bethsaida), then five of
our Lord's apostles—the five always mentioned first in our
New Testament lists of the apostles—were from the same
provincial town" (Hayes, *ibid.*, p. 26).

It was a simple home beyond a doubt, without many
luxuries and without means for higher education. There
were "hired servants" (Mk. 1:20) employed in the business
and eventually John according to the most natural interpretation of John 19:27: "From that hour the disciple took
her to his own home," apparently had a home in Jerusalem (cf. Acts 21:6). But the language may mean simply
(Bernard, Westcott) that John took the mother of Jesus at
once to his Jerusalem lodging and later to his home in
Galilee. In that case no problem is raised about John's
being able to afford a home in Jerusalem. At any rate it is
plain that John's educational facilities were confined to in-

struction in the home and the synagogue, advantages open
to all Jewish boys and taken seriously in every home where
piety ruled. Like Peter, he was termed by the Sanhedrin
"unlettered *(agrammatos)* and unschooled"*(idiōtēs)*, that
is not a student in the rabbinical schools in Jerusalem or
elsewhere. He was not therefore a man of the schools like
Saul of Tarsus, but he was a man of rare intellect and eleva-
tion of soul. He had with Jesus, the greatest of all teachers,
three years of supreme opportunity for growth in knowledge
of the highest things. He came to be the keenest interpreter
in the school of Christ that learned at the feet of the Master.
He took upon himself Christ's yoke and learned of Him
(Matt. 11:29) with a skill unequalled by the others. He
came out of a sympathetic environment and atmosphere and
brought a mind ready for the touch of the Great Teacher.
He responded quickly and surely. His knowledge ripened
and mellowed through a long life till he produced in the end
the greatest book of all time. He had genius beyond a
doubt; he was moulded of the finest clay, possessed of the
noblest moral fibre. "To speak in the language of philosophy, he was not of the lethargic temperament, but of the
melancholic. This is the temperament which beneath an
outward demeanour, somewhat resembling lethargy, conceals
the sweet and swiftest insight; it keeps silence and broods,
but its fire is only suppressed; it is the temperament which
the ancients attributed to their greatest men—to a
Sophocles and a Plato, to the philosopher, the poet, the
genius" (Stalker, *ibid.*, p. 13f.).

6. *A disciple of the Baptist.* It is as a follower of the
Baptist that we catch our first glimpse of John the Beloved
Disciple. He was clearly one of the two disciples who on
two successive days at Bethany beyond Jordan heard the
Baptist describe Jesus, whom he had previously baptized
(Jo. 1:33), as "the Lamb of God that bears away the sin
of the world" (1:29) and "Behold, the Lamb of God"
(1:36). Andrew is named as one of the two (1:40) and
the writer of the Gospel is, by implication, the other, and

with graphic power he tells the incidents here from personal
knowledge (1:14). Twenty times in this Gospel the Baptist
is termed John, while the author not once applies the name
to himself.

The group of four fishermen from the Sea of Galilee (Andrew and Simon, James and John) had heard the echo of
the Baptist's voice all the way from the Jordan. The
people were going in great throngs to hear the new prophet
with his call to repentance, his significant baptism in the
Jordan, and his startling announcement that the Kingdom
of God had at last drawn nigh, that day of days so long
foretold by the prophets and cherished by the people with
wistful longing during the long centuries of oppression by
foreign masters (Assyrian, Babylonian, Greek, Roman).
Perhaps the day of deliverance was at hand. The Baptist
challenged the whole nation to a change of heart and life
and treated them as Gentiles, as he buried them in the
Jordan in token of this new attitude of consecration to the
Messiah now at hand. The message was a searching one
and it reached the heart of young John. "While the worst
sinners are often utterly insensible to their own spiritual
deformity, the whitest souls are sensitively aware of their
own short-comings" (Stalker, *ibid.*, p. 25). John had been
baptized by the Baptist and was standing near the Baptist
when he pointed out Jesus as the Lamb of God that bears
away the sin of the world. Some modern critics are puzzled
over these words of the Baptist in the Fourth Gospel. But
the same idea is in Isaiah 53, and the Baptist had the help
of the Holy Spirit to see what the Pharisees did not see.
God's Spirit can open a preacher's eyes to see what others
have not seen. That is the true function of the prophet—
and such the Baptist was. John was deeply stirred by the
words of the Baptist and cherished them through his long
life as marking an epoch in his own life, recalling the very
hour, the tenth hour (Roman time, ten o'clock in the morning, 1:39) and the whole wondrous day that he and Andrew
spent with Jesus in his abode (tent probably).

Like other Jews of the time John may have looked for a political Messiah who would redeem Israel from the Roman yoke, but in his case the enthusiasm for the new era of national righteousness did not ignore his own personal life. He was not blind to the spiritual aspects of the Messiah's task as the Lamb of God. "Many are willing to reform the world who need first to be reformed themselves" (Stalker, *ibid.*, p. 26). The Baptist himself was not so carried away by the multitude's enthusiasm as to consider himself the Messiah. He saw clearly that he was simply the Voice crying in the wilderness proclaiming the coming of the Messiah. And now he has baptized Jesus and identified Him to a group of his own disciples as the Messiah, the Lamb of God. "He must increase, but I must decrease." So the Baptist found joy in seeing so gifted a disciple as the young John leave him to follow Jesus.

7. *One of the first to follow Jesus.* Andrew and John form the first links between the ministry of the Baptist and that of Jesus. These two were the first who saw for themselves that the Baptist was right, that Jesus was in truth the Messiah of Jewish hope. It was too great a discovery to keep to themselves. Andrew sought out his own brother, Simon, told him the great news and brought him to Jesus (1:40-42). This thing Andrew did before he did anything else. Some of the manuscripts here read *prōtos* (first as adjective) rather than *prōton* (first as adverb). That reading plainly implies that the other disciple (John) followed the example of Andrew and brought his brother James to Jesus also. It is probably true, whatever reading one adopts, that John seized the opportunity to bring his brother James to Jesus. So probably on the next day the four fishermen (two pairs of brothers) are now disciples of Jesus, a nucleus from the vast number baptized by the Baptist. Jesus himself wins Philip, who brings Nathanael to the Master. Here then are six followers of Jesus, all from Galilee and all former disciples of the Baptist. It is a small beginning, but

a start has been made in the movement that is to revolutionize the world.

8. *The most loyal of all the Apostles.* There were differences between the twelve men finally chosen by Jesus to be His apostles to carry on His message and mission, as there always will be in such a group. Judas Iscariot will ultimately turn traitor and betray Him. Simon Peter will deny his Master, but will come back and, under the guidance of the Holy Spirit, will lead the disciples in Jerusalem. They will all leave Jesus in the Garden of Gethsemane and flee in terror (Mk. 14:50) when the Master surrenders to the chief priests and captains of the temple (Lu. 22:52). But John followed by Peter, rallied first and, being known to the high priest, boldly entered with Jesus into the court of the high priest (Jo. 18:15). Peter stopped at the door till John asked the portress to let him in. Even so Peter remained in the open court with the unsympathetic crowd, while John went on into the room where the trial before the Sanhedrin took place. And at the Cross John, alone of the apostles, took his stand with the group of faithful women (Jo. 19:25-27). It was for this loyalty that Jesus committed to John the care of His mother and commended John to her. Christ's own brothers did not as yet believe on Him. John came back to the Cross, after taking the mother of Jesus away, and saw the soldier pierce the side of Jesus (Jo. 19:35). John was the first of the apostles to believe in the fact that Jesus was risen from the tomb (Jo. 20:8). He was one of the first disciples won by Jesus. He loved Him better than all and won the special love of Christ. He loved Jesus utterly and always.

9. *John's later years.* Luke does not mention John after Acts 8:14-25, when Peter and John were sent to Samaria to investigate the work of Philip there. Paul in Galatians 2:9 mentions John as one of the pillars in the Jerusalem church, at the conference there before A.D. 50. After that we see no more of him in the New Testament outside of his Epistles and the Apocalypse. In the Apocalypse he is in

the Isle of Patmos (1:9), while in the Epistles no place is named, though he is apparently in Ephesus. Irenaeus (*Adv. Haer*. III. 1, 1:3, 4) expressly says that John spent his later years in Ephesus, except for the period of exile in Patmos. This Irenaeus tradition is followed by Apollonius, Polycrates, Clement of Alexandria, Origen, Tertullian, Eusebius and Jerome. Irenaeus was a friend and disciple of Polycarp, a friend and disciple of the Apostle John. Irenaeus quotes Polycarp as saying that John lived in Ephesus. This great city had as preachers of Christ, Paul, Timothy, and John. It was the greatest city of Asia Minor. From Ephesus the Gospel radiated to all the regions round, even while Paul laboured in Ephesus (Acts 19:10).

There is a modern theory that John was martyred with James in Jerusalem in A.D. 44—a view without historical foundation, as will be shown in chapters II and X. Jesus had promised the cup of martyrdom to both James and John. James received it in literal fulfilment, and early, but John though he suffered much, lived longest of the twelve. Irenaeus (*Adv. Haer*. ii. 22) says that "John remained among them in Asia up to the time of Trajan." We do not know the year of John's birth, or that of his death. He was apparently younger than Jesus and he was anywhere from ninety to a hundred and twenty years old when he died. Epiphanius says that he was ninety-four. Jerome states that he lived sixty-eight years after the crucifixion. Possibly he died quietly at Ephesus, not far from A.D. 100. The modern name of Ephesus is Ayasalouk, an adaptation of *Hagios Theologos,* Saintly Divine or Holy Theologian.

His writings all belong to the closing years of his life, unless we put the Apocalypse near the time of Nero as some scholars—wrongly in my opinion—still do. This ripe and gifted saint, with hallowed memories of Christ, opens his mind and heart to enrich the world with his treasures of grace and knowledge. Let us follow the course of his life leading up to these great days.

II

THE SO-CALLED PRESBYTER JOHN OF PAPIAS

But first we must dispose of that shadowy figure whom Papias calls "the elder John" according to Eusebius.

1. *The discovery of Eusebius.* "It is certain that Eusebius was the first to discover two Johns in Papias, and he is proud of his discovery. Dionysius the Great had distinguished the Apostle who wrote the Gospel from John, the author of the Apocalypse, and his acute reasonings are reproduced at length by Eusebius, *H.E.* vii. 25" (Dom Chapman, *John the Presbyter*, p. 33). Eusebius finds confirmation for his interpretation of Papias in the story of Dionysius that there were two tombs of John in Ephesus. But there is only one monument to John in Ephesus (Mgr. Duchesne, *Hist. anc. de l' Église,* i., p. 143 note). Warfield, Plummer, Salmon deny the existence of Eusebius's second John in Ephesus. "Keim relegates this 'Doppelgänger' of the apostle to the land of ghosts. There was another mysterious John, the presbyter or Prester John in the twelfth century" (Hayes, *John and His Writings,* p. 141). Bacon, Delff, Dobschütz, Harnack, McGiffert, Schürer attribute the Fourth Gospel to this Presbyter John, and even Lightfoot and Westcott are disposed to admit his existence, though holding strongly to belief in the Apostle John as the author of the Fourth Gospel. It is important therefore to examine carefully the language of Papias to see if Eusebius has correctly understood the mention of John twice by Papias.

2. *The real meaning of Papias.* The words of Papias quoted by Eusebius are: "If, then, any one should come,

having followed personally the elders, I would question him concerning the words of the elders, what Andrew or what Peter said, or what Philip, or what Thomas or James, or what John or Matthew or any one of the disciples of the Lord said, and the things which Aristion and the elder John, disciples of the Lord, say." The mention of "John" twice in this sentence is what led Eusebius astray in his interpretation, if—as now appears—he did not make a mistake. One notes at once that "Aristion and the elder John" are pictured as still living at the time referred to by Papias, for he uses "say," not "said," in speaking of them. If John was still living, while the other apostles had died, that language is easily understood. This fact, if a fact, explains also why John's name is repeated: in his case, as with Aristion, it is not simply a question of what others reported about John's words, but also (note "and," *te*, here and not "or," *ē*, as before and "that which," *ha*, not "what," *ti*) John's own living witness to Papias. In John's case we have both kinds of testimony according to Papias. If it is argued that Papias here calls John "the elder," please observe that he has just before called all the apostles named (Andrew, Peter, Philip, Thomas, James, John, Matthew) "elders" with the same Greek word *presbuteros*. He does not so term Aristion, who is only called a disciple *(mathētēs)* while John is called disciple, apostle, elder like Peter (Lu. 6:13; Matt. 10:1f.; I Pet. 5:1). Some critics would eliminate as a gloss what Papias says about "Aristion and the elder John" (Sanday, *Criticism of the Fourth Gospel*, p. 20).

But that is all pure conjecture. The natural way to take the language of Papias is to identify "the elders" with the apostles named, though Papias does not use the word "apostle" in any extant fragment (Dom Chapman, *John the Presbyter*, p. 59). "At first sight this even appears the only possible meaning, and Dr. Abbott, who does not accept this interpretation, admits that the form of the words is almost irresistible evidence in its favour" (Dom Chapman, *ibid.*, p. 9). The result of this application of the term "the elders" to the apostles named identifies "the elder John" (second mention) with "John" one of the elders previously named. This view co-ordinates "the words of the elders" with "what Andrew or what Peter said, etc." There is another view grammatically possible which subordinates "what Andrew or what Peter said, etc." to "the words of the elders." That is to say, the elders told what they had heard the apostles say and Papias heard not the apostles nor even what the elders said; he only heard one who was a follower of the elders tell what the elders heard the apostles say. This interpretation is grammatically possible, but puts two witnesses between Papias and the apostles. This view gives less value to what Papias reports, but, even so in view of John's old age, it leaves room for the identification made by Papias between the second John and the first. To be sure, if John did not live to the age of Papias, then "the elder John" would be another man.

But there is nothing in the sentence of Papias quoted by Eusebius that demands two Johns and not one. Eusebius argues that the second John is named after Aristion and, therefore, inferior to him. But that by no means follows. The second mention is often a climax. Likewise the use of the article "the elder John" does not have to mean that he is distinct from the apostle John. In 2 and 3 John the use of "the elder" is merely a descriptive epithet and does not mean that he was not a disciple and not an apostle. "We conclude that Papias is not distinguishing between two persons at all, but simply between two methods of gathering his material—one by report of what the apostle had said, and one by hearing the apostle himself" (Hayes, *op. cit.*, p. 139).

3. *Irenaeus's interpretation of Papias.* Irenaeus, born about 140 A.D. and dying about 202 A.D., lived much nearer to the time of Papias (70 to 140 A.D.) than did Eusebius (270 to 340 A.D.). Irenaeus plainly identifies John the elder, the disciple of the Lord with the Apostle John. He calls Papias "the hearer of John" (*Adv. Haer.* v.

33:4), "the disciple of the Lord" (1.8.4, etc.), "he who lay
on the Lord's breast" (iii.1:1), and he attributes to him the
Apocalypse (iv. 20:11), the Fourth Gospel (v. 18:2, etc.),
the First Epistle (iii. 16:8), and the Second Epistle (i.16:
3). Irenaeus does not use the expression "John the Presbyter" just as Papias never uses the word "apostle." Eusebius despised and misunderstood Papias: "Irenaeus certainly
studied him deeply, and quoted him frequently, but he never
found out that Papias knew of two distinct Johns" (Dom
Chapman, *ibid.*, p. 43).

But Irenaeus adds another strong link in the chain of
evidence for the one John in Ephesus. He, himself, had
not known Papias, but he knew Polycarp (martyred Feb.
23, A.D. 155 and born A.D. 69 or 70, according to Lightfoot, *Apostolic Fathers*, II. p. 646; Drummond, *Character
and Authorship of the Fourth Gospel*, p. 188) and Polycarp
was a disciple of John the Apostle. Irenaeus who in his
youth knew Polycarp, three times names John as known to
Polycarp (*Ep. ad Vict.; Ep. ad Flor.; Haer.* iii. 3:4). He
says that he often heard Polycarp tell about what John said.
Irenaeus expressly says: "Then John, the disciple of the
Lord, who also had leaned upon his breast, did himself publish a Gospel during his residence at Ephesus in Asia" (*Adv.
Haer.* iii. 1). So then, we follow the Irenaeus tradition as
clear and historical. He knew only one John just as Papias,
properly interpreted, knew only one. "Critics speak of
Irenaeus as though he had fallen out of the moon, paid two
or three visits to Polycarp's lecture-room, and never knew
any one else. As a matter of fact, he must have known all
sorts of men, of all ages, both in the east and the west,
among others his venerable predecessor Pothinus, who was
upwards of ninety at the time of his death" (Drummond,
Character and Authorship of the Fourth Gospel, p. 348).

4. *Polycrates confirms Irenaeus.* He was a contemporary
of Irenaeus and was bishop of Ephesus. In a letter to Victor, Bishop of Rome, he states that among the great who
have fallen asleep in Asia is the Apostle John: "And more-

over also John who leaned on the breast of the Lord, who
became a priest wearing the *petalon*, both witness and
teacher: he sleeps in Ephesus" (Eusebius, *H. E.* iii. 21).
This is independent testimony to the life of John in Ephesus
and his identity with the Presbyter John.

5. *Testimony of a Vatican manuscript of the ninth century.* "The Gospel of John was revealed and given to the
churches by John while he still remained in the body, as one
named Papias, of Hierapolis, a beloved disciple of John, re-
lated in his five books of Expositions" (Quoted by Hayes,
op. cit., p. 133. See *Thomasius, Works,* Vol. i, p. 344).
This is the unbroken tradition about Papias, except for
Eusebius and those who follow him till the ninth century.

6. *George the Sinful really confirms it.* This writer of
the ninth century has been freely quoted as proving from
Papias that John was put to death by the Jews in A.D. 44,
at the same time that his brother James was slain by Herod
Agrippa I. If that were true, then to be sure John the
Apostle never lived in Ephesus. But the passage from
George the Sinful has been made to mean the opposite of
what he really says as the quotation will show: "After
Domitian, Nerva reigned one year; and he, having recalled
John from the island, dismissed him to live in Ephesus.
Then, being the only survivor of the twelve apostles, and
having composed the Gospel according to him, he has been
deemed worthy of martyrdom. For Papias, the Bishop of
Hierapolis, having become an eyewitness of this one, in the
second book of the Oracles of the Lord, declares that he was
slain by the Jews, having evidently fulfilled with his brother
the prediction of Christ concerning him, and his own confession and consent in regard to this. For when the Lord
said to them, 'Can ye drink the cup which I drink?,' and
when they readily assented and agreed, 'Ye shall,' he says,
'drink my cup, and be baptized with the baptism with which
I am baptized.' So also the very learned Origen, in the
commentary on Matthew, affirms that John has suffered
martyrdom, intimating that he has learned this from the

successors of the apostles. Also the highly learned Eusebius says in the *Ecclesiastical History,* 'Thomas has had
Parthia assigned to him; John, Asia, with whom having
lived he ended his days in Ephesus.' " At once one notes
that George the Sinful quotes Papias in support of his general position that John the Apostle lived on in Ephesus to
the time of the Emperor Nerva, not that he was put to
death in A.D. 44 in Jerusalem, with his brother James. He
does say that Papias reports that John the Beloved Disciple
was put to death by the Jews, as was James. Had Papias
said that John, along with James, was put to death in
Jerusalem, in A.D. 44, George the Sinful would not have
quoted him to support his statement of John's old age and
death in Ephesus.

Unfortunately we do not have the works of Papias preserved save in quotations and cannot therefore verify this
reference by George the Sinful. But we do have the passage
in Origen to which he refers, and it is clear that he misunderstood and misinterpreted Origen concerning the martyrdom of John. Origen, without the slightest hint that
John was killed by the Jews in A.D. 44 or at any other time,
expressly says that John's exile to Patmos was sufficient
fulfilment of the Master's prophecy of the cup for him.
"If George the Sinful misrepresents Origen, may he not
equally misrepresent Papias?" (Hayes, *op. cit.,* p. 133).
Besides, the idea that the appendix to the Gospel (chapter
21) was added to correct the mistaken inference that the
Apostle John lived to a good old age in Ephesus is impossible of tenure. "There would have been no mistaken inference to correct" (Nolloth, *The Fourth Evangelist,* p. 34).
If Luke knew of the death of James in A.D. 44, surely the
death of John at the same time could not have escaped his
knowledge.

7. *Philip of Side cannot be trusted.* "Socrates and
Photius assure us he was a wild historian, who filled nearly
a thousand tomes (his history comprised 36 books, each
containing numerous tomes) with treatises on geometry,

astronomy and geography, all under the name of history, and was unable to preserve any chronological sequence" (Dom Chapman, *ibid.*, p. 99). He wrote about A.D. 430. In 1888 De Boor published (*Texte und Untersuchungen*, V. 2, pp. 182-4) from Codex Baroccianus 142 (seventh or eighth century) a sentence from Papias: "Papias in the second book says that John the Theologian and James his brother were slain by the Jews." This passage agrees with the allusion in George the Sinful to the effect that Papias affirmed that both John and James were put to death by the Jews, but not with the assertion that they were put to death at the same time. It is this latter statement that is the crucial point at issue. Papias, if he was at all informed, could not have said that, for Paul shows (Gal. 2:9) that John the Apostle was alive and active at the Jerusalem Conference about A.D. 50, whereas James was killed A.D. 44. There are various reports as to how John met his death. Papias may have stated that John, as well as James, was put to death, but it is impossible that he said that he was put to death in A.D. 44. Philip of Side clearly had no independent knowledge of Papias and quotes Eusebius incorrectly (Dom Chapman, *op. cit.*, p. 98). He cannot be allowed to twist Papias into opposition to himself.

So then the Irenaeus tradition stands and rightly understood, is the same as the Papias tradition. The so-called Papias tradition for John the Presbyter, in distinction from the Apostle John, "turns out to rest on the most precarious, if not even preposterous, foundation,—if, indeed, it can be called a foundation at all. It is not strange that sober scholarship, represented by such men as Lightfoot and Harnack and Zahn, rejects its validity without any hesitation" (Hayes, *op. cit.*, p. 135).

8. *What if there was another John of Ephesus?* One can hardly hold that two Johns lived on in Ephesus at the same time, either one able to write the Fourth Gospel. Curiously enough Eusebius held that both Johns lived in Ephesus and that the Apostle John wrote the Gospel and the Epistles and

the "Elder" John the Apocalypse. But in 2 and 3 John the writer calls himself "the Elder" (Presbyter), not the Apostle. Delff turns it around and makes the "Presbyter" John the author of the Gospel and Epistles. "This hypothesis must be ruled out of court, for the author of the Gospel claims to be one of the twelve, shows that he was present at the Last Supper, where he asks, as if one of the twelve, who was to be the traitor" (Dom Chapman, *op. cit.*, p. 73). The chief result of admitting a separate "Presbyter John" is confusion. A most interesting and able "Historical Survey" of the Johannine problem in Britain, America, Germany and France is given in W. F. Howard's *The Fourth Gospel in Recent Criticism and Interpretation,* (pp. 33 to 105). Bacon, for instance, in his *The Fourth Gospel in Research and Debate,* dismisses from the picture both the Son of Zebedee and the shadowy "John the Presbyter" (p. 452). One may believe what he will about "John the Presbyter," but with the knowledge at present before us, he passes off the stage. There remains only John the son of Zebedee, Disciple, Apostle, Elder, author of the Gospel, Epistles, and Revelation. We can now proceed with the story of the Apostle John in the New Testament.

III

THE BELOVED DISCIPLE

1. *The tragedy about John.* This beautiful epithet, "Beloved Disciple" applied to him alone, and deservedly so, has become one of the most hotly debated problems of New Testament criticism. It was all simple enough for the aged John looking back over the wonderful years, to tell his story of Jesus as he remembered it and as he had tested it through these years. But today his story is challenged at every point by sincere scholars who are confused by the conflicting details that have come to light.

Then there are some who come to the study of John with prejudiced minds. The usually fair-minded Dr. William Sanday says: "They all start with the 'reduced' conception of Christianity, current in so many quarters, that is akin to the ancient Ebionism or Arianism. But so far as they do this their verdict as to the Fourth Gospel is determined for them beforehand" (*The Criticism of the Fourth Gospel,* p. 29). In a sense every one is prejudiced *pro* or *con* in most matters. Dr. Sanday makes his own confession (*op. cit.,* p. 5): "I cannot but believe that there is a real presumption that the Christian faith, which has played so vast a part in what appears to be the designs of the Power that rules the world, is not based upon a series of deceptions." Certainly no one can accuse Sanday of trying to deceive anyone. In 1872 (*Authorship and Historical Character of the Fourth Gospel,* p. 304) he wrote: "The Gospel is the work of the Apostle, the son of Zebedee; it is the record of an eye-witness of the life of our Lord Jesus Christ; and its historical character is such as under the circumstances might be expected—it needs no adventitious commendation to make it higher." Surely that is as clear as a bell. And yet in 1920 (*Divine Overruling*, p. 6) he laments: "I am afraid there is one important point on which I was probably wrong — The Fourth Gospel. . . . The turning point in my own mind was when I began to take in more directly than I had hitherto done this question of Miracle." He had already prepared the way for this, in 1907, in *The Life of Christ in Research* (p. 222): "I am prepared therefore to believe that there may be some deduction to be made, on historical grounds, from the variations of Miracle in the Gospels."

One has to begin somewhere and not undertake to prove everything. Jesus himself draws a line of cleavage in the minds of men. "One cannot but suspect that some at least of the opposition to the Fourth Gospel has sprung from theological prejudices and presuppositions" (Hayes, *op. cit.*, p. 120). Sufficient proof that John the Apostle wrote the Fourth Gospel will be presented in Chapter XIII. Here the Johannine authorship must be assumed. "Absolute demonstration is from the nature of the case impossible, but it may fairly be said that the external and internal evidences combined are such as would in any ordinary case, and apart from all doctrinal prepossessions, be considered strong, if not conclusive, in favor of the Johannine authorship of the Gospel" (W. T. Davison, Hastings One Volume D B). We shall meanwhile assume that John the Apostle wrote the Fourth Gospel, the Johannine Epistles, and the Apocalypse.

2. *"The disciple whom Jesus loved" only so named in the Fourth Gospel.* There is no mention of John or his brother James by name in the Fourth Gospel. This fact itself arouses interest as to the cause for such omission. If John is the author, one can readily understand the reason for it. A parallel case is the use of "we" and "us" by Luke in the Acts from 16:11 on, and the like omission of any mention of Titus, Luke's brother. Once (21:2) the sons of Zebedee are mentioned as two of the seven by the Sea of Galilee. In

18:15f. the use of the terms, "another disciple," "that disciple," "the other disciple," for the companion of Peter is
another device for avoiding giving the name of John. So
also in 19:35 we have another indirection for the name
John: "The one who has seen has borne witness" and "that
one knows." Some scholars to-day interpret "that one"
(ekeinos) here as an appeal to God, but most likely the
reference is to "the one who has seen" just before. John is
bearing his own personal testimony to the reality of the
human body of Jesus against the Docetic Gnostics and, incidentally, also, to the fact that Jesus died literally of a
broken heart as evidenced by the presence of blood with
water. Then again in 20:2-8 the writer avoids the name
John by the use of the words, "the other disciple" along
with Peter just as in 18:15f., only here (20:2) "the other
disciple" is identified as the one "whom Jesus loved" (hon
ephilei ho Iēsous). This is not inference, but interpretation.
In four other passages we have this same beautiful description of John (13:23; 19:26; 21:7, 20-24)—five in all. In
each of these four cases the verb is ēgapa instead of ephilei
of 20:2.

There is a general distinction between the two verbs that
appears in 21:15-17 where Jesus first uses agapaō and Peter
claims only phileō. Agapaō usually means the higher devotion while phileō (from philos friend) gives the warm personal aspect of love. And yet both terms are used of Christ's
love for John and of God's love for man (3:16 and 16:27).
Both are used of the Father's love for the Son (3:35 and
5:20). Both are employed in telling of Jesus' love for man
(11:3, 5, 36). Both occur in discussing the love of men for
other men (15:12, 17, 19). Both are used for love of men
for Jesus (8:42; 16:27). Agapaō alone appears in speaking of Jesus' love for the Father (14:31). For full lists of
all the passages see Bernard on John's Gospel, Vol. II, pp.
702f. In 11:3 we have hon phileis (whom thou lovest)
used of Christ's love for Lazarus (in the message from

Martha and Mary to Jesus); in verse 5 *ēgapa* is employed
for Christ's love for Martha and Mary and Lazarus.

3. *He claims to be the author of the Gospel.* In one instance the author refers to himself and others by the first
personal plural pronoun: "We beheld his glory" (1:14).
The verb comes just after the mention of the Incarnation,
"the Word became flesh." The reference may be simply to
that great fact. It would then be the literary plural and
would include others besides the author, but certainly it has
to mean that the writer claims to be a personal witness of
the earthly life of Jesus. The use of the word "flesh" answers also the Docetic heresy. But it is possible that the
immediate reference is to the vision on the Mount of Transfiguration when Peter, James, and John (Mk. 9:2) saw the
dazzling glory of the Transfigured Christ (Lu. 9:32) and
when Peter wanted to build three tabernacles *(skēnas)* (for
Jesus, Moses, and Elijah). At any rate John here (1:14)
employs the verb "tabernacled" *(eskēnōsen)*, the very metaphor used by Peter on the Mount (cf. also 2 Pet. 1:16f.).
It is interesting, also, to note that in I John 1:1 we have
the very same appeal to personal acquaintance with Jesus
as we have in John 1:14; and the use of the very same verb
form *(etheasametha,* we beheld) in both is an argument for
identity of authorship in the Gospel and the Epistle. We
have seen already that the avoidance of the name John is
due to the fact that John is the author of the book. The
use of "we" in 1:14 identifies the author with "the disciple
whom Jesus loved."

4. *Identified as the author by John 21:24.* "This is the
disciple who bears witness concerning these things and who
wrote these things, and we know that his witness is true."
The reference here is clearly to "the disciple whom Jesus
loved" of verses 20 to 23. There can be no other meaning
given to this endorsement than that the Beloved Disciple,
himself, is the author of the Gospel (including the appendix
—chapter 21). The use of the plural here ("we know") is
not the literary plural of "we beheld" in 1:14, but is in con-

trast with "I think" of 21:25 by the author himself. We do not know who belonged to this group that added 21:24 to the appendix. No manuscript omits it, though Aleph omits verse 25. The natural inference is that it was added before the book was published.

Apparently it was the elders in Ephesus who gave this endorsement to the Johannine authorship, since John had concealed the fact by the use of indirections like "the disciple whom Jesus loved." There is no need to think of this note being inserted only when denial of the Johannine authorship had arisen, long after the book appeared. B. H. Streeter argues that this addition of verse 24, though it was added to show that the author was the Apostle John, "is a mistaken identification." "And that the Apostle the author had in mind was John can hardly, I think, admit of serious doubt" (*The Four Gospels,* p. 432). That is to say, the author purposely created the impression that the Apostle was the author of the Gospel. So Harnack suggests that verse 24 was added to help on this idea: "The twenty-fourth verse of the twenty-first chapter of the Fourth Gospel, about which we have spoken, will always remain a strong indication of the fact that in Ephesus the Fourth Gospel was deliberately put out, after the death of its author, as a work of the Apostle" (*Chronologie,* p. 679). Sanday, after giving this quotation, pithily adds: "*Facilis descensus.* When once we begin imputing fraudulent actions we may easily find we have to keep on doing so. It should, however, be remembered that the ground of all this is no assured fact, but only the exigencies of a complicated theory which, quite apart from this, has a load of improbability to contend with" (*Criticism of the Fourth Gospel,* p. 64). This greatest and noblest of all books is charged with being put out as a fraud! But in the welter of hostile criticism the fact remains that the Fourth Gospel claims to be written by the Beloved Disciple who is known to be the Apostle John.

There are those, like Dr. A. E. Garvie *(The Beloved Disciple),* who see a triple authorship (the Witness, the

Evangelist, the Redactor). The Apostle John, according to this view, may be the witness and so, in some sense, the source for much of the Gospel. But that is certainly not the purport of the book itself. It purports to be, and means to be received as, the work of the Beloved Disciple. In simple truth, the style of the book, as a whole, is the same and leaves no room for such a divided authorship. The opponents of the Johannine authorship of the Fourth Gospel agree only in this denial. The alternatives offered are manifold and contradictory. We are concerned chiefly with the claim of the book itself as to authorship, and that is plain enough, as all admit, however some may seek to get rid of the claim.

5. *Clearly one of the Twelve Apostles.* To begin with, the disciple whom Jesus loved of 21:20, identified as the author in 21:24, is one of the seven named in 21:2 and is the one who recognized Jesus first in 21:7. Three names are given (Peter, Thomas, and Nathanael) and the sons of Zebedee (James and John) and "two other of his disciples" (almost certainly Andrew and Philip). These are all "apostles," for the word "disciples" here has this specialized group in mind. This fact does not itself determine which one of the seven apostles is the Beloved Disciple, the author of the book. This disciple whom Jesus loved "was at the table, reclining on Jesus' bosom," (Jo. 13:23) at the last supper "with the twelve disciples" (Matt. 26:20), expressly called "the apostles with him" (Lu. 22:14). So then Peter beckons to this apostle "whom Jesus loved" (Jo. 13:24) that he shall ask concerning the betrayer of the Lord. There is no escape from this identification, save to say either that the author of the Fourth Gospel has misrepresented the facts and claimed to be present when he was not, or that Luke is wrong in saying that Jesus "sat down, and the apostles with him," when, as a matter of fact, another was present who was on even more intimate terms with Jesus than the apostles themselves. This latter alternative is the way out indicated by Delff, and allowed by Sanday as practically

equivalent to the Johannine authorship. Sanday sees clearly that the Beloved Disciple is the author of the Fourth Gospel and was present at the last supper. "I propose to defend the traditional view, or (as an alternative) something so near the traditional view that it will count as the same thing" (*Criticism of the Fourth Gospel*, p. 3). But Sanday is mistaken about its "counting as the same thing"; there is no room for this other bosom friend and disciple of Jesus at this last supper unless we juggle with the Gospel records which make no reference to such another friend. Dr. Garvie is perfectly justified in punching a hole in Sanday's argument at this point (*The Beloved Disciple*, p. 205). Indeed, even Sanday says: "It is not, on the face of it, certain that 'the disciple whom Jesus loved' must have been one of the Twelve. He may have been what might perhaps be called a sort of *supernumerary* Apostle" (*op. cit.*, p. 98). But even here Sanday is compelled, in the face of Luke 22:14, to use the word "Apostle," though he adds (italics his) *"supernumerary"* to it. But both Mark (14:17) and Matthew (26:20) employ the words, "the Twelve"—and that leaves no room for Sanday's gratuitous "supernumerary." With all due regard for Sanday's great learning and love of fairness, it is plain that Homer nodded at this point. It is a needless hypothesis contradicted by the Gospels themselves.

We must either bluntly admit that the Beloved Disciple was one of the Twelve Apostles or assume that the Gospels have not correctly presented the facts. Streeter sees clearly that the Beloved Disciple is meant to be understood as the Apostle John: "The Beloved Disciple, then, will be an Apostle; but he is that Apostle transfigured into the ideal disciple. And that the Apostle he had in mind was John can hardly, I think, admit of serious doubt" (*The Four Gospels*, p. 432). Streeter, to be sure, holds that verses 24 and 25 of chapter 21 are a late addition and that the Beloved Disciple did not write the book. That the author (whoever he was) meant by the "Beloved Disciple" to picture John

the Apostle, he agrees, admits of no doubt. But he feels
driven to get rid of verses 24 and 25 to give room to the
theory of non-Johannine authorship. He sees clearly that
with these verses intact there is no room for his view.

Granted that the Beloved Disciple is one of the Twelve
Apostles, as the untampered with records compel one to
acknowledge, it is not hard to eliminate all but John. Peter
drops out and certainly Judas Iscariot does. Only
Peter, James and John form the "inner circle" around Jesus.
He would surely be one of these three. With Peter out,
only James and John are left. But James was put to death
A.D. 44 by Herod Agrippa I. So then, John remains the
only possible one to whom the appellation can be applied.
Why not admit it? Well, most scholars still do, but there
is a strong array of names against it to-day. There are
those who reject utterly the Johannine authorship; men like
Bacon, Bauer, F. C. Burkitt, Percy Gardner, H. J. and Oscar
Holtzmann, Jülicher, Loisy, Reville, E. F. Scott, Schmiedel,
Schwartz, Soltau, Streeter, Wellhausen, Wernle, Wrede.
There are some who, with redactions and partition theories,
admit Johannine portions; men like Bernard, Bousset, Car-
penter, Delff, Garvie, Harnack, McNeile, Moffatt, Schuerer,
Spitta, J. Weiss, Wendt, Windisch. But there are still great
scholars that champion the entire Johannine authorship (the
Beloved Disciple) such authorities as Ezra Abbot, Askwith,
Burch, James Drummond, C. R. Gregory, Hayes, Lightfoot,
Nolloth, Peake, Sanday (with an alternative), J. Armitage
Robinson, Scott-Holland, Scott Moncrieff, Stanton (at first),
Strachan, R. H. Vedder (in revision), Watkins, B. Weiss,
Westcott, Theodore Zahn.

It is sometimes assumed to-day that the Johannine question is settled adversely, once and for all, but this cannot
justly be said with so many names of great weight still on
the side of the Beloved Disciple. The real facts are open
to all; and each one has to decide for himself in the light
of all the known facts. Each critic approaches the problem
with his own prejudices and predilections. Loisy, though

denying the reality of the Beloved Disciple and taking the epithet to mean "the young church" (*Le Quatrième Évangile,* pp. 125-129), yet admits (p. 132) that, taken literally, the Beloved Disciple can only be one of the twelve. Nolloth (*The Fourth Evangelist,* p. 29) rightly insists that for the writer of the Fourth Gospel to pose as John would be "a deliberate attempt to mislead." "In order to be taken for an Apostle and eye-witness of Christ he would be aping a scrupulous modesty, arraying his deceit in the garb of one attractive virtue." Believe it who can, with this Gospel before you.

6. *The pride of John in calling himself "the disciple whom Jesus loved."* The author of the Fourth Gospel is sometimes criticized for arrogating to himself a title which would show that Jesus loved him more than he did any of the apostles. In particular would this criticism be applicable if the Apostle John is the author, since he omits his own name and that of his brother James always, save by inference in "the sons of Zebedee" (21:2). "The reticence and modesty with which in his Gospel St. John refers to himself and his relatives" (Stalker, *op. cit.,* p. 34) are thought by some to make improbable that he would use the epithet here under discussion. "In estimating the character of St. John this reserve should be noticed as a prominent characteristic; and it harmonizes well with the other qualities of his exquisite nature" (*ibid.*). It was not conceit on John's part to use this praise of Jesus to describe himself, but pardonable pride, not inconsistent with true humility. In the Synoptic Gospels John is not a prominent figure; "always he is mentioned in connection with others who are more prominent than he" (Hayes, *op. cit.,* p. 59). "He was naturally a modest man, of a retiring disposition. It was only when the others had died that he came to primacy in the church. Even then he bore himself with simple dignity and was unassuming in conduct and speech" (*ibid.*). Even so, it is noted that the other Gospels never call John "the disciple whom Jesus loved," but left it for him to use that phrase.

That is true, but John's employment of the epithet is due to something very far from the modern spirit of self-advertisement. "John was the very opposite of the man who is forever talking about himself, vaunting his own deeds, and blowing his own trumpet" (*ibid.*, p. 60).

Beyond a doubt he cherished the memory of the special love which Jesus held for him all during his long life and now, as he looked back upon the mystery and wonder of that fellowship, it is precisely the memory of that sacred life which is the outstanding honour of his own life. He ventures to record it as an expression of his appreciation. John's feeling is that the Master understood him when others did not and took him to his heart in a way that even Peter recognized as a thing apart to itself (Jo. 13:23f.). "That which the Saviour loved in him was produced by Himself; and here we come upon the deepest reason of the attachment between them. Perhaps no one whom Jesus ever met so much resembled him in natural configuration; but Jesus brought out all that was best in John, and repressed or destroyed what was evil" (Stalker, *op. cit.*, p. 16). But no more than Paul (I Tim. 1:12-16) did John understand how Jesus could pick him out for such fellowship and service. Dr. Garvie, though he does not identify "the disciple whom Jesus loved" with the Apostle John (*The Beloved Disciple*, p. 202), yet sees no impropriety in the use of the phrase by "the witness," as he terms him, in distinction from "the redactor" and "the evangelist": "But even in his later years he did not reveal his name, and probably it was out of respect to his wishes that the disciple who reported what he had taught did not betray his secret, but gave as a tribute of his affection the description of him as 'the disciple whom Jesus loved,' if that description is not itself a humble self-confession, and a grateful adoration of Christ on the part of the witness."

We can agree with Hayes (*op. cit.*, p. 63f.) on this point: "He assumes it, because he deserved it. It belonged to him by right of conquest. He had achieved the place nearest the heart of the Incarnate One. That was the greatest honour he ever had had or ever could have." John treasured that secret all through the years and unbosomed his heart with it in lieu of telling his own name. I cannot agree with Stalker (*op. cit.*, p. 80) that "St. John's was a refined and reserved nature, and *pride was his besetting sin.*" He was refined and reserved, but I see no proof that "pride was his besetting sin." He had ambition, as comes out clearly in his request with James for first place in the Kingdom, but there is no real proof of pride in his use of the phrase "the disciple whom Jesus loved."

7. *The disciple who loved Jesus.* Love begets love. There is no finer illustration of this truth than in John's devotion to Jesus. "John loved him with a love surpassing that of women" (Hayes, *op. cit.*, p. 64). In time John came to be called "the apostle of love" because he has so much to say in his First Epistle concerning love. There is no one passage in John's writings that compares with I Corinthians 13 as a picture of love, but all through his Gospel, in the Epistles, and in Revelation love is the dominant note. John himself came to be a noble illustration of the love which he discussed. One of the legends about John's old age is that he was too weak to walk and had to be carried to the church services where, seated in a chair, he would only say: "Little children, love one another." Asked why he repeated these words so often, he explained: "Because, if you have learned to love, you need nothing more."

In his Gospel the very heart of his conception of Christ's mission is found in 3:16 where love is given as the motive behind God's gift of his Son for us. "We love him, because he first loved us" (I Jo. 4:19). Plutarch calls one of the friends of Alexander the Great *Philo-Basileus* (the friend of the king or of the monarch) and the other *Philo-Alexandros* (the friend of Alexander or of the man). "So Grotius calls Peter, *'Philo-Christos,'* the friend of Christ, and John, *'Philo-Jesus,'* the friend of Jesus" (Hayes, *op. cit.*, p. 65). Both John and Peter were personal friends of Jesus and took

Him to be the Messiah. The difference between the relationship is more in the personal touch and affinity than in any official aspect. No one has ever loved Jesus Christ with more unalloyed love and understanding than the Apostle John. Stalker is clearly right when he says that "it is the personal bond that holds the heart. The most profoundly Christian spirits have loved the Saviour, not for His benefits, but for Himself alone" (*op. cit.*, p. 101). Whatever may have been true of Peter, John entered into the very holy of holies of Christ's personality.

IV

A SON OF THUNDER

1. *This epithet used only once.* That is in Mark 3:17, in connection with the choosing of the twelve apostles by Jesus. After naming "James the son of Zebedee and John the brother of James" and before mentioning "Andrew, etc.," Mark inserts as a parenthesis: "And he placed on them (i.e. James and John) a name 'Boanerges,' which is Sons of Thunder." He had already noted (verse 16) that Jesus had given a nickname to Simon: "And Simon he surnamed (*epethēken onoma*, gave an added name to) Peter," the very idiom used of James and John. The giving of the surname to Peter is recorded in John 1:42 and also in Matthew 16: 18f., but nowhere else in the New Testament is there an allusion to this surname for James and John. Mark does not tell us when Jesus gave them this epithet, nor why. He can scarcely mean to say that it was given at the time when the twelve were chosen.

In all the four lists of the apostles (Mk. 3:16f.; Matt. 10:2f.; Lu. 6:14f.; Acts 1:13f.) the first four names are Peter, James, John, Andrew, though they are not always given in the same order. Acts follows Mark's order here—that of rank, with Andrew last of the four—while Matthew and Luke give the pairs of brothers together (Peter and Andrew, James and John). It is probable that Mark obtained his information about the giving of this surname to James and John from Peter who, himself, had received one from Jesus. The word Boanerges, or "Sons of Thunder" is a modified transliteration of the Hebrew *Benē Regesh*, though *Regesh* literally means tumult or uproar. There is

42

a Hebrew word *rogez* (Job 37:2) which apparently means
the rumbling of a storm. "This seems to point to the quar-
ter where a solution may be found" (Swete). Others have
sought the origin in Syriac and Armenian roots. The explanation given by Mark is all the real light on the subject
that we possess.

2. *Probably a note on the temperament of John and
James.* This characterization "Sons of Thunder," was given
to these two brothers by the Master Himself and there must
have been real ground for it, even if we do not see clearly
why it was given. It may seem surprising to us for the
Apostle of Love to be so described by Jesus who loved him
so supremely. We know less about James than about John
because of his early martyrdom, but he, too, is included in
the picture. Some have dared to say that James and John
were called Sons of Thunder because they were disciples of
the Baptist whose preaching echoed like a clap of everlasting
thunder over the hills of Judea. Surely that is not a pertinent explanation for applying the word to James and John,
for Peter and Andrew were also disciples of the Baptist.
Others say that James and John won the epithet because
they preached in a loud voice and in a boisterous manner.
There *are* preachers whose voice and manner remind one of
a thunderstorm, but we have no ground whatever for thinking so of James and John. Certainly it was not true of John
in his old age. In the Gospels and early part of the Acts it
is Peter, not John, who "speaks out"! There must be
some other reason for this description of these two apostles.

We are left to think that the Sons of Thunder were so
called by Jesus "from the impetuosity of their natural character" (Swete), an impetuosity that in the case of James led
to his death in A.D. 44 at the hands of Herod Agrippa I, an
act that greatly pleased the Jews (Acts 12:1-3). Peter at
that time was arrested and thrown into prison. One wonders
why John was not involved on this occasion, as he had
formerly been put into prison with Peter by the Sadducees
in the Sanhedrin. He may have been out of the city at this

time or for some unknown reason James may have been
more antagonistic to the Jews just then. But both James
and John "could flash fire at times. A man cannot flash
fire unless he has some flint in him. It runs up and down
his backbone and it shows in his face" (Hayes, *op. cit.*, p.
47).

3. *An instance of intolerant zeal in John.* The twelve
apostles had been disputing as to which of them should be
the greatest in the kingdom of heaven. Both John and
James were involved in this unseemly wrangle. The
Master gave them all a severe rebuke by pointing to the
little child as an object lesson in humility and real greatness, "for he that is least among you all, the same is great"
(Lu. 9:48). This time, John, not Peter, speaks up to re-
lieve the embarrassment that they all felt or, perhaps, to put
himself in a favourable light with Jesus after the rebuke.
Whatever the motive, this is the only remark attributed by
the Synoptic Gospels to John alone. Swete *(Comm. on
Mark)* thinks that "it creates an impression of candour and
conscientiousness not unworthy of the future *theologos*."
John involves others with him without naming them, probably James, and even Peter and Andrew, as on another occasion (Mk. 13:3). But, as the spokesman, John assumes
responsibility: "Teacher, we saw one casting out demons in
thy name, and we tried to hinder him, because he was not
following us." Some manuscripts have "with us," and that
is what the other reading means. This irregular worker,
who used Christ's name as some non-Christian exorcists
later did in Ephesus, (Acts 19:13) seems actually to have
cast out the demons by the power of Jesus. He was not a
professional exorcist like those in Ephesus, but apparently
a sincere believer in Christ, though not following the group
around Him. Undoubtedly John expected the approval of
Jesus for his zeal and loyalty to the Master. Stalker keenly
suggests (*op. cit.*, p. 88) that John had been doubtful at the
time about this narrow zeal to which he reluctantly assented,
that his conscience was stung by the rebuke of Jesus, and

that he now tells the incident by way of confession. That may be true. Stalker has an almost uncanny insight into people's motives. If this is true, "it is to his honour that he was so prompt both to feel the prick of conscience and to make a public acknowledgment of his mistake." But John was certainly wrong when he tried to put clamps on one who though not in the apostolic group, was doing the Master's work in the Master's name. There is a vivid lesson here for all modern Christians who seek to limit the power of Christ to their own circle. At any rate Jesus pointedly rebuked John: "Stop hindering him: for there is no man who will do a mighty work upon my name and be able quickly to speak evil of me. For he who is not against us is for us." There is room enough in the world for many groups to follow Christ in their own way, just so they really follow Him. At the time John probably felt jealousy for the honour of the apostolic circle, but the words of Jesus turned a new light on his conduct.

4. *The desire for instant vengeance on the Samaritans.* Both James and John are involved in this display of temper. Race hatred and religious prejudice flare up on this occasion. Jesus was on His way, a bit late, to the feast of tabernacles in Jerusalem. Instead of going with the caravans down on the east side of the Jordan through Perea, He, with the apostles, went south from Galilee through Samaria. The old hatred of the Samaritans towards the Jews (Jo. 4:9) blazed up: the Samaritan villagers in a certain town refused to receive Jesus "because his face was going toward Jerusalem." That fact alone was enough for these prejudiced Samaritans. They would have speeded Him on His way had He been going north to Galilee away from Jerusalem, as once they did in Sychar. (Jo. 4:39-42). Besides, this was not Sychar. It is significant that Luke tells of this incident immediately after recording John's narrow intolerance (9:49f.). This time both James and John speak to Jesus: "Lord, dost thou wish that we bid fire to come down from heaven and consume them?" (Lu. 9:54). John and

James had recently seen Elijah with Jesus on the Mount of Transfiguration (Lu. 9:30f.) and this fact probably reminded them of the way that Elijah twice called down fire from heaven, that consumed the embassies (fifty-one each time) from Ahaziah, King of Israel, because he worshipped Baalzebub, the god of Ekron, instead of Jehovah (II Ki. 1:1-16). There was justification for the anger of James and John, but not for likening themselves to Elijah, who had been specifically directed in this act of vengeance by the angel of Jehovah.

There was a bit of naiveté in the assumption of James and John that they really had the power to call down fire from heaven on this village that had rejected Jesus. There was also presumption in proposing an act of vengeance before Jesus Himself had spoken. "They were confident that they could have produced the lightning. Yet almost unconsciously they felt that their proposal was unchristlike" (Stalker, *op. cit.*, p. 92). It certainly was "unchristlike," for Jesus "turned and rebuked them." Some manuscripts add here: "And he said, Ye know not of what spirit ye are." This saying is found in the *Codex Bezae* and is probably not a part of the Gospel of Luke. But it is almost certainly a genuine saying of Jesus, for it is wholly like Jesus—and like no one else. A few manuscripts also add: "For the Son of man came, not to destroy the souls of men, but to save"; an adaptation of Matthew 5:17 and Luke 19:10. It was a natural burst of thunder on the part of James and John, and they longed also for the flash of lightning to smite the Samaritans who had, as they felt, given an insult to the Master as well as to themselves. *Quid mirum filios tonitrui fulgurare voluisse?* (Ambrose). But Jesus bade them to cease thundering and not to flash any lightning at all. It was like the rebuke administered to Simon Peter in the Garden of Gethsemane when Jesus told him to put his sword back into the sheath and then calmly healed the ear of Malchus. The old man of hate spoke in James and John, not the new man of love in Christ Jesus. We all have cause to remember what Jesus did on this occasion when we are tempted to persecute those "rude fanatics" who do not welcome the Lord Jesus. Some day John will see things in a clearer light.

5. *The ambitious request of James and John.* Mark (10: 35) relates how James and John came to Jesus immediately after the tragic experience which took place as they went up to Jerusalem for the last time. "And Jesus was going on before them, and they were amazed, but those that were following him were afraid" (Mk. 10:32). There was a strange look on the face of the Master that was soon explained. He took the twelve to one side and said: "Behold, we are going up to Jerusalem; and the Son of man will be handed over to the chief priests and to the scribes, and they will condemn him to death, and they will hand him over to the Gentiles, and they will mock him and will spit upon him and will scourge him and will kill him, and after three days he will rise again." Matthew explains (20:19) that the death will be by crucifixion and the resurrection on the third day. Luke adds (18:34) that "they understood not one of these things and this saying was concealed from them and they kept on not perceiving the things that were being said."

In the case of James and John it is plain that their minds were running on their own selfish ambition even at the very moment when Jesus was portraying his own dreadful death in Jerusalem. The Master's words ran counter to their own ideas of a political kingdom with high places of preferment for each of them in it, so that the terrible, ominous words of Jesus left no impress on them at all. Their minds were closed to the ideas of Jesus. They were amazed at his tragic look and sorrowful words, but they did not resent them as Peter had done at the time when Jesus called him Satan for offering Him a worldly crown (Matt. 16:23). Indeed, Jesus has recently promised that "in the regeneration when the Son of Man shall sit on the throne of his glory, ye also shall sit upon twelve thrones, judging the

twelve tribes of Israel" (Matt. 19:28). That prophecy they
had interpreted in the sense of literal thrones here on earth.
They cherished the promise and were actually dividing out
the positions among themselves, oblivious to the depression
in the present mood of Jesus. So James and John, accom-
panied by their mother (Matt. 20:20), who made obeisance
to Him as to a king, came boldly to Jesus with a blunt request: "Teacher, we wish that thou do for us whatever we
ask of thee." The mother's ambition is pardonable, especially if she is the sister of Mary the mother of Jesus.
She was loyal to Jesus and had given him her two sons, her
best treasures. She wanted the greatest places for them.
But it is pathetic to see this group of mother and sons,—
closest of all to Jesus,—make such a selfish request in the
presence of the other ten especially at this time when the
shadow of the Cross lay heavy on the heart of Jesus. Alas,
how often has the Lord Jesus, in crucial moments in the history of Christianity, seen selfish ambition lift its head in the
circles of His followers. Matthew represents the mother as
speaking while Mark portrays James and John as making
their own request. Probably both accounts are true. At
any rate, the Master according to Mark, without rebuke,
patiently asks: "What would ye that I should do for you?"
They do not recoil, but say: "Give to us that in thy glory
we may take our seats, one on thy right and one on thy left."
There it is in the raw, the personal ambition of these sons
of thunder. Jesus explains kindly with a gentle rebuke:
"You do not know what you are asking." The request was
based on sheer misconception of the kingdom as being political. Then Jesus went on with a challenge: "Are you able
to drink the cup that I drink ("about to drink," Matthew),
or to be baptized with the baptism that I am baptized
with?"

This challenge carries the ambitious apostles into the very
heart of Jesus. In Gethsemane James and John along with
Peter, will come to know what this "cup" is as he cries out
for it, if it be possible, to pass from him (Mk. 14:36). The

Incarnation was already the cup: the Cross but the fulness of its suffering. Jesus had already (Lu. 12:50) spoken of His death under the metaphor of baptism. (See Paul's symbolism in Romans 6:3.) The reply of the two brothers is astonishing in its crass simplicity and blind audacity: "We are able." How little they knew of the meaning of Christ. There was "immense egotism in it, but there was immense loyalty as well" (Hayes, *op. cit.*, p. 50). After all the Master's patient teaching and fellowship to get "such a light-hearted and eager reply" (Swete) from the Beloved Disciple was a cut to the quick. Tenderly the Master goes on: "The cup that I drink you shall drink and the baptism that I am baptized with you shall be baptized with." This meant little to them then, but James will be the first of the twelve, to get the martyr's crown. John will be the last to go and apparently will not die a violent death—though he will suffer a thousand deaths while alive.

We have seen that there is no historical basis for the notion of Georgius Hamartolus and Philip of Side (the De Boor Fragment) that Papias states that John was put to death by the Jews. "The stories that he drank poison and was immersed in burning oil without being harmed cannot be relied upon, though they go back to the second century" (Plummer). "There is no sufficient evidence to cast serious doubt on the universal tradition that John died peacefully at Ephesus in extreme old age" (J. Arm. Robinson, *The Historical Character of St. John's Gospel*, p. 79). But the rest of the Master's words dashed their ambitious hopes to the ground: "But the sitting on my right hand or on my left is not mine to give, but it is for those for whom it has been made ready." "The Lord disclaims the right to dispose in an arbitrary manner of the higher rewards of the kingdom" (Swete). He will distribute according to the Father's will, "prepared of my Father," Matthew adds. The Master does not explain on what basis the Father makes such selection among the elect. It is a destiny and a reward according to character and work and the inner fitness of things. It is the part of loyalty to leave the decision to the Father's love and to trust him wholly.

The door is thus definitely shut in the face of the selfish ambitions of James and John. Ambition in itself is not wrong; only it should be ambition to do one's best and to please Christ (II Cor. 5:9), not to have one's way or to get high preferment. John and James were silenced, but the others had something to say. "The ten began to be indignant concerning James and John." They were bound to hear of it, even if they were not actually present. Possibly Peter voiced the feeling of the ten about this attempt by private influence to gain the advantage over the rest of them. Jesus had already rebuked this jealousy among the twelve as to who among them was the greatest (Mk. 9:33-37); now it had broken out again. The ten may have felt that Jesus was not severe enough towards James and John. Jesus saw the envy flashing as the ten stood apart and gave vent to their wrath. He called the apostles to him and spoke a revolutionary word to them: "You know that those who are reputed to rule over the Gentiles lord it over them and their grandees wield power over them. But it is not so among you. So whoever wishes to become great among you shall be your minister; and whoever wishes to be first among you shall be slave of all. For the Son of man also did not come to be ministered unto, but to minister and to give his life a ransom for many." There was no reply to this profound philosophy of life. Both the ten and the two are silenced for the present. "Never, surely, did Christ utter a more revolutionary word or characterize more clearly the differences between the world and Christianity" (Stalker, *op. cit.*, p. 87). But, alas, how often the spirit of the Gentiles creeps into the hearts of the followers of Jesus and wipes out the root difference here outlined. On this occasion John is revealed as a son of thunder in an unpleasing light, but at least there is energy and action though in the wrong direction.

6. *John's courage at the trial at Jesus.* It is true that,

when Jesus startled the apostles by saying that one of them would betray him, John was as puzzled as were the others. "The disciples began to look on one another, at a loss concerning of whom he was speaking" (Jo. 13:22). It was Peter who suggested to John that he ask Jesus who it was. "It was the acknowledgment by St. Peter of St. John's primacy in the love and confidence of Christ" (Stalker, *op. cit.*, p. 97). Whether John asked in a whisper or not, the reply of Jesus together with the request was not quickly grasped by the others and is recorded only by John. But "two now knew the terrible secret. Jesus had relieved his heart of the burden by making John partaker of it. Judas knew that John knew" (Stalker, *op. cit.*, p. 98). Judas "hated Jesus for telling; he hated John for knowing" *(ibid.)*. Satan gripped the heart of Judas afresh and he went out straightway into the night. John, along with the others, expressed undying fealty to Jesus even unto death (Mk. 14:31)— and then in Gethsemane fled with the rest in panic, upon the arrest of the Master (Mk. 14:50).

But it must be put down to his credit that he was the first to rally from that panic. At any rate, he showed more courage than did Peter, who followed Jesus afar off (Mk. 14:54). Both Peter and John recovered themselves enough to follow Jesus to the court of the high priest (Jo. 18:15), but John, being known to the high priest, went boldly on into the court, while Peter halted, and lingered at the door without till John spoke to the portress to let Peter come in also (Jo. 18:16). Mark (14:54) and Matthew (26:58) do not explain how Peter was unable to enter into the court. But Peter again remained beneath in the court with the officers, the maids and other servants, while John found a place in the room where Jesus was on trial. At the Cross John alone of the apostles stood with the Mother of Jesus and some other women, sharing with Jesus the peril and shame of the Cross.

It is a bit curious that the most feminine of the apostles in temperament is precisely the one who with the women stands fast to the Master in this darkest hour of all. Men are supposed to be stronger for life's burdens, but it is actually the women who carry earth's sorrows more readily. When the shadows fall, they rise to the emergency with more elasticity of heart and simple trust in God. John comes back to the Cross, after a brief departure with the mother of Jesus, in time to see the Roman soldier pierce the side of the body of the Master, whence both blood and water came out (Jo. 19:34). There is a possible allusion to this experience of John in I John 5:6. On these occasions the Son of Thunder reveals a courage and loyalty quite in keeping with the surname given him by Jesus. It manifestly refers not to mere uncontrolled explosiveness in John but to an element of power and strength. "John never lost the Boanerges spirit, and Jesus never desired that he should. He was the boldest of the twelve at the time of the crucifixion. He was the first to recover from the panic of the Gethsemane garden. He was the one man among all the followers of Jesus who seems to have been near him at the trial in the high priest's palace and nearest him during the last hours of the Cross. He was the first of them at the empty tomb on the morning of the Easter day, and he was the first to attain to the resurrection faith" (Hayes, *op. cit.*, p. 54). It is small wonder that Jesus loved John in such a special manner.

7. *The denunciation of sin in the Epistles.* In John's later years—the other apostles, including Paul, all gone— he stood alone in the defence of the Gospel Message against Gnosticism. The Gnostics degraded Jesus Christ either by separating the *aeon* Christ from the man Jesus (the Cerinthian Gnostics)—like the modern Jesus of history and Christ of faith—or by denying real humanity to Jesus and making him all *aeon* with only a shadow body (the Docetic Gnostics). They considered flesh as sinful in itself and one wing of them gave way to gross sensuality on the plea that the soul was immune from the sins of the flesh. This situation must be clearly understood, in order to see why the

aged John uses such plain terms in denouncing these licentious heretics. He calls a spade a spade: he brands as "liars" those who profess personal knowledge and intimate fellowship with Christ, if they hate their brothers and live on in known sin (secret or public).

John has not lost his temper or become petulant like an irritable old man. These men are like the Pharisees whom Jesus branded as hypocrites because their piety was mere pretence. Even Diotrephes calls for exposure by John for his dictatorial assumptions and presumptions. Cerinthus was one of the outstanding Gnostics towards the close of the first century. One of the many stories told about John is to the effect that on a certain day he was in one of the public baths in Ephesus when Cerinthus came in. John at once fled, and urged others to do so for fear that the walls of the bath might fall on them.

This spirit is in keeping with the narrow zeal that tried to hinder the man that was casting out demons in Christ's name, and with the heated intolerance that wished to call down fire from heaven on the Samaritans. Clearly John had great provocation from Cerinthus and the Gnostics. All his writings (the Gospel and the Epistles in particular) refer to them. In the above mentioned incident at the bath in Ephesus (if it be true) he apparently let his indignation get the better of his self-control. Stalker (*op. cit.*, p. 8) hopes "that the education imparted in the school of Christ had long before the arrival of old age made St. John more charitable in his judgments and more watchful in his words." But he may have been at that time already an old man.

We should bear in mind that people in glass houses had best not throw stones. "It is not easy to find the golden mean between Sadducean laxity on the one hand and Pharisaic censoriousness on the other. We may be censuring the disciples at the safe distance of the centuries and doing the same thing ourselves" (Stalker, *op. cit.*, p. 89). John is not a compromiser in creed or in conduct. He is the apostle of purity as well as of love. "To him Judas is a devil and the

son of perdition. The Jews are the children of the devil.
Every professing Christian who walks in the darkness is a
liar, and makes God a liar. The antichrist is a liar. Every
sinner is a child of the devil. Whoever hateth his brother
is a murderer. False teachers are to have no lodging in
their homes and no greetings in their streets. This is the
spirit of a Boanerges—vehement, irreconcilable, uncompro-
mising, intense in conviction and intense in denunciation, a
face like flint, a backbone inflexible, straightforward in dealing, handling all subjects and all people without gloves,
calling things by their right names" (Hayes, *op. cit.*, p. 53).
The colors are here a bit overdrawn, but in the main it is
true.

8. *Final mellow self-control.* It was not so in the beginning that the fiery and impetuous young John was able to
restrain himself. The fine steel had to be tempered before
it was able to carry a fine edge and not be turned. Surely
the rich love of Jesus for John was so rare and radiant a
response that his very heart was transfigured into the love
which burned there with a steady flame. Like the Baptist,
whose first disciple he was, he became a bright and shining
light. Even when John learned to control the intensity of
his indignation the fire still slumbered within the volcano.
"The self-suppression of St. John's later writings may be
only the self-assertion of his youth in a ripened and sancti-
fied form; and the intolerance of his youth may in his old
age have mellowed into the firmness of principle and the
perseverance of tireless love" (Stalker, *op. cit.*, p. 83). In
the mellowness of a ripe Christian old age John was not
effeminate, not a mere sentimentalist as most of the artists
—even Leonardo da Vinci in the Last Supper—represent
him. His was not a girlish face, but that of a true apostle
of love who knew the sin and suffering and sorrows of men,
and whose love shone through the great deeps of his soul.
He had the strength of the eagle and could soar to the
heights above the storms to the serene calm in Christ. He
knew what it was to face and breast the storm and to fight

the wild beasts within and without. Hayes (*op. cit.*, p. 23) feels that the Synoptics are hardly fair to John: "These three rebukes for the spirit of selfishness and the spirit of revenge and the spirit of intolerance are all that the synoptics have seen fit to record of the Apostle John and his individual relationship to the Lord." The Fourth Gospel makes amends by presenting to us the Beloved Disciple with his wondrous charm and spiritual insight.

A CLOSE COMPANION OF PETER

1. *Early associations together.* John and Peter were apparently from Bethsaida and later in business as fishermen in Capernaum (Jo. 1:43; Lu. 5:10; Mk. 1:29). One may safely conjecture that the understanding friendship between these two men, so different in many ways, was formed when they were boys. It had its roots in childhood fellowship and was strengthened by business contacts and camaraderie. Peter's buoyant boyishness was appreciated by John's quiet and quick sensitive apprehension. Stalker (*op. cit.*, p. 153) suggests that as boys they went together to the feasts in Jerusalem as Jesus did when twelve. They, together with their brothers, James and Andrew, were both drawn to the Jordan by the preaching of the Baptist. They both were won to Jesus on the same day or on successive days. Peter was brought to Jesus by his brother Andrew while John brought his brother James. They both, along with their brothers, gave up their fishing business, at the same time (Lu. 5:10f.). Peter was admitted to the inner circle of Christ's friends (Peter, James and John) as appears several times in the Gospels. This item calls for more discussion in a separate chapter. We shall here consider the various incidents that occur when John and Peter appear together without the other apostles. "It would be difficult to conceive two characters by nature more unlike than St. Peter and St. John" (Stalker, *op. cit.*, p. 61). And yet by grace their hearts are knit together like those of David and Jonathan.

2. *Probably sent together on the tour of Galilee.* We know that they were sent out "by two and two" (Mk. 6:7).

It is not stated how they were grouped on this first preaching tour. Swete thinks that they were paired according to the list in Matthew 10:2-4. If so, John went with his brother James and not with Peter. This is purely conjectural; and one guess is as good as another. My own opinion is that Peter and John went together on this epochal tour. Each would supplement the other in a wonderful way.

3. *Probably the two sent to prepare for the triumphal entry.* The Synoptics all (Mk. 11:1; Matt. 21:1; Lu. 19:29) mention the fact that Jesus "sends two of his disciples" to go into the village and secure the colt for Jesus to ride on the occasion of His triumphal entry into Jerusalem. Here again it is simply a natural inference that the two sent are Peter and John. Swete feels sure that Peter is one of the two: "The minuteness of Mark's account suggests that Peter was one of the two selected on this occasion." Broadus (on Matt. 21:1) thinks Peter and John are "very likely" the two apostles sent on this mission. I agree with the opinion of Broadus.

4. *The two sent to prepare for the last passover meal.* Here there is no conjecture, for Luke (22:8) expressly says: "And he sent Peter and John, saying, Go and make ready for us the passover, that we may eat." Mark (14:13) mentions that "he sends two of his disciples" but he does not give their names, probably because Peter was one of them and it was from him that Mark secured his information. Both Mark and Matthew (26:17) show that the disciples were sent in response to an inquiry as to where they were to eat the passover meal. The undoubted association of Peter and John here renders it probable that they are the two unnamed disciples sent to secure the colt for the triumphal entry. In both instances Mark merely states that "two" were sent, without giving their names. One begins to have a suspicion that Peter was quick to offer his services on such occasions, but that Jesus trusted more the skill and efficiency of the quiet John who said little, but did more to bring things to pass. Peter's aggressiveness and John's

steadiness made an ideal combination. They readily secured the colt for Jesus and promptly obtained the use of
the guest-chamber from "the goodman of the house." It is,
of course, possible that this is the house of Mary the mother
of John Mark, where the disciples met later for prayer
(Acts 12:13), though there is no real proof to that effect.
This was apparently on Thursday afternoon and the passover meal was to be observed at sundown. The Synoptics
plainly picture Jesus and the apostles eating the passover
meal at the regular time at the beginning of the 15th of
Nisan (sunset of Friday). The lamb was slain on the
afternoon of the 14th of Nisan. There are scholars who
insist that John's Gospel puts this meal eaten by Jesus and
the apostles a day ahead, and that Jesus, Himself, was put
to death at the time of the slaying of the paschal lamb.
But the natural meaning of the five passages in John (13:
1f., 27; 18:28; 19:14, 31), when properly understood, is in
harmony with the language of the Synoptics. For the proof
see my *Harmony of the Gospels for Students of the Life of
Christ* (pp. 279-284).

5. *The only two Apostles at the trial of Jesus.* Apparently John took the initiative after they had all fled from
Gethsemane, for "Peter followed him afar off" (Mk. 14:54).
However, John (18:15) puts it as if Peter was the one who
rallied first: "now Simon Peter followed Jesus, and so did
another disciple." This may merely be an instance of John's
customary method used in the Fourth Gospel of concealing
himself and his own activities. At any rate it was John who
was known to the high priest and who got Peter into the
court of the palace. The others do not seem to have come
near the trial of the Master. We are not surprised that the
great love of John for Jesus made him dare danger for himself and push on into the very court room where the trial
went on. It is common to throw stones at Peter for his
shameful denials of his Master when confronted by the
maids and the men gathered around the firelight and the
open door. Peter, however, did, at least, have courage

enough to come that close to the Master in His hour of need, whereas the ten held entirely aloof. To be sure, Peter had boasted more than the others of his loyalty and devotion even unto death, though they all chimed in and asserted theirs also. John, however, went further than Peter and was not ashamed to be known, even in the palace of the high priest, when his Master was on trial there for His life, as the friend and follower of Jesus. Ridicule and sneers may have been thrown at John for all that we know, but, if so, they glanced off without harming him. His very courage may have won him immunity from the rabble. Besides, John had not used a sword in Gethsemane as Peter did.

It is interesting to observe how these two bosom friends behave in the hour of peril. It is the more shrinking and retiring one who, like Joseph of Arimathea and Nicodemus, at the burial of Jesus, is fearless and bold, while Peter, who talked most and loudest of his courage, is the coward who slinks away with a broken heart before the pitying look of Jesus. We have seen already how at the Cross John, alone of the apostles, comes and takes his place with the women there. And yet it is to be noticed that John gives in his Gospel little concerning the trial of Jesus before the Sanhedrin, but chiefly supplementary important details of the trial before Pilate. Perhaps John had little heart to enlarge upon the report of the Synoptics concerning the conduct of Caiaphas and the Sanhedrin.

6. *The first two Apostles at the empty tomb.* Events have moved with suddenness to the fatal end of all the hopes of the apostles. The gloom of the night settled on their hearts heavily and they failed to recall the promise of Jesus that He would rise again on the third day. Only the Pharisees remembered that (Matt. 27:62). It would seem that Mary Magdalene ran ahead of the other women, as they approached the tomb on that fateful Sunday morning, wondering how to get the stone rolled away from before the tomb. She saw the stone pushed to one side and instantly concluded either that the enemies of Jesus had robbed the

grave of His body or that Joseph of Arimathea and Nicodemus had removed it to another place. Without waiting to investigate further or to discuss it with the other women Mary Magdalene, (not to be confused with Mary of Bethany or with the woman that was a sinner, Lu. 7:36-50) ran at once with speed to tell the story of the empty tomb to Peter and John. We have John's own account of this incident told with great vividness (20:1-10).

A verse of doubtful genuineness in Luke (24:12) mentions the fact that Peter visited the tomb, but no mention is made of John, though further on (verse 24) allusion is made to the visit of certain brethren who went to the tomb and found it empty. The use of the preposition *(pros)* twice in John seems to indicate that Peter and John were not stopping at the same place in Jerusalem. It is a wonder that Mary Magdalene was able to find Peter. His terrible denials may not have been known to her, though most likely Peter had told John his sad story. "Possibly Peter, after weeping bitterly by himself, had sobbed out his contrition on the bosom of this disciple whom Jesus loved; and John's forgiveness may have been to him a confirmation of the forgiveness of the Lord" (Stalker, *op. cit.*, p. 113). At any rate Mary Magdalene went to Peter, and John was willing to join with him in meeting the new strange crisis reported by Mary. It was a man's job and Mary knew instinctively to whom she should turn. As John tells it, Peter "went forth" first and "the other disciple," both the objects of the same personal affection by Jesus (Westcott), at once joined him. In silence "they were going on to the tomb" (John pictures the action by the use of the imperfect tense). In fact, it developed into a race between the two: "Now the two were running together" (descriptive imperfect again). The eager heart of each disciple gave wings to his feet as he ran. But "the other disciple ran ahead more swiftly than Peter and came first to the tomb" (aorist tenses this time). John was the younger, fleeter of foot and with a deeper love for Jesus to drive him on. The use of the superlative "first," when only two are compared, is common enough in the vernacular then, as well as now. On arriving John "stoops down beside the tomb and glanced at the linen clothes lying within," but true to his instinctive shrinking nature "did not enter in." "A natural feeling of awe would arrest one of the character of St. John" (Westcott). But Peter, following John and seeing his hesitation at the mouth of the tomb, went boldly in, as one would expect him to do, and "looked carefully at the linen clothes lying there, and the napkin that had been upon his head not lying with the linen clothes but rolled up in a place apart." Peter saw all this by careful scrutiny, but drew no conclusion from the facts observed. The courageous impulsiveness of Peter overcame John's timidity so that then he also went on into the tomb "at once without a look or a pause" (Westcott), the last to enter though the first to arrive as John rather proudly repeats.

"This strongly suggests that we are dealing with the narrative of an eye-witness" (Bernard). John, of course, saw precisely what Peter had already seen, but the result on his fine sensitive nature was different. John at once "believed." Believed what? Certainly not just that the body had been removed by foe or friend as Mary had said. "In great crises of experience the mind is preternaturally active and into minutes can crowd the thinking of years" (Stalker, *op. cit.*, p. 118). John drew an inference from the orderly arrangement of the headkerchief that showed that no rude or rough hand had removed it. Only the living Lord Himself could have thus slipped out of this head bandage and left it undisturbed. "The undisturbed grave-clothes shows that the Lord had risen through and out of them. The facecloth carefully rolled up, the action of the living Lord" (Westcott). There was no evidence of haste. "The deserted tomb bore the marks of perfect calm. It was clear, therefore, that the body had not been stolen by enemies; it was scarcely less clear that it had not been taken away by friends" (Westcott).

We do not know whether John at this moment opened his heart to Peter or not. Stalker (*op. cit.*, p. 117) inclines to think so: "This was the most revolutionary moment of their lives, though both of them experienced other moments, both before and after, of vast importance. There, standing alone in the tomb in the morning light, they saw the glory of their Master as they had not seen it even on the Mount of Transfiguration; and they saw, in a flash, the course of their own future history." John saw all this, but one does not feel sure that Peter did, just yet. In fact, John mentions his own belief as a thing apart. Here, before he saw the Risen Christ, he "believed" that He was alive. In his old age he cherished this item in his life as one that gave him joy. He did not wait, like Thomas, for ocular demonstration before he believed. He believed without seeing.

Peter soon received a special message from the Risen Lord (Mk. 16:7) and the Master appeared to him alone (Lu. 24:34; I Cor. 15:5), an event of great importance. But John anticipated all these proofs and was the first of the apostles to believe that the Master was alive. One is entitled to think that John did not regard the report of the women as "idle talk" (Lu. 24:11) and did not "disbelieve" (Mk. 16:11) the words of Mary Magdalene. From the nature of the case, the circumstances that induced belief in John were not such as to convince others. John explains here that it was only "belief" on his part as yet and not "knowledge," because "as yet they knew not the scripture (probably Ps. 16:10), that he must rise again from the dead." They all should have known it, of course, for Jesus had repeatedly told them that on the third day He would rise from the dead. It was now the third day (Lu. 24:21), but the light did not yet shine into their hearts. John saw the glimmer of hope and his heart leaped in faith to greet it. John appears at his very best in this scene by the empty tomb of Jesus, and the new day of hope dawns for him then and there. If Jesus was indeed alive again, the Kingdom of God was alive also. There was a future for John and for all the rest. The death of Christ left the disciples "without a head or a plan; and nothing remained for them but to return to their lowly occupations, disillusioned and discredited men" (Stalker, *op. cit.*, p. 121). John was the first of the apostles to revive his faith from the wreck of their hopes. He was himself along with the others to see the risen Lord this very night (Jo. 20:19-25), when his faith became the knowledge of actual experience.

7. *Peter's interest in John by the Sea of Galilee.* The sons of Zebedee are mentioned as in the group of seven disciples by the Sea of Galilee (Jo. 21:2) and it is "the disciple whom Jesus loved" who recognizes the Lord Jesus on the shore (verse 7). It seems clear that John also heard the immortal dialogue between Jesus and Peter concerning Peter's love for Jesus (21:15-19), for it is reported in life-like fashion. So then, when Jesus pointed out to Peter that he would in time glorify God by a martyr's death, "Peter, turning about, sees the disciple whom Jesus loved, following, who also at the supper leaned upon his bosom and said, 'Lord, who is the one who betrays thee?' Peter, therefore, seeing this man says to Jesus, 'Lord, and of this one, what?'" (21:20f.). Apparently, when Jesus had said to Peter, "Keep on following me," Jesus and Peter moved away from the group. "And as they moved away from the others, John went after them, not doubting that he was welcome whenever Jesus called his close friend Peter" (Bernard).

The whole picture is alive, if the reference to the scene at the last supper when John reclined on the bosom of Christ "is added here to explain the close connection of St. John with St. Peter, and the confidence with which St. John ventured to follow even without a special invitation" (Westcott). The query of Peter about the destiny of John is quite natural after what Jesus had just said about Peter's own destiny. "The fact that St. John was following was itself an unspoken question as to the future, and asking of the Lord's will" (Westcott). The question of Peter was singularly short, almost abrupt, but not unkind, though full of

curiosity on Peter's part about the future of his closest
friend. The reply of Jesus implies that Peter's curiosity had
gone too far, to the neglect of his own imperative duty to
keep on following Jesus that he might not repeat his previous back-sliding: "If I wish him to remain while I am coming, what is it to thee? Do thou keep on following me"
(21:22). The Master repeats the command to Peter as his
own deepest concern, and emphasizes it by the juxtaposition
of the personal pronouns, "thou me" *(su moi)*. The condition (third class with uncertainty involved) does not mean
that Jesus does actually wish John to live on till He comes
back again. Note the precise idea, "while I am coming,"
not "till I come." But there is a distinct rebuke to Peter
for his idle curiosity concerning the destiny of the Apostle
John. Stalker quotes "a deep student of human nature"
(op. cit., p. 138) pertinently: "There are two great vanities
in man with respect to knowledge—the one to neglect to
know what it is our duty to know, and the other a curiosity
to know what it does not belong to us to know." Peter was
here confronted with both of these "vanities." He was in
peril of covering up the sense of his own duty to keep on
following Christ by his eager curiosity about the future of
his intimate friend. Jesus sharply calls Peter back to the
atmosphere of the episode immediately preceding, when He
had probed his heart in order to equip him for his own work
as shepherd of the sheep.

John tells about this rebuke of Peter's curiosity, out of
no desire to depreciate his friend, but to correct a misinterpretation of Christ's words that was still current when he
wrote his Gospel: "There went out therefore this saying
among the brethren that that disciple dies not." It is not
strange that the word of Jesus should have been thus twisted
by constant repetition, especially as John lived on after all
the other apostles had died. Augustine notes that even in
his day some people said that they had seen the earth over
John's grave in Ephesus move as if he were still alive.
John wishes to correct a false impression by repeating pre-

cisely what Jesus did say. At the time of writing John was
still alive. Incidentally this correction is proof that the
apostle John wrote the appendix (chapter 21) as well as the
rest of the book. Whether he wrote it near the time of
Nero or in the reign of Domitian, he was still alive long
after A.D. 44, when his brother James was put to death
by Herod Agrippa I. If John was not alive when the appendix was written, there was no need for the story to be
corrected. This interpretation disposes also of any theory
that any one else than the Apostle John, the Beloved Disciple, wrote the Gospel. Bernard on verse 24 says: *"Prima
facie,* this indicates that the Beloved Disciple wrote the
Gospel with his own hand, including the appendix, and not
only that his reminiscences are behind it." But Bernard
thinks that *graphō* (write) can mean "dictation," which is
true; the word is used in John 19:19, when Pilate ordered
the writing of the title on the Cross, and in Romans 16:22
where Tertius wrote at Paul's dictation. That interpretation is possible, of course, though quite improbable. Bernard concludes: "The elders of the church certified that the
Beloved Disciple caused these things to be written. They
were put into shape by the writer who took them down, and
afterwards published them, not as his own, but as 'the Gospel according to John.'" Yes, but why, if John was long
dead already, publish the correctness of a false report that
he was not to die? The theory vanishes into thin air.
Streeter (*op. cit.,* p. 432) sees the situation more clearly
than does Bernard. He pointedly says: "But if the verse
(xxi. 24), which identifies the actual author with the Beloved Disciple is a later insertion, it is open to us to surmise
that it is a mistaken identification." The elders of Ephesus
themselves, according to Streeter, blundered in saying that
the Beloved Disciple wrote this Gospel. That is a serious
charge to make against the very men in Ephesus who knew
the facts about the life and death of the Apostle John and
who also knew all about the so-called Presbyter John—if
there was such a man. But Streeter goes further still, and

charges the actual author of the book with posing as John even though John was long dead: "And that the Apostle the author had in mind was John can hardly, I think, admit of serious doubt." So then this point of contact between Peter and John in the appendix throws a real light, not only on the men themselves, but also on the problem of the authorship of the Gospel. The critics who deny the Johannine authorship of the Fourth Gospel are hard put to it to explain the appearance of the words of Jesus to Peter about John's destiny, if John was already long dead when the Gospel was written. Harnack, indeed, holds that the elders at Ephesus are guilty of a deliberate untruth (*Chronologie,* p. ix). This is the last direct glimpse of John that we get in the Gospels and it comes from the Beloved Disciple himself.

8. *John with Peter at the Gate Beautiful.* John was, of course, with the disciples on the mountain in Galilee when Jesus appeared to more than five hundred; and on Olivet, near Jerusalem, when he ascended on high. He is named as one of the group that waited for the promise of the Father (Acts 1:13), but he is not described as taking an active part on the great day of Pentecost, except indirectly in the statement that "Peter stood with the eleven" as the spokesman for them all. In the Acts thereafter, whenever John is mentioned, it is in connection with Peter. So here in Acts 3:1-26—"Peter and John were going up into the temple for the hour of prayer the ninth" (3 P.M.). We have already become used to the idea of seeing Peter and John together in the life of Christ in the Gospels. The same holds true in the early part of the Acts. Furneaux does not think that there was much difference in their age, "for the idea that Peter was older rests only on the fancy of artists. . . . The contrast in character and disposition—the one ardent and impulsive, the other quiet and thoughtful—may, as often happens, have drawn them together. Their intimate companionship at the close of the Gospel story and at the beginning of the apostolic history is a connecting link of great value." Kirsopp Lake and H. J. Cadbury (Vol. IV

The Acts of the Apostles) raise the question whether by John here Luke does not mean the John Mark of Acts 12: 12, 25. But that is an unlikely hypothesis.

John in the Acts does not anywhere play an active part. It is Peter who speaks to the lame man (3:4, 6) when "together with John" he gazed at the beggar. And in verse 11, when the crowd gathered, the now healed man held on to both Peter and John—holding Peter with one hand and John with the other—as together responsible, in some sense, for his cure. So also in verse 12 Peter includes John, as he did in verse 4, as a participant in what was done by God's power in Christ the Risen Lord (verse 16). And in 4:1 Luke adds that "while they were speaking to the people" the Sadducees and officers of the temple came upon them. This obviously means that John had some part in the speaking, or at least that he heartly approved of what Peter said. Certainly, John was as full of the Holy Spirit during those days as was Peter or any one else. Peter stands out more sharply in Luke's narrative, but John is there also and he counted for much.

9. *John with Peter before the Sanhedrin.* Both were arrested by the officers (Acts 4:3) and put in ward against the morrow, for it was already evening, "because they were teaching the people and proclaiming in Jesus the resurrection from the dead" (4:2). John shares with Peter the distinction of being the first of the apostles to be placed in prison for Christ's sake. Jesus had foretold that fate for them and now it is become a reality for Peter and John. As usual the spokesman, Peter, makes the defence next day before the Sanhedrin, but he includes John in his statement of the case (4:9). He said skilfully: "If we to-day are being examined for a good deed done to an impotent man." We have no word from John in the Acts, but the Sanhedrin, we read (verse 13), "beholding the boldness of Peter and John and having perceived that they were unlettered and common men, began to marvel and to recognize them that they were with Jesus." It is possible, of course, that

some of the Sanhedrin may have recalled at this moment that they had seen both Peter and John in that very hall on the morning of the crucifixion" (Furneaux). Besides, John was himself known to Caiaphas (Jo. 18:15). They were not recognized on the day before (Acts 4:2), but the very boldness of the men drew close attention to them and led to the recognition. But all the more they were astonished at the courage and skill of their defence since they were plainly not educated rabbis, not schoolmen at all, but unlettered *(agrammatoi)* and without official position of any kind, merely private men *(idiōtai)*, former fishermen, as we know, who were defying the highest ecclesiastics of the Jewish people.

The Sadducees were angered because Peter and John had been publicly proclaiming the actual resurrection from the dead of Jesus, the very man whom they, with the help of the Pharisees, had persuaded Pilate to crucify. The Sadducees as over against the Pharisees, denied the possibility of resurrection for any one, and so they take the initiative in this arrest. But, instead of disproving the fact of Christ's resurrection by showing that his body was still in the tomb, they curtly arrest Peter and John for preaching about it. The worst of the situation from their standpoint was that the once lame man was standing before them all, walking and leaping and praising God. It was therefore useless to deny the miracle.

In their predicament the Sanhedrin threaten Peter and John and order them "no longer to speak in this name to any one." But both Peter and John replied to them: "We are not able not to go on speaking what we saw and heard." That is to say, they defy the authorities who have stepped in between them and their duty to God. So after more threats they were released and "went to their own folks and announced what the chief priests and the elders had said to them" (4:23). It was Peter and John's first experience in prison and they came out nobly, but with a wholesome fear that drove them to earnest prayer to God for more courage

and proof of God's favour. That proof came in the shaking
of the house "and they went on speaking the word of God
with boldness." John is present in all this picture, though
it is Peter who is the leading speaker. Later all the apostles
will know what it is to be in prison for Christ (5:18-42)
when they are delivered by the skill of Gamaliel, the Pharisee, in scoring a point against the Sadducees. Once more
they were commanded "not to go on speaking in the name
of Jesus" (5:40), but this time they rejoiced "that they
were counted worthy to be dishonoured for the Name. So
every day in the temple and from house to house they did
not cease teaching and preaching (evangelizing) Jesus as
the Messiah" (5:41f.).

For a time John appears no more in the picture in Acts,
but he had learned how to suffer. His brother James will
become so bold a champion of Christ that Herod Antipas I,
to please the Jews, will slay him by the sword. At the same
time he put Peter in prison (12:1-3). Why John escaped
on this occasion we do not know. No doubt it was the
boldness of James in his testimony for Christ that made him
the shining mark as the first of the apostles to die for Christ.

10. *John sent with Peter to investigate the work of Philip
in Samaria*. It is noteworthy that it was Philip, the evange-
listic deacon, who brought the gospel to Samaria at the time
that the Jerusalem Christians were scattered by Saul's persecution (Acts 8:4f.). The rest were preaching as they fled
from the wrath of Saul. Jesus had preached in Samaria
once with notable results, but the apostles shared the an-
tipathy of the Jews towards this mongrel race (half Jew,
half Gentile). Technically Jews, they were not admitted
to full fellowship. Naturally, therefore, the report of what
Philip had done in starting a church in Samaria called for
investigation by the apostles who in spite of Saul's persecution, were still in Jerusalem. So they sent Peter and John,
the outstanding leaders among them, to see how matters
stood in Samaria (Acts 8:14f.).

To both it was a strange experience, since on their first

preaching tour Jesus had forbidden them to go into a Samaritan city (Matt. 10:6). John, moreover, would recall how he and his brother were so angry with a Samaritan village (Lu. 9:54). "He was sent to the very people on whom, a few years before, he had wished to call down fire from heaven, to invoke the falling of another flame, which should burn indeed, but not consume" (Furneaux). At first it would seem that John and Peter were puzzled over what to do. "They prayed concerning them that they might receive the Holy Spirit."

Hackett takes this passage to mean that they prayed that the faith of the Samaritans might be confirmed by the baptism of the Holy Spirit, since they had only been baptized in the name of the Lord Jesus. But, more plausibly, Furneaux holds that "the prayer was for the restoring of their own doubts. Though their Master had commissioned them to be His witnesses in Samaria (1:8), He had earlier forbidden them to enter into 'any city of the Samaritans' (Matt. x. 5). How were they to know that these old enemies were now indeed one with themselves? They would leave the solution with their Lord. If the Spirit descended on these converts, their doubts would be answered. He would testify to the expansion of the Church, as He had testified to its formation." They had been converted by the Holy Spirit before baptism, but what Peter and John prayed for was some demonstration like that at the great Pentecost and such as came later to Peter's surprise on the household of Cornelius in Caesarea. "To the Apostles this was the dawn of a new day—the day when others than Jews as proselytes were first admitted to the church" (Furneaux). Peter and John laid their hands on them as on the deacons in Acts 6:6 and as Paul did in Acts 19:6. But there was no laying on of hands when the Holy Spirit came upon the believers at Pentecost in Jerusalem (Acts 2:4, 33; 4:31) and in Caesarea (10:44). Simon Magus "saw" that the converts of Philip now received the Holy Spirit, apparently because they spoke with tongues.

John and Peter were wholly satisfied with the genuineness of the work of grace in Samaria and on the way back to Jerusalem to make their report, they themselves preached the gospel in many villages in Samaria. They were now as much involved in this departure as was Philip. The novelty was more in the overcoming of prejudice than anything else, for the Samaritans had been circumcised and were technically Jews. The problem of preaching the gospel to real Gentiles was to come up later to Peter, Barnabas and Paul in Caesarea and Antioch.

This is the last time that John appears in the Acts and it is in connection with Peter. Luke drops them to take up the story of Paul's missionary campaigns, but it is plain that Peter and John were preparing the way for the spread of the gospel into the wide world. Peter will have his struggles over the problem whether the Gentile Christians are to become Jews, also, but he will be led into the freedom that is in Christ. In due time John will take his stand with Peter by the side of Paul and Barnabas in Jerusalem in favour of Gentile freedom. We are, however, told nothing concerning the coming of John into this open road. He must have known the story of Peter's own experiences at Joppa and Caesarea, as he gave them to the church in Jerusalem when the Pharisaic wing of the church there arraigned Peter for entering the house of Cornelius (Acts 1:1-18). Beyond a doubt John stood with Peter on that occasion and rejoiced in his vindication. These two great apostles, the two stars among the twelve, understood one another on this occasion, as always. That, of course, is not to say that John approved Peter's cowardly and shameful denials of his Lord, but that he understood Peter's weakness and sympathised with his struggles and helped him to come back and to strengthen the brethren as Jesus had charged him to do. Peter had by now forged ahead to leadership in Christianity, but John ere long will soar above him as the eagle, the theologian. Peter will in later centuries come to be thought of in an artificial ecclesiastic sense as the first pope and the sole custodian of the keys in a way never meant by the Lord Jesus. But John's greatness will be quite independent of ecclesiasticism. There was no jealousy between Peter and John. "St. Peter must have known all the time that in this friendship he was getting more than he could give. . . . The things of Christ were shown to him (John), the character of Christ was put upon him, the spirit of Christ was breathed into him. And this gave to his friendship a priceless value; for all other advantages which friendship can confer grow small in comparison with the charm and the influence of the beauty of holiness' (Stalker, *op. cit.*, p. 153f.).

VI

ONE OF THE INNER CIRCLE

We are trying to get into the actual life of John, as far as practicable, by the help of the meagre materials at hand. So then we come back and look at him from another angle.

1. *Three stages in John's relation to Jesus.* Stalker (*op. cit.*, p. 5) has sharply indicated this aspect of John's life as Believer, Disciple, Apostle. He was, first a believer when he turned from the Baptist to Jesus and accepted him as the Messiah at Bethany beyond Jordan (Jo. 1:35f.). Stalker calls him disciple when he left all to follow Jesus (Lu. 5: 1-11), and apostle when Jesus formally called the twelve and named them apostles (Lu. 6:13). This is a convenient way of looking at the matter, but not strictly correct, since John calls the first six believers "disciples immediately after they became believers (Jo. 2:2, 11, 12, 22; 3:22; 4:2, 9, 27, 31, 33) and before the four left all to follow Jesus. The point in the call by the Sea of Galilee is that these four are now called to follow Jesus permanently, renouncing entirely the business of fishing. The term disciple overlaps two stages of the process. There were three transitions in John's career as a Christian but perhaps disciple, personal follower, and apostle might suit the facts a shade better.

2. *The two pairs of brothers.* Before the twelve apostles were set apart, and even among the first six disciples (Andrew and Peter, John and James, Philip and Nathanael), the first two pairs of brothers stand out and apart. They were the first to come to Jesus from the Baptist and to own him as the Messiah. They are the first to be called to continuous following of Jesus. They are named first in all the

73

four lists of the twelve apostles (Mk. 3:16f.; Matt. 10:2f.; Lu. 6:14f.; Acts 1:13f.). It is possible that another pair of brothers existed among the twelve, James the son of Alphaeus and Judas the brother of James (Lu. 6:15; Acts 1:15), though this is not certain. The Greek has simply "James's Judas." But these two, if brothers, play no such part in the ministry of Jesus as do Andrew and Peter, James and John. These four are the apostles, according to Mark (13:3), who on the Mount of Olives ask Jesus privately to explain what and when will be the things of which He so solemnly spoke, as they left the temple for the last time. There was a bond between Jesus and these brothers because they were the very first who stepped out from the crowd and took an open stand by His side. So then, in choosing the twelve apostles, it was only natural that the Master should pick these four out first.

"In choosing the Twelve, Jesus was determining not only their life but also His own. If they were to be with Him, He was to be with them" (Stalker, *op. cit.*, p. 58). It is often a matter of wonder why Jesus did not select school men. The scribes opposed him. Nicodemus and Joseph of Arimathea hesitated for long. Paul was called by Jesus later to do what these twelve had not done, to take the gospel to the Gentiles. One has to believe that Jesus made the best choice possible with the material at hand. He did it after a night of prayer about it. Stalker thinks that at the same time John was praying about it at the foot of the mountain. Perhaps! At any rate John was to be the one who would enter into the closest fellowship with the Master and who would be able to give to the world the highest examples of His teaching. These men Jesus chose "that they might be with him" (Mk. 3:14). They were to preach and to heal, but they were first to be with Jesus, to listen to His tabletalk, to hear His sermons, His parables, to see His miracles, to see men turn from sin to eternal life, to see the Master in action at close quarters. "The followers of a Socrates, the catechumens of an Ambrose, the students of a Tholuck, the pupils of an Arnold, have informed the world of the magnetism with which their teachers held them; but no man ever spake and no teacher ever charmed like this One" (Stalker, *op. cit.*, p. 55).

3. *A circle within the circle.* The twelve apostles formed a circle that inevitably marked them off from the other disciples of Jesus. There was, as we have seen, the still narrower circle of the two pairs of brothers. Some even think that James and John were cousins of Jesus on the assumption that Salome, the mother of James and John, was the sister of the mother of Jesus. If true, that would inevitably make a close tie between Jesus and the sons of Zebedee. One of these brothers, John, was "the disciple whom Jesus loved" most of all. But Peter was drawn into the circle with James and John on several occasions when Andrew is not included. Why this still narrower circle of three was drawn, leaving Andrew out, we cannot tell. Two of this circle (Peter and John) were undoubtedly the most gifted of all the twelve, and James was clearly a man of energy and force, since he was the first martyr among the twelve. One does not wonder that Peter with all his impulsive versatility and warm-hearted humanness was included with John and James; but why was not Andrew, also, taken into this sacred circle? It was Andrew who brought his brother Simon to Jesus, the greatest deed of his whole life, and one would not expect Peter to brush Andrew aside so that Andrew would be known and named as the brother of Simon Peter (Lu. 6:14). No doubt Peter did outshine Andrew in sheer ability and aggressiveness, but Andrew wins our admiration by the poise and balance of his character. However, on the three occasions when the inner circle of three appear in the Gospels, Jesus selects them and it is clear that there is no private clique at all. Jesus beyond a doubt had His reasons for selecting these three men and these alone on these important occasions. It is a high honour, one of the highest ever given any men, to be thus

chosen by the Master. John is in this group each time and wears his crown with Peter and James.

(a) *In the home of Jairus.* Luke (8:51) names them "Peter and John and James" while Mark (5:37) has "Peter and James and John, the brother of James." For a while, just as Andrew was spoken of as "the brother of Peter," John was known as "the brother of James," though he, like Andrew, had brought his brother to Jesus. But in the long run men seek their real level in history as in life. It was a solemn occasion when Jesus reached the home of Jairus. The little daughter of the ruler was dead and the mourners were raising a tumult and weeping and wailing greatly. They laughed Jesus to scorn when He insisted that the maid was not dead (to stay dead), but was sleeping. Calmly Jesus said: "Fear not: only believe, and she shall be made whole. And having come to the house he did not allow any one to go in with him except Peter and John and James and the father of the maid and the mother" (Lu. 8:51).

Why did Jesus pick out "the chosen three" (*eklektōn eklektoteroi*, Clement of Alexandria calls them, "more elect that the elect")? Clearly it would not have done to take the entire twelve in. That would have been confusion for the father and mother who were in agony of heart. Jairus had already the definite promise of Jesus that He would raise his daughter from the dead. Plummer suggests that these three apostles are admitted for the sake of the twelve. He adds: "Moreover, they were in character most fitted to profit by the miracle." At any rate, John with Peter and James saw this amazing thing. They saw Jesus take the maid by the hand and bid her arise. To the astonishment of all, they saw her arise, walk, and eat. Jesus commanded the parents not to tell "to keep them from letting the effect of this great blessing evaporate in vainglorious gossip. To thank God at home would be far more profitable than talking it abroad" (Plummer). We may be sure that this tremendous miracle left its mark on the mind and heart of

John, who so often speaks of Jesus as having power of life over death.

(b) *On the Mount of Transfiguration.* Each of the Synoptics states that Jesus "took with him Peter and James and John" (Mk. 9:2; Matt. 17:1; Lu. 9:28); only Luke, as before, has it "Peter and John and James," possibly (Plummer) because when Luke wrote, John had become better known than James who was now dead. Jesus chose this same inner circle to go with Him up into the mountain where He was to pray (Lu. 9:28). It was a high privilege for these three apostles to share His fellowship in time of prayer. Sometimes the Master went into the mountain alone and communed with His Father. But this night—the sleepiness of the apostles, the bright light, and "on the next day" prove that it was night—Jesus felt the need of fellowship and took along this inner circle to be witnesses also (Tertullian) of His glory. "To the Three it was a great privilege to see their Master in this hour of exaltation. Two of them refer to it in their writings as a crowning mercy of their experience" (Stalker, *op. cit.*, p. 71). So Peter (II Pet. 1:16f.) speaks of being an eye-witness of Christ's majesty and majestic glory on the mount and records the message of the Father for the benefit of the Three. John (Jo. 1:14) may have this great event chiefly in mind when he says that "we beheld his glory." We cannot say that the three apostles behaved in the most becoming fashion while the Master prayed and was transfigured with the glory of heaven; talked with Moses and Elijah about His coming death *(exodus)* in Jerusalem, which was in truth to be His real glorification (Gould) as Jesus terms it in John's Gospel (13:31f.). But they "were heavy with sleep." It was Peter, not John, who made the foolish proposal about the three tabernacles, but even John on this occasion failed to be of special comfort to the Master in His hour of high exaltation and preparation for the Cross. Nevertheless he and the other two had at least seen the glory of Jesus as the Son of God, and they could treasure the memory of this glory in their hearts "until the Son of Man be risen from the dead" (Matt. 17:9). They were not to tell the nine as yet what they had seen, but "the conviction wrought in their minds by what they witnessed would impart itself to all, through their tone and general influence" (Broadus). Certainly that was one purpose of the Master in having them with Him on the Mount. Alas, in the dark hour to come they failed miserably in holding fast to this proof—for themselves, not to speak of others! John, it is true, did rally enough to go to the courtroom and to stand by the Cross, but he did not show any evidence of supreme confidence, or of belief in the resurrection as sure to happen in three days. Stalker (*op. cit.*, p. 71) felicitously observes: "All who meet with Christ on the heights will, in some degree, share in the same privileges" of the three chosen apostles. Yes, but let us hope that better use will be made of them.

(c) *In the Garden of Gethsemane.* Judas, after being exposed in the upper room at the last passover meal, had gone upon his hellish mission of betraying his Lord. The Master had opened His very heart in words of comfort and cheer to the remaining eleven (Jo. 13 to 16) and, after leaving the upper room, had made the intercessory prayer for them and for all who will believe on Him (Jo. 17). He crossed over the brook Kidron into the garden called Gethsemane, as His custom was (Lu. 22:39), a custom known to, and taken advantage of by, Judas. He asked eight of the apostles to sit by the entrance "while I go yonder and pray" (Matt. 26:36). Then once again He took with Him Peter and James and John (Mk. 14:33) "and began to be grieved and distressed" (Matt. 26:37) (literally "not at home"—German *unheimlich*—). He had already prayed for a return to the glory with the Father (Jo. 17:5). Mark (14:33) uses the same verb *(adēmonein)* with the addition of "greatly amazed" *(ekthambeisthai)*.

The Master Himself was amazed at His emotions as He faced the crisis in Gethsemane. He confesses to the three

His sorrow of soul "even unto death" and urges that they pray that they enter not into temptation like this (Lu. 22: 40). "Abide ye here and watch with me," He pleads. Then He went forward about a stone's throw and fell on His face on the ground and prayed "that, if it was possible, the hour might pass away from him"; He said: "Abba, Father, all things are possible to thee; bear this cup away from me: howbeit, not what I will, but what thou wilt" (Mk. 14: 35f.). Jesus was in the throes of His greatest temptation, namely, to turn back from the Cross. He did not know till now that the hour, when it did come, would bear so heavily upon this heart with the burden of the world's sin. It is small wonder that this outcry came, but there was instant acquiescence in the Father's will. He would go on to the Cross. He would drink the cup to the lees. Jesus had sought solitude in His hour of suffering and He longed for sympathy. Hence He did not go far from the three chosen ones. Paraphrasing freely: It was a golden opportunity for the Three. What insight might they not have obtained into the heart of their Master. What service, divinely recompensed, might they not have borne Him! What matchless opportunity here offered to prepare themselves to play the man in the scenes about to ensue! But it was a lost opportunity (Stalker, *op. cit.*, p. 73f.). They were near the Master, but they were not with Him in spirit. They were "sleeping for sorrow," even John. Jesus excused them on the ground that "the spirit indeed is willing, but the flesh is weak." The second time He found them sleeping and ashamed. "They knew not how to answer him." The third time they were still asleep, but it no longer mattered. "Sleep on now and take your rest; it suffices; the hour has come; behold, the Son of man is betrayed into the hands of the sinners. Arise, let us be going; behold the one who betrays me has arrived" (Mk. 14:41f.).

It was all over. The Master had won His victory over Satan without their help, at least, without their active sympathy. It was a tragedy that even the disciple whom

Jesus loved failed Him in this supreme hour. "The opportunity was passed; and nothing could ever recall it" (Stalker, *op. cit.*, p. 74), that is the tragedy for Peter and James and John. Would the eight waiting by the entrance to the Garden have done any better? There is no proof of it. These three were the inner circle of Christ's chosen friends and they fell down lamentably when He needed them most. Do we do better when Christ takes us with Him into Gethsemane? The three failed Jesus worse here in His hour of agony, when He needed sympathetic support, than on the mountain top of privilege, when they beheld His glory. Both experiences concerned the death of Jesus on the Cross for the sin of the world, that atoning death the mysteries of which still baffle the greatest minds of earth. It was natural for Jesus to wish to have these dear friends with Him in His hour of triumph, but it was "still more an instinct of the heart to wish this in the season of sorrow" (Stalker, *op. cit.*, p. 73). They fell asleep on both occasions. But Jesus did not cast John off for this shortcoming. Though he had missed his greatest opportunity, though he had failed our Lord in His highest moments and deepest agony, John remained still the disciple whom Jesus loved most of all.

VII

A MAN OF SPIRITUAL INSIGHT

1. *A Johannine style and type.* The Johannine books
reveal a man of a special type. There is a Johannine style
and a Johannine type of teaching. "Now of all the New
Testament writers St. John is the most peculiar. He cannot make a remark, or describe a scene, or report a conver-
sation or a speech, without doing it as no one else could"
(Stalker, *op. cit.*, p. 14). Indeed, so definite is this Johannine style and method of approach that it differentiates to
some extent the reports of the sayings of Jesus in the Fourth
Gospel as compared with the words of the Master in the
Synoptic Gospels. Each Gospel exercises a certain amount
of freedom in the report and translation of the words of
Christ from the Aramaic in which they were usually spoken.
And yet there is a distinct Johannine flavour in Matthew
11:25-30 (Lu. 10:21-24), "a Johannine aerolite" according
to some scholars. The same note appears in Matthew 28:
18-20. Sometimes, as in John 3:16, 31, it is not easy to tell
whether John is giving the words of Jesus or reflections of
his own on the teaching of the Master. But the Johannine
style is indisputable in the Gospel, the Epistles, and also in
the Apocalypse—though less so in this last because of the
subject matter.

Incidentally, this is an internal argument for identity of
authorship and for the unity of the Fourth Gospel. Streeter,
though rejecting the Johannine authorship of the Gospel,
is strong for the unity of the book: "From the considerations I have adduced it would seem clear that the hope that
by critical analysis sufficiently refined we can reconstruct

sources used by John is chimerical." "Simplicity and unity are its two characteristics. There is nothing vague or abstract about it; it is altogether clear and concrete. The spiritual and the practical are at one with John" (Hayes, *op. cit.*, p. 69). Simple words carry profound meanings and reach the highest heights, words like light, life, love are contrasted with darkness, death, hate. He is fond of repetition as well as contrast. He expects you to gaze long and see deep into the crystal lake, to gaze until you do see what you do not see at a mere superficial glance. "This Gospel speaks a language to which no parallel whatever is to be found in the whole compass of literature; such child-like simplicity, with such contemplative profundity; such life, and such deep rest; such sadness, and such serenity; and above all, such a breadth of love, are eternal life which has already dawned, a life which rests in God, which has overcome the disunion between the world that is and the world to come, the human and the Divine" (Tholuck, *Commentary on John*, p. 18).

2. *The first to believe in the resurrection of Jesus.* We have already seen how John reveals pardonable pride in the fact that, though Peter entered the tomb first, he was the first to believe that Jesus had risen from the dead (Jo. 20: 8). He believed before he saw the Master, believed without seeing—according to the beatitude of Jesus to Thomas, who had not done so (20:29). This priority of faith on John's part was due to his fine spiritual insight. He was able to see what Peter did not, namely, the meaning of the orderly arrangement of the graveclothes of Jesus. Peter saw the facts, but John perceived the meaning of the facts. John was here "enlightened," and not Peter, also, as Benham states (*St. John and His Work*, p. 36). But Benham (p. 35) rightly observes that the description indicates "the minute observation and absolute recollection of the eye-witness."

It is precisely because John betrays this keenness of perception into the reality of things that we care so much to

know who the author of the Fourth Gospel is and all that
we can learn about him. "It *must* make a difference
whether works that have profoundly affected Christian
thought in every age proceed from one who stood by the
side of Christ and wrote from recollection of an ineffaceable
experience, or whether they are from the hand of some unknown collector of stories, current in Christian circles long
after every eye-witness of the Saviour had passed away. It
is no mere question of literary or antiquarian interest. It
concerns the measure of security we feel, when reading these
writings, that we are in touch with one who knew, from
direct personal experience, the mind and will of Christ"
(Nolloth, *The Fourth Evangelist,* p. 6). Certainly in this
incident the Beloved Disciple means to tell his own experience as the first of the apostles to believe that Jesus had
risen from the dead. If it is merely some one else of a
later time posing as the Apostle John, the truth fades from
the picture and reality becomes romance. It is a crown of
glory for John and a rainbow of hope for us, if true. If not,
it is a mere will-o'-the-wisp.

3. *John's quick recognition of Jesus.* As early that wonderful morning Jesus stood on the beach by the beloved lake
in Galilee, "the disciples knew not that it was Jesus" (Jo.
21:4). It was some distance to the shore from the boat in
which, with no luck at all, they had been fishing all night.
They did not apparently recognise Him by His voice or
manner when he directed them to cast the net on the right
side of the boat. But, when "they were not able to draw it
for the multitude of fishes, that disciple therefore whom
Jesus loved, says to Peter, 'It is the Lord.'" Whatever the
others thought, John needed no proof. He remembered that
other wonderful draught of fishes from this same lake after
a like failure (Lu. 5:10). Some unimaginative critics actually charge Luke and John with confusing the one incident
—as if Jesus could not or would not work similar miracles.
The two occasions are wholly different in time, place, circumstances. John's quick insight recalled what Jesus did

then. Even though he cannot see Him clearly in the early
dawn, he knows that this is the Lord Jesus now. Here again
it is John who *sees* first, while Peter *acts* first and leaps into
the water to go to the Master. "The entire scene is emi-
nently characteristic. It was St. John, the man of affection
and insight, who *discerned* Christ first; it was St. Peter the
man of passion and energy, who *reached* Him first. Each
was before the other in one respect, and both were the
leaders of the rest" (Stalker, *op. cit.*, p. 132). If John is
"the disciple whom Jesus loved," as we know to be the fact,
surely it is not strange that he should recognise the Risen
Christ before any of the others. He had not only a quick
and sensitive nature, but a surpassing love, as well, that
could tell the Master's presence almost without seeing Him.

4. *John the seer.* A seer is a prophet who sees what is
present and sometimes, in rapt vision, what is to come. In
the Apocalypse we have the seer in ecstatic rhapsody, but he
is the same seer in calmer mood in the Fourth Gospel. In
John 19:35 he alludes to himself as the witness of the blood
and water coming out of the pierced side of the Saviour:
"He who has seen has borne witness." This is characteristic
of John, who always could see what the others did not. He
could see further and deeper and higher than all the rest.
The eyes of his heart were illuminated more brilliantly; his
intellect had a clarity that was transparent. "John saw with
his heart and with his intuitions as well as with his eyes.
He saw deeper into the being and personality of Jesus than
any one else. The Fourth Gospel is the proof of that statement. He saw further into the future than any other
disciple, discerned the whole cause of the contest, and
glimpsed the triumph of the end. The Apocalypse is the
proof of this" (Hayes, *op. cit.*, p. 66). "The Fourth Gospel is remarkable for the new light it throws upon the ministry of our Lord. It regards that ministry from a new
point of view. It looks upon it with new eyes, the eyes of a
seer and a saint. John listened to the words of Jesus as the
others did; but his ears were opened to hear as they did

not hear. He heard the hidden harmonies. He saw into the very heart of things. He realized the supreme marvel of it all, and he gave it a most beautiful setting when he undertook to put it into writing for others to read and enjoy" (*ibid.*, p. 97).

5. *John the mystic.* He was a mystic as was Paul, and as every true Christian must be. Stalker calls mysticism John's distinctive peculiarity: "His peculiarity has been described by calling him a mystic: he does not deal much with the outside things, but lays hold of everything from within. A scene or occurrence is only interesting to him on account of the idea which it embodies. His thinking is intuitive: he does not reason like St. Paul, or exhort like St. Peter, but concentrates his visions on the object, which opens to his steady gaze" (*op. cit.*, p. 14). Streeter sees this clearly about the author of the Fourth Gospel (*op. cit.*, p. 366): "The starting point for any profitable study of the Fourth Gospel is the recognition of the author as a mystic—perhaps the greatest of all mystics. . . . His mysticism, like that of Paul, is a mysticism centered, not on Absolute Being, but on the Divine Christ. . . . The author of the Fourth Gospel stands between two worlds, the Hebrew and the Greek, at the confluence of the two greatest spiritual and intellectual traditions of our race. In him Plato and Isaiah meet. To call John a mystic is only correct so long as one remembers that in the Hebrew tradition the prophet is the counterpart of him whom elsewhere we style the mystic." According to Streeter, we must never forget that John "is a Jew first, and never quite a Greek." Jerome could say: "John excels in the depths of the divine mysteries." But John is a mystic whom the average Christian can understand. He can almost make us feel as if we too have reclined on the bosom of the Saviour.

In the Fourth Gospel John takes us into the very Holy of Holies as A. T. Pierson (*Keys to the Word,* p. 103) says: "It touches the heart of Christ. If Matthew corresponds to the Court of Israel, Mark to the Court of the Priests, Luke to the Court of the Gentiles, John leads us past into the Holy of Holies." Hear Philip Schaff also (*Addresses on John*, p. 482): "The Gospel according to John is the most original, the most important, the most influential book in all literature." Culross (*John Whom Jesus Loved*, p. 212) bears his witness to the blessed mystical power of this Gospel: "I believe the writings of John have been blotted by more penitents' tears and have won more hearts for the Redeemer than all the rest put together." Culross (p. 106f.) quotes also Matthias Claudius: "I am far from understanding all I read, yet often John's idea seems to hover before me in the distance; and even when I look into a place that is entirely dark, I have a possession of a great, glorious meaning, which I shall some day understand, and hence I catch so eagerly at every new exposition of the Gospel according to John." The greatest minds of earth are humble and reverent as they gaze at the pictures of Christ in the Fourth Gospel. Even James Drummond, the Unitarian scholar, feels this keenly (*Character and Authorship of the Fourth Gospel*, p. 1): "And when we remember how it has moulded the faith, and touched the heart, and calmed the sorrows of generations of men, we must approach it with no ordinary reverence, and with a desire to penetrate its inmost meaning, and become more thoroughly imbued with its kindling power." One of the clearest pictures of the Christ of John is drawn by the brilliant blind preacher of Edinburgh (*St. John's Portrait of Christ*) whose inner light was clearer than that of most men who can see with their eyes.

6. *John the theologian.* The early Christian writers called him, *ho theologos.* In fact, the Gospel of John is "confessedly determined, not by a purely biographical, but by a theological interest" (Drummond, *op. cit.*, p. 3). John says (20:30f.) "Many other signs therefore Jesus did before the disciples, which are not written in this book, but these have been written that ye may keep on believing that Jesus is the Messiah, the Son of God, and that believing ye may keep on having faith in his name." This apologetic

purpose does not tarnish or diminish the historical worth of
the book, but merely indicates the purpose of the author in
the selections made out of the vast amount of material at
hand. "This leads us to say next that John is the greatest
theologian and the most profound philosopher of the early
Christian church. . . . Even Baur agrees with this verdict.
He says, speaking of the Johannine type of thought: 'In it
the New Testament reaches its highest plane and its most
perfect form'" (Hayes, *op. cit.*, p. 68).

Paul is the great missionary statesman and constructive
theologian who battled successfully with Pharisaic narrowness in Christian circles and Gnostic speculations that
threatened to undermine Christianity. John rose to higher
heights than Paul, but was without Paul's argumentative
prowess. John "looks at everything from the standpoint
of the eternal life and light and love, but he sees these at
home in the human heart and incarnate in human history.
The riddle of the universe is no riddle to him. He has the
key which will unlock all its mysteries" (Hayes, *op. cit.*, p.
69). And even when our own eyes do not see so clearly as
John we can at least see that he sees and that he sees with
the steady gaze of one who knows. He is prophet (seer),
mystic, theologian. His "theology is reasonable and reasoned, but the processes of its reasoning are seldom in evidence. It is of the contemplative, intuitive and mystical
type. It sees life as a whole" (*ibid.*, p. 68).

7. *The Eagle.* The ancient Christian writers also called
John the Eagle because of the fanciful application of the
four living creatures in Revelation 4:7 to the Four Gospels.
Mark was the Lion, Matthew the Man, Luke the Calf, John
the Eagle. Augustine in his discussion of the Gospels
(*Harmony of the Gospels,* 1:6; *Nicene and Post-Nicene
Fathers,* Vol. VI, p. 81) says of John: ". . . . Whereas
John, on the other hand, soars like an eagle above the clouds
of human infirmity, and gazes upon the light of the un-
changeable truth with those keenest and steadiest eyes of

the heart." Adam of Saint Victor likewise pictures John as
the Eagle:

> "John, the eagle's feature having
> Earth on love's twain pinion leaving,
> Soars aloft, God's truth perceiving,
>   In light's purer atmosphere."
>   (Schaff's *History of the Christian Church,*
>   Vol. I., p. 588).

The instinct is right, however fanciful its origin, that sees
this in John. Like the eagle John rises with tireless wings
into the ether and is at home on the heights with Christ.
He can dare look at the Sun of Righteousness and tell us
what he sees of the Glory of God in Christ. We feel instinctively that we are on hallowed ground when we walk
with John through the guidance of the Holy Spirit who took
of the things of Christ and revealed them unto John.

VIII

RECEIVING A HOLY TRUST FROM JESUS

1. *The mother of Jesus by the Cross.* She stood there
(Jo. 19:25), not far from the rough Roman soldiers who
were gambling for the tunic of Jesus, her son. She was
there because she had to come. No fear could keep her
away. The sword that the old prophet Simeon had fore-
seen and foretold (Lu. 2:35) was piercing her soul. Then
she had understood but little what the words meant, now
she knew. But he had spoken other words also: that her
Babe would be set for the falling and rising of many, for a
sign now, alas, come true, spoken against, that the thoughts
of many hearts might be revealed. But the darkness of this
hour was too dense for Mary to see clearly. *Stabat Mater*
can be understood by us better in Palestrina's great oratorio
than in mere words. Besides, what had become of the
promise of Gabriel about the Child Jesus: that He was to be
called the Son of the Highest; that He was to sit on the
throne of David and reign over the house of Jacob for ever;
that there would be no end to His kingdom (Lu. 1:32f.).
The message of the shepherds about the song of the angels
she had cherished in her heart (2:19), brooding over all the
wondrous events attendant on the birth of Jesus, knowing
that the Power of the Highest had overshadowed her and
that the Holy Spirit had begotten this Child (Matt. 1:20).

All this she knew. True, once she feared that Jesus was
over-wrought by nervous strain in his Messianic work and
she had tried to take Him home for rest (Mk. 3:19-21, 31-
35). Her son had claimed to be the Messiah, the Son of
God (as she knew Him to be)—and this was the end of all

her hopes and of God's promises to her. Surely no mother in all the history of the race ever had her dreams so rudely dashed to earth as were Mary's on this terrible day of woe. Calumny was heaped upon calumny. He was accused by the ecclesiastics of being a blasphemer against God and a rebel against Caesar. He was condemned to die on the cross as a common criminal, the most shameful death on earth. In my little book, *The Mother of Jesus: Her Problems and Her Glory,* I have tried to picture Mary as she went on into this great catastrophe. It was night in her soul and John does not attempt to remove the veil from her broken heart. She stood by the Cross on which her Son was slowly dying. She knew that he was innocent of any wrong to God or man. She knew that he was still the Messiah. If she had heard him foretell his death on the Cross and his resurrection on the third day, the words were not comprehended by her any more than by the twelve apostles whose minds were blinded by their own ambitions. The chances are that Mary did not hear these strange (to the apostles) predictions of his death and resurrection. At any rate she stood by the Cross, the picture of utter grief and sheer despair. No rainbow of hope was on this storm cloud for her. It was black night and there were no stars. She had human sympathy, such as it was, in the presence of a small group with her.

2. *The other women there.* "Now there stood beside the Cross of Jesus his mother and the sister of his mother, Mary the wife of Clopas and Mary Magdalene." This looks like four women in two groups, though it is possible Mary the wife of Clopas is the sister of the mother of Jesus. If there are four of them, three besides the mother of Jesus, then the sister of the mother of Jesus may be Salome (Mk. 15:40; 16:1) and Salome may be the mother of the Sons of Zebedee (Matt. 27:56). This is a probable, but by no means, certain, interpretation of the names of these women. If Salome, who is the mother of James and John, is also the sister of the mother of Jesus, then the mother of Jesus has her own sister

by her side in this dreadful hour. In any event, it is a faithful band of women, who had ministered unto Jesus in Galilee (Mk. 15:41). Some of whom stood afar and watched the sad end (Lu. 23:49), some of whom came and stood with the mother of Jesus by the Cross (Jo. 19:25). Where were the twelve apostles in this hour? Judas was dead and Peter had denied him, but there were ten others. "Striking it is that, in this hour of peril, when the men of Christ's following were conspicuous only by their absence, the women were so loyal and fearless; and the only man who stood with them was the most womanly spirit in the apostolic company. But there is an infinite difference between the feminine and the effeminate. Woman may in some respects be weaker than man, but she is stronger in love" (Stalker, *op. cit.*, p. 102).

3. *The Beloved Disciple there also*. It is just like John, whom Jesus loved so dearly, to show his love for Jesus at this hour, whatever the other apostles did. If Salome was his mother and the sister of the mother of Jesus, then John stood here with his own mother. That view gives added piquancy to his presence, but it is intelligible enough in any case. "It was in the strength of his love that John was like a woman, while in mind and character he was a thorough man. The women may have been protected by their sex; he had no such protection, and yet he was there. No doubt in the service of Christ all kinds of power are necessary, and the masculine virtues have a part of their own to play; but for the supreme efforts of sacrifice and devotion which Christianity requires it must ultimately depend on the strength of love" (Stalker, *op. cit.*, p. 102). That is, Christianity depends on the love of women for Christ and of men who love Christ the way women do. Hence it is entirely consistent with the nature of his character to see John here at the Cross of Jesus with this small band of loving and believing women. And Jesus saw this faithful group.

"Amid the howling sea of evil passions with which his cross was encompassed the dying eyes of the Saviour rested with a sense of profound relief on this little group of loyal and loving hearts" (Stalker, *op. cit.*, p. 103). They had no words of cheer to offer to the Master, but they were there. Has Christ a word for them? "At the very moment when his executioners fulfil the last part of their office, Christ in calm sovereignty works for others. The soldiers at their will dispose of His raiment, but He Himself, even from the Cross, determines the relationships of life" (Westcott).

4. *Christ's gift to His mother.* "Jesus, therefore, seeing His mother and the disciple whom He loved standing by" (beside her as well as beside the Cross) speaks to His mother. "All who were present at the scene acted according to their true nature: priests (v. 21), soldiers (vv. 23, 24), Jews (v. 31); and so Christ fulfilled the last office of filial piety" (Westcott). Jesus loved His mother. He had always loved her and now, in His supreme hour of anguish for the sin of the world He thinks of her in this her hour of sorrow. She could not comprehend what He was undergoing. What theologian to-day understands the depths and heights of meaning in the Cross of Christ? But the Son remembers His mother with loving care. He calls her "Woman" as He did at the wedding in Cana of Galilee (Jo. 2:4), but it was not a term of disrespect then nor is it so now. It is here a title of respect rather than of parentage. The glances of the Master "rested on His mother and His favourite disciple. These were the two dearest souls to Him on earth; His eyes lingered on them" (Stalker, *op. cit.*, p. 103). What can Jesus say to His mother that will brighten her heart in this hour of gloom? She was losing her chief earthly stay and support as well as the son of her pride and glory. The other sons were still ambitious. Bernard thinks that these other sons were not Mary's sons at all, but merely "step-sons," sons of Joseph by a former marriage. In that case, (an unlikely one as I think), John was really closer kin by blood to Mary, as her nephew, than such stepsons. Besides, if John was her nephew, Salome, John's mother, was her sister. But, all this aside, Jesus commands His mother to

regard John as her son: "Behold, thy son." The word "behold," is here an interjection (exclamation), not a verb, as the nominative case proves, but Jesus meant it as a dying request or command for His mother, to look on John as her son and to look to him for support. "To Mary this was a splendid gift. It assured to her a home for the rest of her days in which she would breathe the same peaceful and hallowed air as Jesus had breathed into the home at Nazareth, and it gave her the protection of a Greatheart to stand between her and the world" (Stalker, *op. cit.*, p. 104). Mary made no reply to these gracious and precious words. None was needed. The legacy of Jesus to His mother was John as a son.

5. *The charge to the Beloved Disciple.* Swiftly Jesus "then speaks to the disciple: 'Behold thy mother.' " This command to John did not, of course, mean that John was to renounce his own mother, whether Salome who may have been standing by at the time or not, but that he was to regard and treat the mother of Jesus as a second mother, to love her and to care for her as he would his own mother. The legacy of Jesus to John was the care of His own mother. Jesus did not call John by name, but He spoke the command directly to him. "To St. John the Lord stood in the same relation as before" (Westcott). John's task was a holy one, to comfort Mary, even when his own heart was breaking. It was, indeed, a precious gift to John, for Mary, on her own account, would have been an ornament to any home; but, even if her presence had involved inconvenience, she would still have been thrice welcome to him as the mother of his Divine Friend. Friend? Jesus had called His own mother 'thy mother'; was not this to adopt him as a brother? This was a supreme honour: and all the trouble which it might involve was light to a heart which loved with such fervour as his" (Stalker, *op. cit.*, p. 104). There would be joy to John in doing this blessed service for the Master, joy in the midst of unspeakable sorrow for them both. But even John's grief was not to be mentioned beside

that of Mary. What after all could John say? But he
could act. He could carry on with Mary. We know
that Peter was married, but there is no evidence that John
was married, at this time or at any time. Some of the early
Christians called John "the Virgin" *(ho Parthenos)*, since
he never married.

6. *The new home for Mary.* "And from that hour the
disciple took her to his own." The Greek idiom *(ta idia,*
his own things, literally) is the same that occurs in John
1:11 (and Jesus came to His own land or home) where it
is followed by "His own people" *(hoi idioi)* who received
Him not. Then again it appears in John 16:32: "Behold,
the hour comes and has come that ye may be scattered, each
to his own home (or affairs), and leave me alone." The
idea is clear here that John at once accepted the sacred trust
from Jesus and led Mary away from the Cross, for she had
already endured all that she could stand. He took her to
his place of abode in Jerusalem, whatever it was, whether
tent or cottage. The language does not necessarily mean
that John had a settled home in Jerusalem. He was acquainted with the high priest, we know, but he could have
gained this acquaintance on his visits to the city. His
father had hired servants in his business at Capernaum and
this fact argues for a competence, but not necessarily
wealth. It has been argued by some that the words here
used compel us to understand that the Beloved Disciple had
a Jerusalem home and hence John is ruled out because he
could not afford such a luxury. But that is setting up a
man of straw and then being unable to knock him down.
All that the words here mean is that the Beloved Disciple
took Mary to his abode in Jerusalem. Whether this was
temporary or permanent we do not know.

John took Mary to his abode and quickly returned to the
Cross, for he was anxious to see the tragedy to the end.
When he arrived, the Master was already dead, for he saw
blood and water burst out from His side when the Roman
soldier pierced him (Jo. 19:34f.). John bears his personal

witness to this effect as a refutation of the Docetic theory that Jesus did not have an actual body of flesh. How long Mary lived we do not know. She was present in the upper room and was one of the 120 waiting for the coming of the Holy Spirit with power. Now her time of glory has come and her vindication. No one could have quite the joy of heart in the Resurrection of Jesus that was hers. She was, of course, living in Jerusalem with John, who remained here, like the other apostles some years. One could wish that Mary lived on till Luke came with Paul to Caesarea, but we cannot tell. The first two chapters of Luke's Gospel have touches that could only come from her directly or indirectly. And there is in them an Aramaic flavour that argues for a document written by her or by some one who got his information from her orally. To be sure, some of the women of her circle may have been seen by Luke, if he did not actually see her. There is one story that she lived on some twelve years and died and was buried in Jerusalem before John went to Ephesus to live. Another story is that she went with John to Ephesus and died there. We simply do not know. We may be sure that John was loyal to his Lord and faithful in his discharge of this precious trust and that Mary, on her part, cherished this legacy of her Risen and Glorified Son. The Roman Catholics have legends galore about how Mary received heavenly "assumption" and "glorification." These they invented when they came to worship her. Mary has been neglected by Protestants because the Romanists enthrone her. She is Christ's point of contact with our human nature, but she is not an object of worship. Let us respect her for her surpassing nobility of character and service. She deserves honour from every Christian in the world.

IX

ONE OF PAUL'S "PILLAR" APOSTLES

The mention of John by Paul (Gal. 2:9) gives a most interesting further sidelight on his career.

1. *The great issue at Jerusalem.* My views on the Jerusalem conference one will find set forth at length in chapter VII, "Paul's Doctrinal Crisis," in *Epochs in the Life of Paul,* and in chapter XV "Peter the Co-worker with Paul," in *Epochs in the Life of Simon Peter.* Here a summary statement is sufficient. Paul and Barnabas on their return to Antioch from the first great mission tour had been challenged by the Judaizers from Jerusalem for not having the Gentile Christians circumcised (Acts 15:1ff.). It was the same circumcision party that made charges against Peter on his return from Caesarea concerning his attitude towards Cornelius. Paul and Barnabas had refused to circumcise the Greek Christians in Antioch before the tour and they stoutly denied the right of these self-appointed regulators from Jerusalem to Judaize the Gentile Christians. Paul realised the tremendous issue raised by this demand to make Christianity merely one form of Pharisaism. So he and Barnabas determined to bring this problem squarely up before the Judaizers in the Jerusalem church and to face them with duly accredited representatives from the church of Greek Christians in Antioch.

The Jerusalem church was wholly Jewish, but Paul did not believe that the majority were Judaizers. Peter has been vindicated of the charge made against him by the Judaizers (Acts 11:1-18). Besides Paul and Barnabas, there went from Antioch Judas and Silas and Titus (Greek Chris-

tian who represented in himself the whole issue). It was a
solemn moment for the future of Christianity which now
stood at the cross-roads, the parting of the ways between
a spiritual and evangelical message or a mere ceremonial
and sacramental system—freedom or bondage for the Gentile Christians. "It was the one great crisis in the history
of the church, on the issue of which was staked her future
progress and triumph. Was she to open her doors wide, and
receive all comers, to declare her legitimate boundaries co-
extensive with the limits of the human race? Or was she to
remain forever narrow and sectarian, a national institution
at best, but most probably a suspected minority even in her
own nation?" (Lightfoot). Paul's contention for Gentile
freedom is best expressed in the Epistle to the Galatians.
Martin Luther rightly perceived that this Epistle best expounded his contention of justification by faith, not by
works. Hence he expounded it at length in a great commentary. The Epistle to the Galatians is a bugle note of
the freedom that is in Christ.

2. *The presence of John with James and Peter.* James is,
indeed, named first by Paul in Galatians 2:9, "James and
Cephas and John." Burton thinks that this is due to the
prominence of James, the half-brother of Jesus, in the work
of the conference. He presided over it, made the deciding
address, offered the resolution for Gentile freedom from the
Mosaic ceremonial ritual, and apparently wrote the circular
letter to the Gentile churches guaranteeing to them this
liberty (Acts 16:4). It is not surprising to see Peter and
John together as in the earlier part of the Acts, but by this
time it is plain that James has come to be the outstanding
figure in the Jerusalem church, while the apostles are mainly
engaged in their mission campaigns in different directions.
When Peter after his escape from prison in Jerusalem, left
"another place," he gave directions that those in the home
of Mary should go and "announce these things to James and
the brethren" (Acts 12:17). This place of leadership in
Jerusalem James still occupied on Paul's last visit to the

city (Acts 21:18). Paul names "James and Cephas and John, the recognised pillars," not merely "the reputed pillars" of the Jerusalem church. They were "the men of repute" beyond a doubt, though they added nothing to Paul in the way of authority, prestige or knowledge on the subject of Gentile freedom. "Some commentators attribute a depreciatory sense to *dokountes*, 'the so-called leaders.' This is not justifiable. The Greek word means 'the recognised or accepted leaders.' Lightfoot quotes examples of a depreciatory sense for *dokountes*, but in them all the depreciatory innuendo comes from the context and not from the word. To attribute such a meaning to it here is out of keeping with Paul's courteous attitude to the leaders, and is also opposed to the spirit which we have recognised in this narrative" (Ramsay, *Paul's Epistle to the Galatians*, p. 300f.).

The men whom Paul describes as "false brethren who slipped in to spy out our freedom which we have in Christ Jesus, to enslave us" (Gal. 2:4) are the Judaizers, not the "pillar" apostles, for James was an "apostle" (Gal. 1:19), though not one of the twelve. He was an apostle in the general sense like Barnabas. Paul claimed equality with the twelve because of his direct call from Christ. He does not acknowledge the superiority, ecclesiastical or personal, of these three "pillars" of the Jerusalem church. Clement of Rome and Ignatius likewise term the apostles "pillars" (cf. Eph. 2:20). Paul demands recognition from them, perfect equality with them for Barnabas and himself and independence for each group of leaders, they for the work among the Jews, Paul and Barnabas among the Gentiles. This demand was made after frank discussion in the private conference and firm refusal on Paul's part to yield to the demand of the compromisers, who were frightened by "the false brethren" (the Judaizers), that Titus be circumcised because he was a Greek. James and Cephas and John were not among the compromisers. The rather, they saw clearly the wisdom of Paul's contention for liberty for the Gentile Christians

and gladly gave Paul and Barnabas the right hand of fellowship and freedom. They championed Paul's cause in the
open conference which followed the private one, urging only
respect for certain Jewish ideals of morality and worship, which Paul readily agreed to. "It was a memorable
day when these four men met face to face. What a mighty
quaternion. Amongst them they have virtually made the
New Testament and the Christian church. They represent
the four sides of the one foundation of the City of God. Of
the Evangelists Matthew holds affinity with James; Mark
with Peter; and Luke with Paul. James clings to the past
and embodies the transition from Mosaism to Christianity.
Peter is the man of the present, quick in thought and action, eager, buoyant, susceptible. Paul holds the future in
his grasp, and schools the unborn nations. John gathers
present, past, and future into one, lifting us into the region
of eternal life and love" (Findlay). Lightfoot in his commentary on Galatians has an illuminating essay on "St. Paul
and the Three." Rendall properly denies that James, Peter
and John were "at first lukewarm and hesitating in their
support of Paul and Barnabas." They were cordial, in contrast with the coldness of the compromisers.

3. *John's only contact with Paul.* Only that is to say, so
far as we know. Paul expressly states that he did not see
John on his return from Damascus to Jerusalem, but only
Cephas and James, the Lord's brother, of the apostolic circle
(Gal. 1:18f.) and also, according to Luke, Barnabas (Acts
9:27). John had been with Peter to Samaria and had returned to Jerusalem (Acts 8:14, 25), but at this juncture,
along with the rest of the apostles, save Peter, he was absent
from the city on a preaching tour. Now, however, John is
again in Jerusalem and meets Paul of whom he had heard
so much. John may have seen Saul the persecutor when he
was laying waste the church in Jerusalem, and certainly he
knew of his conversion and his work with Barnabas in Antioch and on the recent great mission campaign. But in none
of John's writings does he mention or refer to Paul, who had

long been dead, when he wrote. Peter, as we know, does
mention and praise Paul, and Paul mentions Peter several
times: he had once to rebuke him to his face (Gal. 2:11-14).
Here Paul calls John one of the pillars of the Jerusalem
church. So then "we are happy from this notice to learn
that the two great teachers of Christianity met at least once
face to face" (Stalker, *op. cit.*, p. 155).

In the early part of the Acts we see John "standing silent
in Peter's shadow" (Findlay). There is a "holy reserve"
surrounding John in the Acts as in the Gospels, for his hour
of aggressive leadership had not yet come, but already "his
name ranked in public estimation amongst the three fore-
most of the Jewish church" *(ibid.).* We may be sure that
John was glad to greet Paul who had already shown that
the Risen Jesus made no mistake in calling him to be the
apostle to the Gentiles. And Paul would be equally rejoiced to meet John. "Paul's fellowship with Peter and with
James was cordial and endeared. But to hold the hand of
John, 'the disciple whom Jesus loved,' was a yet higher satisfaction. That clasp symbolized a union between men most
opposite in temperament and training, and brought to the
knowledge of Christ in very different ways, but whose com-
munion in Him was deep as the life eternal. Paul and John
are the two master minds of the New Testament. Of all
men that ever lived, these two best understood Jesus Christ"
(Findlay, *Epistle to the Galatians*, p. 127f.). The eyes of
these two Christian giants met in understanding love and
confidence.

4. *John takes Paul's side against the Judaizers.* He did
it at once and whole-heartedly. It is a complete misinterpretation of Paul's language in Galatians 2:1-10 to take it
as ridicule of "the recognised pillars" who only reluctantly
came over to Paul's view against the Judaizers. James and
Peter and John "entirely acquiesced" (Benham) and gave
Paul and Barnabas the right hand of fellowship. We are
not told anything that John said, but we can feel sure that
"he exercised a powerful, though quiet, conciliatory influ-

ence in the settlement of the Gentile question. The personality of Paul excited, we may be sure, the profoundest interest in such a mind as that of John. He absorbed and yet in a sense transcended, the Pauline theology. The Apocalypse, although the most Judaic book of the New Testament, is penetrated with the influence of Paulinism. The detection in it of a covert attack on the Gentile Apostle is simply one of the mare's nests of a suspicious criticism. John was to be the heir of Paul's labours at Ephesus and in Asia Minor. John's long life, touching the verge of the second century, his catholic position, his serene and lofty spirit, blending in itself and resolving into a higher unity the tendencies of James and Peter and Paul, give us the best assurance that in the Apostolic age there was indeed 'one, holy, catholic, Apostolic Church' " (Findlay, *op. cit.*, p. 127). There was no breach between John and Paul.

5. *John disappearing from the New Testament records save in the Johannine writings.* John had no Luke to write his life. His own writings were all done toward the close of the first century unless the Apocalypse be dated shortly after Nero's reign, a view now held by only a few scholars. But we are not to think of John as idle, or restless, or ineffective. His personality and power are evident in the writings that he has left. They constitute an immortal memorial. The Gospel is regarded by many, probably by most, Christians as the profoundest book of all time. It is significant that much time elapsed before John wrote. Paul and Peter and James had all passed on. Jerusalem and the temple were destroyed. The Jewish nation was no more. Persecution of Christians by the Roman emperor had come from Nero and now once again under Domitian. The Gnostic heresy had grown apace, but John lived on, growing riper and richer in the grace and love of Jesus Christ.

X

JOHN LINGERING ON IN EPHESUS

1. *According to the general tradition.* We have already seen in chapter II on "The So-called Presbyter John of Papias" that Papias was misunderstood by Eusebius about "the Elder John" being another than "the Apostle John." The witness of Papias, Polycarp, Irenaeus, and Polycrates is clear-cut as to the Apostle John's residence in Ephesus and authorship of the Fourth Gospel. George the Sinful, properly understood, expressly states that John was recalled by Nerva from the Isle of Patmos, whither he had been banished by Domitian, to live in Ephesus. The statement of George the Sinful that John and James were both put to death by the Jews is another matter. We know of the death of James in Jerusalem A.D. 44. Clearly George the Sinful cannot mean that John was put to death at that time, else he would have said nothing about the Isle of Patmos and Ephesus in the time of Nerva. One is bound to feel that those modern scholars who have taken up this obscure item in George the Sinful about the death of John, while overlooking his plain statement concerning Nerva and Ephesus, have allowed their prejudice against the Johannine authorship of the Fourth Gospel to blind their historical judgment, to make room for a possible, not to say mythical, "Presbyter John" of Ephesus as the author.

It is not the first time that scholars have wandered into a bog after a will-o'-the-wisp of pure hypothesis. It will take something more convincing than the misinterpretation of George the Sinful of a dubious remark of Papias about John's death at the hands of the Jews, (confirmed by the

102

De Boor Fragment with no details), to overthrow the clear-cut testimony of Irenaeus (*Adv. Haer*. III. 1, 1; 3, 4) that the Apostle John lived in Ephesus, a statement supported by Apollonius, Polycrates, Clement of Alexandria, Origen, Tertullian, Eusebius, and Jerome. Unfortunately we cannot even with the help of the early church fathers, trace John's life in detail after the Jerusalem conference. One report is that John remained in Jerusalem till the death of Christ's mother about A.D. 50 (just after the Jerusalem conference), "loyally and lovingly fulfilling the charge which the Saviour had imposed on him with his dying breath" (Stalker, *op. cit.*, p. 155). Augustine refers to a legend that John preached to the Parthians. Both Renan (*L' Antichrist*, xxx) and Salmon (*Introduction*, p. 396) think it probable that John was with Peter in Rome before Peter's martyrdom there and that he escaped from Rome to Ephesus. Benham (*op. cit.*, p. 49) thinks that John reached Ephesus about A.D. 65, after the war with Rome broke out. One tradition is that he brought the mother of Jesus with him to Ephesus. Both Jerusalem and Ephesus claim to possess the tomb of Mary. If John did reach Ephesus about A.D. 65, he found the church full of the memories of Paul's work there. Paul had spent three years there and had influenced all the province of Asia as a result. But even Paul was violently driven out of Ephesus at the close of the three years by the uproar caused by Demetrius.

Some modern scholars think that Paul was thrown into prison in Ephesus, and that he wrote his prison Epistles there. There is no actual evidence for the first supposition and the latter is only speculative hypothesis. Paul had foretold to the elders of Ephesus at Miletus on his way to Jerusalem, A.D. 56 or 57, that grievous wolves would come upon them (Acts 20:29). They had come at this time—as John discovered. One of the great tasks of John's ministry in Ephesus and Asia will be to fight off the ravages of these Gnostic wolves. This fierce struggle will be apparent in all his writings. Ephesus was the centre of the worship of Artemis, in her magnificent temple, and of all the mystic cults with their magical books (Acts 19:19). At first Jerusalem was the headquarters for the apostolic campaigns, later Antioch, but now towards the close of the century Ephesus is the place of power. The city was the largest and most influential in Asia Minor. It had had great preachers of Christ: Aquila and Priscilla, Apollos, Paul, Timothy, and now John. Paul laid the chief foundations here, and towards the close of his life (I Tim. 1:3), left Timothy in charge. That fact is one point against Benham's view that John came to Ephesus as early as A.D. 65. My own feeling is that it was nearer A.D. 70 when Paul was dead and Timothy gone, though out of prison (Heb. 13:23). There is point in the message of Jesus to the angel of the church of Ephesus in Revelation 2:1-7, in that this church of great privileges and great leaders has left its first love and first works and has fallen to the plane of mere lip orthodoxy. We may be sure that, while John lived in Ephesus, he kept up the great traditions of Paul's work with some added touches of his own. The modern name of Ephesus is *Ayasalouk* from *hagios theologos* (Holy Divine), one of the titles given John in Ephesus.

2. *Some stories about John in Ephesus.* Some of these stories have more verisimilitude than others. They at least reflect the impressions made by John's life and work in Ephesus. Irenaeus (*Adv. Haer.* III. iii. 4) says that Polycarp states that "John, the disciple of the Lord, going to bathe at Ephesus, and perceiving Cerinthus within, rushed out of the bathhouse without bathing, exclaiming, 'Let us fly, lest even the bathhouse fall down, because Cerinthus, the enemy of the truth, is within.'" "Do you know who I am?" said Cerinthus. "I know thee for the first-born of the devil," was the reply of the Son of Thunder. Cerinthus was the champion of the kind of Gnosticism that made the Christ an *aeon* that came upon Jesus the man at his baptism and left him on the Cross; somewhat like the modern Jesus of history and Christ of faith or theology. John was

a Son of Thunder, as we know, and may very well have said something like this to show his disapproval of the heresy of Cerinthus.

Clement of Alexandria (*Ante-Nicene Fathers*, Vol. II., p. 603) tells a moving story of how John was invited to come from Ephesus to an adjoining city where he found a fine youth "powerful in body, comely in appearance, and ardent," and committed him to the bishop thus: "This youth I commit to you in all earnestness, in the presence of the church, and with Christ as witness." Then John went back to Ephesus. Years afterwards John was sent for again to come to the same city. John said: "Come now, O bishop, restore to us the deposit which I and the Saviour committed to thee in the face of the church, over which you preside, as witness." The bishop, with great embarrassment had to confess his own remissness and that he had let the young man fall into evil companionship and wicked ways till now he was leader of a robber band. "He is dead to God. For he turned wicked and abandoned, and at last a robber; and now he has taken possession of the mountain in front of the church, along with a band like him." John rent his clothes and said: "It was a fine guard of a brother's soul I left! But let a horse be brought me, and let some one be my guide on the way." John was arrested by the robber's outpost and demanded to be brought before the captain of the robbers who, on seeing the aged Apostle, fled in shame. But John, in spite of his age, ran after him crying: "Why, my son, dost thou flee from me, thy father, unarmed, old? Son, pity me. Fear not; thou hast still hope of life. I will give account to Christ for thee. If need be, I will willingly endure thy death, as the Lord did death for us. For thee I will surrender my life. Stand, believe, Christ hath sent me." The robber stood, looking down, threw away his arms, trembled, wept bitterly, and fell into the arms of John, who finally restored him to the church whose bishop had let him slip through his hands. This story is certainly good enough to be true and is like the Apostle of Love.

There is another story told by Jerome, which may be true, to the effect that John in his extreme old age was unable to walk and had to be carried to the church where, instead of a sermon, he would only say: "Little children, love one another, love one another, love one another." His disciples grew weary of this repetition, but John said that, if they really loved one another, it would be enough, for it was the Lord's commandment. The Fourth Gospel and the Epistles illustrate John's insistence on love. There are many legends like the stories about the tame partridge, the deadly poison, the bugs in the caravanserai, the boiling oil in the cauldron, the rising and falling of the ground on John's grave in Ephesus. Let them pass away.

3. *The picture of John in his Epistles.* Assuming that "the elder" in 2 and 3 John, like "the elder John" in Papias, is the Apostle John—as I believe to be true—we are justified in catching what personal glimpses we can in his Epistles. In the First Epistle the aged apostle is greatly concerned that followers of Christ shall walk even as the Master walked and that they love one another as God loves them. Stalker (*op. cit.*, p. 186) terms " 'God is love' the greatest sentence which man ever uttered. All these possessions, however, and God himself, are brought nigh to men in Christ, and it is by abiding in Him that we enjoy them. In this blessedness St. John had lived for a lifetime, and the purpose of his writings was that others might have fellowship in the same blessedness." The Epistle itself has absolutely no personal items about author or readers. But the second Epistle to the Elect Lady is full, brief as it is, of delicate personal touches about the lady's children in Ephesus and John's desire to talk with her face to face as the reason for the brevity of the letter. The Third Epistle is to a brother (Gaius) and shows concern about the success of the missionaries sent forth by John, with a warning against Diotrephes for his opposition, and praise of Demetrius for his cordial support of these travelling preachers of Christ. We here catch a glimpse of John carrying on missionary

operations over Asia Minor after the fashion of Paul. "It reminds us of St. Paul's brief Epistle to Philemon; and, like it, supplies a specimen of apostolic courtesy, as well as a glimpse of the changes which Christianity was introducing into the social relationships" (Stalker, *op. cit.*, p. 185).

4. *The endorsement of the Elders of Ephesus to the Gospel.* It is generally believed that verse 24 of chapter 21 of the Fourth Gospel was added by the elders of Ephesus before the book was sent out, as their endorsement that the witness borne about Jesus is true and in order to identify as author the Beloved Disciple, hence the Apostle John. Streeter (*op. cit.*, p. 431f.) quite agrees that the Beloved Disciple can only be the Apostle John ("only John is left"), but he considers the identification of this Beloved Disciple with the author in 21:24 "a mistaken identification." But it is difficult to see how or why the elders in Ephesus, who knew the facts of John's later years in Ephesus and the authorship of the Fourth Gospel, could or would make such a mistake. For one who reads it carefully, the identity of the Beloved Disciple with the Apostle John is plain in the book, itself. What is here added is the clear statement that he is the author of the book. Whether this identification was added before publication, while John was still living, or after John's death is not very material. The point is that it is the approval and identification of those in Ephesus familiar with the facts. The early writers say that the elders of Ephesus besought John to write down his recollections of Jesus lest they should be lost. If this is true, it is easy to see why they had such an interest in the book and also why they endorsed it and identified the author. Dr. Percy Gardner (*Ephesian Gospel*, p. 43) denies that there is any evidence that the author of the Fourth Gospel and the First Epistle was named John. "We find at Ephesus a veritable confusion of Johns." The confusion, I submit, is in the mind of the critics, not in the historical evidence. In his posthumous volume, *The Gospel of the Hellenists* (1933), B. W. Bacon gleefully notes the recantations of Sanday, the

BIRDVILLE BAPTIST CHURCH LIBRARY

hesitation of Stanton, the rejection of Charles, the advocacy of a "witness" by Bernard, Garvie, Carpenter, and Inge, and seems to think that the Johannine authorship of the Fourth Gospel is overthrown. He sets up "the Ephesian Elder," not the "Presbyter John," but a great unknown who "has left us masterpieces of religious literature," an imaginary genius who wrote the greatest of books. But John's Gospel has been attacked before and still stands.

5. *The exile in Patmos.* The author of the Apocalypse calls himself John (1:1, 4, 9; 22:8) and says that he was in the Isle of Patmos (1:9) when he saw the visions. Apparently it was there that he wrote the book. This island is one of the group called the Sporades, in the Aegean Sea not far from Ephesus. It is only a few miles in length, rugged, and beautiful, a lonely spot with only a few hundred inhabitants to-day. John explains that he was there "because of the word of God and the witness of Jesus." That can mean in order to receive God's word and the witness of Christ, but more naturally that he was sent here because of his preaching the Word of God and because of his witness to Jesus Christ (objective genitive). That is to say, he was banished here from Ephesus by Domitian during the Domitianic persecution of the Christians. Lonely islands were often used as places of banishment, but God overruled the punishment in John's case for good. "Possibly in Ephesus St. John had been working so hard that he had little time to think and no time to write; but, when banished to this solitude, he found ample leisure. So it was that when Milton's public life was violently ended by the death of Cromwell, and his outward activity limited by his blindness, he "mused" the greatest epic of the world; and it is indirectly to those who kept Bunyan for twelve years in Bedford jail that we owe the *Pilgrim's Progress.* Prison literature has greatly enriched mankind, and at the head of all such productions we must place the Book of Revelation" (Stalker, *op. cit.*, p. 160). So then this little island will always be linked with the Apostle John who here was given to see the

bright side of the terrible persecutions of the martyrs and other saints.

6. *The death and burial of John in Ephesus.* The story as we get it, is that Trajan allowed John to return to Ephesus where he died a natural death. But there is a tradition that he met a violent death at the hands of the Jews. It is just as well that we do not know the circumstances of John's death any more than we know the details of the martyrdom of Peter and of Paul. If John was actually put to death by the Jews, then he, like his brother James, was a martyr for his faith in Jesus. The prophecy of Jesus about them both may be the origin of the story that John also met a violent death. But surely John suffered a virtual baptism of blood in Patmos and drank enough of Christ's cup there to fulfil the forecast of the Master about him. It is even said that two tombs of John are pointed out to-day in the ruins of Ephesus. Probably neither one is genuine. What is certain is that here died the last of the twelve apostles, the greatest of them, the greatest of all the disciples of Jesus through the ages save the Apostle Paul, who alone rivals him in genius and service.

XI

JOHN FIGHTING GNOSTICISM

(The First Epistle)

1. *The author.* As already indicated, the Johannine authorship of Gospel, Epistles, and Apocalypse is accepted here as proven. There are difficulties, to be sure, as in all historical problems, but the balance of evidence both external and internal, is, in my judgment, decidedly in favour of the Johannine authorship of them all. Ancient testimony is practically unanimous in attributing to the Apostle John the First Epistle. Modern opinion is nearly unanimous that the First Epistle and the Fourth Gospel are from the same hand even if that hand is not that of the Apostle. A few, indeed, credit the Second and Third Epistles to another, but on the flimsiest grounds.

The author of this Epistle does not call himself "the elder," as in the other Epistles or "John," as in the Apocalypse, but he often says "I write unto you" (3:1, 12-14, 26; 5:13). Sometimes he uses the literary plural (1:1-5) and often the plural including the readers with the writer (1:6-10; 3:1f., 16-24; 4:7, etc.). The author claims to have been a personal witness of the life and ministry of Jesus Christ (1:1-3). There is no one to challenge the uniform testimony up to the time of Eusebius (except Marcion and the Alogi) that the Apostle John wrote this Epistle. If he wrote the Gospel, he wrote this Epistle. Holtzmann (*Jahrbuch für Prot. Theologie,* 1882, p. 134) argues for imitation of the Gospel in the First Epistle and separate authorship. Brooke *(Int. Crit. Comm.)* holds for identity of authorship as probable, but is unwilling to take sides as to the author: "We are always on safer ground when we speak of the 'Ephesian Canonical Writings' than when we assign them definitely to S. John, Apostle, or Elder."

2. *The date.* There is nothing to indicate either the absolute or relative date of the First Epistle in relation to the other Johannine Epistles, the Fourth Gospel or the Apocalypse. Findlay *(Fellowship in the Eternal Life)* treats II and III John before I John. There is no reference in the two shorter ones to the longer Epistle nor *vice versa.* Which was actually written first we really do not know nor does it matter for our understanding of either of them. "The only certainty is that the Epistle presupposes its readers' acquaintance with the substance of the Gospel (otherwise such expressions as 'Word of life,' 'new commandment' would have been unintelligible); but that does not imply its posteriority to the composition of the Gospel in literary form" (Robert Law, *Int. St. Bible Encyl.*). They all three seem to come before the Apocalypse, if the Domitianic date for the Revelation is accepted as is the case for my part.

There remains the date of the First Epistle in relation to the Fourth Gospel. Here again we possess no clear data. The undoubted resemblances, to be noticed directly, can be argued either way as to precedence in time. The First Epistle can be regarded as a preparation for the Gospel, as a summary of the Gospel written afterwards, or even a resumé sent forth simultaneously with the Gospel (Lightfoot). On this point one follows the mood of the moment for there are no critical data that are at all conclusive. Hayes *(op. cit.,* p. 176) considers this Epistle "the last book in our Scriptures to be written," but there is no real evidence for so dogmatic a position. As a guess, one may hazard the suggestion that these Epistles preceded both Gospel and Apocalypse and that they were written in the earlier stages of John's residence in Ephesus, probably not later than A.D. 85. But any year between A.D. 80 and 90 suits all that we really know on the subject.

3. *The readers.* There is no indication as to the residence

of the recipients of the Epistle. Since John writes from
Ephesus, one naturally thinks of the churches in Asia Minor
(cf. I Pet. 1:1) as those likely to be in the mind of John.
It is not a personal letter like II and III John, nor written to
a single church like Paul's Epistles to the churches in
Thessalonica, Corinth, Rome, Philippi, but like James, Galatians, I and II Peter, Jude, is addressed to the Christians
of a wider area. There would naturally be both Jews and
Gentiles among the readers of the Epistle, and John closes
with a warning against idols (5:21) which shows that at
this point he has Gentile disciples in mind.

4. *Kinship to the Fourth Gospel.* So close and vital is
the connection in language and thought between the First
Epistle and the Fourth Gospel that it is actually proposed
by a few scholars that the First Epistle is written in imitation of the Fourth Gospel by another hand. But that is
rather crude criticism and misses the heart of the matter.
No mere imitation could catch so precisely the tone and
spirit, not to say idiom, of the Fourth Gospel. Only the
same man (cf. Ephesians and Colossians) could make them
so alike and yet so independent. They both come out of the
same mind and heart, have the same outlook and meet
largely the same situations. At once one is struck by the
likeness in language and thought between I John 1:1-5 and
John 1:1-18 in the use of "Beginning," "Word," "Life,"
"Light," "Darkness," "Witness," "Manifest," "Behold,"
"Father." Other words of similar tenor run through both
books like walk, know, true, confess, children of God, cleansing, sin, propitiation, love, boldness, flesh, believe, Paraclete,
etc. There is no occurrence of *oun* (then, therefore) in the
Epistle, a word which, mainly in a transitional sense, is used
200 times in the narrative portions of the Gospel only, and
not at all in chapters 14-16. The independence of the Epistle
in its method of treatment exists along with this kinship of
thought and language, and justifies "the first-rate importance" (Law) of the Epistle itself. It stands high on its
own merits. There are natural differences between the

Fourth Gospel and the First Epistle, but "not enough to compel us to assume different authors" (Brooke, *op. cit.*, p. xviii). Certainly identity of authorship in this case is far more probable than imitation.

5. *The Gnostic background of the Epistle.* It is possible, since the Epistle was written after the destruction of Jerusalem, and not far from the date of the Fourth Gospel in which "the Jews" are so often presented as the enemies of Christ (primarily, the Jewish rulers), that the hostile element of the Jews is in the author's mind at times. It is possible, as Wurm argues, that in 2:22f. those Jews, who deny that Jesus is the Messiah, are pictured. But this language applies equally well to Cerinthus, exponent of the type of Gnosticism which distinguished between the man Jesus and the *aeon* Christ (Messiah) who by this view came on Jesus at the baptism and left him on the Cross. "The 'master-lie' is the denial of the true nature of the Incarnate Christ, as the writer and his fellow-Christians had come to know Him. Cerinthianism may be included, in the conception, but Cerinthus is not *ho antichristos*" (Brooke). There is no doubt of the presence in Asia Minor of Gnostic teaching which was disturbing the churches. Incipient Gnosticism is met by Paul in Colossians, Ephesians, and the Pastoral Epistles. This oriental syncretism made a subtle appeal to cultured minds touched by Plato's idealism. Its philosophy held to the essential evil of matter and contended that the good God could not directly create it. Hence the world of matter was created by a subordinate *aeon* or emanation from God with power enough to do it and yet too far removed to contaminate God. There were very practical results on those Gnostics who accepted Christianity and amalgamated it with their philosophy. One was the problem of sin, since the flesh is matter.

Two views prevailed among these Gnostics about sin. One view, asceticism, taught that the body must be kept under control by severe discipline. This led to separation and monasticism. The other view advocated licentiousness, on the plea that the sin of the flesh did not affect the soul, which is all that counts. We see this peril in 1:6, 8, 10; 2:4f. Dionysius of Alexandria says "that, as Cerinthus was a voluptuary and wholly sensual, he conjectured that Christ's kingdom would consist in those things which he so eagerly desired, in the gratification of his sensual appetites, in eating and drinking and marrying" (Robert Law). The person of Christ presented a grave problem to these Gnostics which they met in two ways.

The Docetics denied the actual humanity of Jesus and held that he had only a phantom body and was in reality all *aeon*. This error, plainly combated by Ignatius, John opposes in 1:1-3 when he appeals to the evidence of the senses (hearing, sight, touch) in proof of the actual humanity of the Word of Life. We see his opposition to it, also, in his insistence on the witness of the blood of Jesus (1:7; 3:16; 5:6-8) and His "walk" (2:6) and His "coming in the flesh" (4:2). The Cerinthian Gnostics distingished between the man Jesus and the *aeon* Christ and John insists on the oneness and identity of Jesus Christ the Son of God (1:3; 2:1f.; 2:22f.; 3:23; 4:2, 9, 14; 5:6-11, 13, 20). The Epistle becomes much more intelligible when we perceive the vital contest with error that threatened the very life of Christianity and had already brought an inevitable cleavage (2:19). John uses plain terms for the leaders (liars, antichrists) in his effort to save the loyal followers of Christ from these plausible and perilous purveyors of speculative philosophy that sapped its victims of all spiritual life and energy.

6. *The purpose of the author.* That should be plain enough. "It is probably true that the writer never loses sight altogether of the views of his opponents in any part of the Epistle. But it is important to emphasize the fact that in spite of this, the real aim of the Epistle is not exclusively, or even primarily, polemical. The edification of his 'children' in the true faith and life of Christians is the writer's chief purpose" (Brooke). That is true and we

must not forget that "St. John's method is to confute the error by the exposition of the truth realised in life. His object is polemical only so far as the clear unfolding of the essence of right teaching necessarily shews all error in its real character" (Westcott). Yes, but we should not be so "pacifistic" that we are afraid of the word "polemical" in our attitude toward Satan and his devices. Martin Luther was extreme in many of his ways, no doubt, but he was not afraid of polemics and he made possible modern civilization and progress by firmly fighting the pope and breaking all his bonds on the human mind and spirit. Robert Law does not hesitate to speak of "The Polemical Aim of the Epistle," because John was meeting in open, front-on opposition "the fantastic caricature" of "the Divine reality," this "acute Hellenizing of Christianity," "that strange, obscure movement, partly intellectual, partly fanatical, which, in the second century, spread with the swiftness of an epidemic over the Church from Syria to Gaul." Some were obscene like Cerinthus, some of the leaders were intellectually acute. "The great Gnostics were the first Christian philosophers." There was finally "a bewildering multiplicity of Gnostic sects."

John faced this "unethical intellectualism" bravely and blazed the way for all who have to meet modern imitations of Gnosticism, like so-called Christian Science. There are a few who even charge that the author of the Fourth Gospel was himself a Gnostic and that the First Epistle was written to confute him. But surely that view fails utterly to comprehend the Fourth Gospel. Westcott rightly observes that the Fourth Gospel assumes the humanity of Jesus (against the Docetics) and proves his deity (against both Docetics and Cerinthians) identifying Jesus and the Christ (Messiah) or Logos, while the First Epistle assumes the deity of Jesus Christ and proves his humanity (1:1-3, 7; 4:2, 9; 5: 6-8). Bacon, in his posthumous book, *The Gospel of the Hellenists* (1933), thus describes the Fourth Gospel, which he denies to the Apostle John as he did in his *The Fourth*

Gospel in Research and Debate. John's answer to the Gnostics is not less knowledge, but more. He is not an obscurantist. "He writes to them not because they do not know, but because they know" (Brooke).

7. *Stylistic peculiarities*. Some of these have already been indicated. Like the Fourth Gospel this Epistle is Hebraistic in tone with very few actual Hebraisms, quite in contrast to the Apocalypse. In the Epistle there is a sparse use of the Greek particles (*oun* not at all) and conjunctions, save *kai, hoti,* and *hina*. The author is very fond of repeating words and phrases but with important additions each time like the figure in a woman's crocheting. One may note also (Holtzmann) the infrequent use of the relative, the disconnected sentences, the use of parallelism with both positive and negative statements, the use of the demonstrative before a conjunction, the limited vocabulary, the similarity of ideas with those in the Fourth Gospel like the Incarnation, eternal life, abiding in Christ and in God, God's love shown by sending His Son, the command to love one another, believers as children of God, the stress on witness, the series of contrasts (light and darkness, love and hate, life and death, truth and falsehood, the Father and the world, children of God and children of the devil, knowing God and not knowing God). Note also the Paraclete of John 14:16, 26 and I John 2:1, the Parousia and Judgment in John 5:26-29; 6:39f. and I John 2:18f., propitiation in John 3:16 and I John 2:2; 4:9f. There is a gentleness in the affectionate tone of the aged apostle as he writes with consuming passion to his "little children" (2:1). He is the Apostle of love, but with a burning heart. He is still the Son of Boanerges as he faces Cerinthus and all other defamers of Jesus Christ, the Son of God. John longs that those who have received the Anointing (*Chrisma*, 2:20, 27) may know the truth and be free from every lie. Bishop McDowell (*Iliff School Studies*, p. 72) has said: "John does not argue against people living in the dark. He simply floods

the world with light, and a heretic must hunt a hole if he wants darkness."

8. *The development of thought in the Epistle.* Westcott voices the feeling of every interpreter of First John when he says: "It is extremely difficult to determine with certainty the structure of the Epistle. No single arrangement is able to take account of the complex development of thought which it offers, and of the many connexions which exist between its different parts." And yet there is movement, progress, climax. All the threads are gathered together by the close. But meanwhile truth is presented, now from this angle, now from that, with a new focus, a fresh facet that like the diamond flashes light at every turn. The thought is not rambling, not disjointed, not disconcerting, but the author's quick intuitions of parallel lines of thought call for keen attention on the reader's part. The reward, however, is worth the trouble. No theme is announced and no separate outline is offered. There is no salutation and no farewell.

The author plunges at once into discussion of the reality of the human personality of Jesus Christ so that in 1:1-4 we have the heart of the whole matter set boldly before us in a series of abstract phrases (the neuter singular relative *ho*, that which, like *pan ho*, all that, in Jo. 6:37, 39 and 17:24 for the totality of the redeemed), but with repeated emphasis on the writer's personal experience "concerning the Word of Life." Clearly the author has in mind John 1:1-14 or is familiar with the truth stated about the *Logos* as Life becoming flesh. In John 1:1 we have *en archēi* (in the beginning) and here *ap' archēs* (from the beginning). In John 1:14 there occurs the very verb form (*etheasametha*, we beheld) that we find here is verse 1. There it apparently refers to the glory on the mount of Transfiguration while here it is applied to the Incarnation. Here we three times (verses 1, 2, 3) have another verb for seeing (*heōrakamen*, we have seen), also referring to the Incarnation (the Word of Life) just as in John 1:18 this verb in

the perfect form (*heōraken*, has seen) is used of seeing God.
Three times also here (verses 1, 3, 5) we have *akēkoamen*
(we have heard) defining John's certainty that he (literary
plural "we") actually has heard and retains as a permanent
possession (perfect active indicative) his knowledge of the
Lord Jesus himself.

He goes further and appeals to the sense of touch, "our
hands handled, touched, felt" (*epsēlaphēsan*) the Master,
the very word used by Jesus in Luke 24:39 to prove to the
astonished disciples that He in His risen form was not mere
spirit, a telling thrust at the Docetics who denied that Jesus
had an actual human body. John here interjects a parenthetical explanation to the effect that Jesus in His Incarnate
body was the Life manifested, a word (*ephanerōthē* twice in
verse 2) used in John 2:11 of the manifestation of the glory
of Jesus at the miracle in Cana, by Paul (Col. 3:4) and
John (I John 3:2) of the manifestations of the Messiah in
His second coming and of our likeness to Him. There is the
note of certainty in the words of John who speaks calmly of
his own personal knowledge of the Word of Life and he
bears witness (*marturoumen*, verse 2, another common Johannine word) in a public way (*apaggellomen*, we announce
as a messenger *aggelos*, used three times as showing the
urgency of John in speaking his message, verses 2, 3, 5).
He proclaims "the eternal life which was with (*pros* as in
Jo. 1:1 "with God") the Father." In John's Gospel and
Epistles we have *aiōnios zōē* 23 times and here a picture of
the eternal life manifested in Christ and which, like Christ
(the Logos), was with the Father before the manifestation.
After the parenthesis John repeats his witness of his personal experience and declares his purpose to be "that ye also
may keep on having partnership with us" in this rich and
glorious experience of John's. The word "partnership"
(*koinōnia*) which John uses here four times (verses 3, 4, 6,
7) carries the idea of active participation as partners (from
koinōnos, partner, Lu. 5:10). So then John is not merely
answering the Gnostics; he desires to enrich believers in

Christ with his own experience of Christ. He hastens to explain that his "fellowship" (partnership) is "with the Father and with his Son Jesus Christ." That is to say, in order to share John's experience, one must get in contact with the Father through His Son who is "Jesus Christ" (one person, not two). He is both divine and human and he is the Revealer of the Father as is so clearly explained in John 1:1, 18; 14:9). Jesus claimed to be the Life (Jo. 14:6) and the Logos was the Life (Jo. 1:4). Now John plainly states why he is writing these things, "that our (or, your, the mss. vary) joy may remain full" (perfect passive periphrastic subjunctive), no spasmodic outburst soon over, but a settled state of joy that will go on for ever. This high purpose runs through all the stirring words of this Epistle.

The next idea in the Epistle is that "God is Light" (1:5), with no darkness in him. It is set forth in characteristic Johannine fashion. He picks this item out as in "the message which we have heard from him (the Son, who is the Light of men, John 1:5, as well as the Life, already discussed). Jesus Christ, the Son of God, the Word, is both Life and Light as the Father is. John claims to have obtained this message directly from the Son and here passes it on to his readers. In this opening paragraph he emphasises life, manifestation, fellowship.

This fact has a vital bearing on the "partnership" with John just mentioned (verse 3) and to be obtained from God in Christ. Profession ("if we say," three times, verses 6, 8, 10) of such partnership or fellowship with God is empty unless it is borne out by the life. Some of the Gnostics who made such loud claims to special "knowledge" and initiation into sacred secrets were notoriously loose in their lives and walked in darkness rather than light. Claiming to have such "fellowship" while going on walking in darkness is plain lying because "we are not doing the truth," which is far more effective than just speaking the truth, good as that is when not given the lie by the life. On the other hand, walking in the light, as God ("he") is in the light, shows,

as all can see, that we are having "fellowship" with one another, for we all have the common partnership of walking
with God in the light. God is Light and walks in light un-
approachable (I Tim. 6:16). Another thing is made clear
and it is that "the blood of Jesus His Son is cleansing us
from all sin." That blood alone, not Gnostic or any other
sacramental rites or rules, can do that great thing, but the
blood of Jesus does cleanse us. Here again John brushes
aside the Docetic denial of the real humanity of Jesus
Christ and insists on the atoning value of His death on the
Cross. Each of us must get the blessing of this sacrifice on
God's own terms. And we do have a sinful nature that needs
this cleansing by Christ's blood and it is folly to deny that
sin exists. We lead ourselves astray by such a self-delusion
and deceive no one else, least of all God. The truth is not
in us then. On the other hand confession of our sins to
God makes it possible for God to forgive our sins and to
cleanse us from all unrighteousness. Full provision for such
forgiveness is made by the blood of Christ for us and God
"is faithful and righteous" to do it when we let Him.

Here is the same gospel that we have in John 3:16 and in
Romans 3:25. John clears the ground from all misapprehension about inherent goodness that makes the atonement
unnecessary. Again, he takes up the case of those who
admit the possession of a sinful nature, but deny the commission of sinful deeds, those who claim complete and final
victory over all sin. "If we say that we have not committed sin (acts of sin), we make him (God) a liar and his
word is not in us" (1:10). Some of the Gnostic initiates
affected immunity from all sinful thoughts, words, or deeds.
John will return again to this denial of any sin and claim to
absolute perfection and holiness, but he bluntly states his
point here. There are those to-day who claim that sin is a
mere notion of mortal mind with no basis in fact, that what
people call sin is mere animal inheritance or due to ignorant
environment and custom and lack of enlightenment and
liberty. Some even imagine that they have attained absolute

perfection in personal holiness. Paul denied it for himself
(Phil. 3:12) and John here denies it for us all.

John is anxious that we may not lose heart in our struggle with sin as did those Gnostics who took refuge either in
asceticism or in licentiousness. "My little children," he
pleads with an old man's affectionate tenderness, "I am
writing these things to you that you may not commit sin"
(2:1). One thinks of Paul's hypothetical objector about so
much grace, who wanted to know if one should not sin a bit
extra to use up some of the over-supply of grace (Rom.
6:1f.). "But," John adds, "if one commit a sin (ingressive
aorist subjunctive, *hamartēi*), we have an Advocate
(*Paraklēton,* John's word for Jesus and the Holy Spirit in 14:
16, 26; 16:7) with (*pros,* face to face with, as in Jo. 1:1)
the Father, Jesus Christ, Righteous One" (as the Father is
"righteous," I Jo. 1:9). "There must be character and
competency in the Paraclete" (Findlay). There is no need
for despair or for licence. We have a sinful nature (1:8)
and we occasionally commit acts of sin (1:10; 2:1) in spite
of our struggling against it, but we are not to lose heart. It
is a winning fight and we have the Holy Spirit's anointing to
help us (2:20, 27), God's Paraclete on earth, and Christ as
our Paraclete in heaven. We are bound to win if we remain
loyal to Christ with such a God-given redemptive plan
(Rom. 8:26f.).

Jesus has the right to speak for us with the Father, because the Father so willed it (Jo. 3:16; Rom. 3:25) and because the Son voluntarily (Jo. 10:18; Heb. 9:14) offered
himself as a "propitiation" *(hilasmos)* for our sins and for
those of the whole world. It is not God who has to be
propitiated, though His sense of justice has to be satisfied
(Rom. 3:26, "that he may be just and justify"). "His
advocacy is valid, because He can Himself bear witness that
the only condition on which fellowship between God and
man can be restored has been fulfilled, i.e. the removal of
the sin by which the intercourse was interrupted" (Brooke).
John's doctrine of the atonement is precisely that of Jesus

(Mk. 10:45; Matt. 20:28), though Jesus used "ransom" *(lutron)* while John has "propitiation" *(hilasmos)* and Paul "curse" *(katara,* Gal. 3:13) as well as "propitiation" *(hilastērion,* Rom. 3:25). In the Gospel (Jo. 1:29) the Baptist pictures Jesus as "the Lamb of God who bears the sin of the world."

John now turns directly on the Gnostics who claim (2:3-6) such intimate "knowledge" of Christ (or God). "Some claimed a knowledge of God, as some claimed a fellowship with God (1:6), irrespective of a Christ-like life" (Westcott). John gives a pointed test for these claimants to superknowledge, who glibly and even flippantly pop up and say, "I have gained special knowledge (*egnōka,* perfect active, state of completion, and experimental knowledge) of him (Christ apparently)." There is no harm in such claims, if they are true. But some of these Gnostics with slick tongues were notoriously immoral or non-moral, as some would say to-day. The test for them and for true Christians is the same, "if we go on keeping his commandments." Bluntly John affirms that this professional babbler of his own secret knowledge of Christ can be called to book, "the one who goes on not keeping his commandments" (the licentious liver), "he is a liar" (*pseustēs,* the very word used of the devil in Jo. 8:44). He is all liar "with no truth in him at all." "But whoever goes on keeping his (God's word), truly in this one the love of God has been perfected." That is to say, "knowledge is not the possession of a few 'pneumatic' (Gnostic) individuals" (Brooke), but this prize of the perfection of love is open to all, and is exhibited by the life, not by loud claims. This "love of God" is the love that God has for us, and it becomes effective in us and leads us to love Him and one another. "We love him, because he first loved us" (I Jo. 4:19). "God abides in us and his love is perfected in us" (4:12). Our keeping God's commandments is continual proof of our vital union with God, as Jesus taught in the parable of the vine and the branches (Jo. 15:1-7). "In this we know that we are in him." Then

John adds a telling and illuminating comment: "He who says that he is abiding in him ought himself also to go on walking just as he (*ekeinos,* that one, emphatic *he* as in Jo. 9:12, etc.) walked."

This use of *peripateō* for the walk or life of the Christian is thoroughly Johannine as is the use here of *ginōskō* (know) and *menō* (abide). C. M. Sheldon's remarkable little book, *In His Steps,* has been translated into many tongues with a circulation of over twenty million. If all nominal Christians only walked in the steps of the Master, we should have a new world, one without so much sin and crime, without war, without hate, without selfishness, with the Golden Rule in actual operation in business and in statecraft. This verse sums up John's idea of the ideal follower of Jesus.

John runs true to form in 2:7 and 8. He had spoken in 2:5 of "the love of God" as "perfected in this one who keeps on doing his Word." He now takes up that phrase for further comment and will revert to it again at length (4: 7-21). The point here is that such perfected love involves love for one another, as he brings out clearly in 1:9-11. While called by Jesus "a new commandment," (Jo. 13:34), it is in reality "an old commandment which they had been having (*eichete,* imperfect) from of old, from Moses in fact. In was old in Christ's day, the call to love their neighbours and even their enemies. It was new to the disciples when Jesus "gave it them in a new form and with a new sanction" (Westcott)—old in command but left on the shelf unused. So John repeats that, while "ancient" (*palaian*) in date or origin, it is "new" or "fresh" (*kainēn*) in practice with each of them. It is in the Old Testament, Jesus taught it and lived it, John urges it. There is need to-day that we keep on preaching it and doing it. It found a "new" and "true" expression "in him" (Christ) and it should find the same expression "in you" (the readers, and that includes "us" to-day).

There is hope in this conflict between light and darkness (1:5f.; Jo. 1:4-13), "because the darkness is passing by and the true light is already shining." In spite of the power of Gnosticism to confuse and mislead, John is an optimist. This optimism may include the hope of the early coming *(Parousia)* of Christ to earth again (2:17f.), as appears plainly in the Apocalypse, though one should always bear in mind that time phrases in all eschatological language (cf. Mk. 13 and Matt. 24 and 25) must be interpreted in relative terms and from God's standpoint, not according to our measurements. Einstein's contribution to the language of science, of time as the fourth dimension (relativity), is pertinent here. But "the darkness" is pictured as temporary and drifting by like the fog of sin that it is. The sun is shining all the while and will in the end dispel the darkness with its blight of fog.

Then tenses, as always, are important in this Epistle. John has in mind here (2:9-11) the continuous braggart: "The one who keeps on saying that he is in the light and keeps on hating his brother is in the darkness up to this moment." Light does not have to say anything, but it simply shines on. The light shines all around the one who keeps on loving his brother so that there is no danger of one stumbling over him as a trap or obstacle *(skandalon)*. On the other hand the one who keeps on hating his brother is not only in the dark, but he keeps on walking around in the dark, as if he were in the light. "He does not know where he is going, because the darkness blinded his eyes." He is in dire peril himself and a menace to all who meet him. See this double use of *skandalon* in Revelation 2:14. Some of the phrases here are identical with John 12:35. The blinding power of sin occurs in Isaiah 6:10 (quoted in Jo. 12:40) and in II Corinthians 4:4. It is terrible to walk in the dark. Jesus Himself (Mk. 15:14) had described the Pharisees as blind guides leading the blind and both falling into the pit.

John is constantly aware in this Epistle that he is addressing a definite class of people. He calls them " 'you' thirty-six times. He says 'I write' or 'I wrote' thirteen times. He calls them 'my little children' six times. He calls

them 'beloved' six times. He evidently recognises a personal
relation existing between himself and his readers. He has
an apostolic, prophetic, and paternal interest in them. He
knows the little children, the young men, and the fathers
among them, and he has a word of counsel for each and all"
(Hayes, *op. cit.*, p. 161). In a way he is here (2:12) explaining why he is so urgent and why he is writing to them
at all,—apology in the original sense. There is an affectionate tone in his use of "little children," whether here meant
in the general sense for all his readers (2:1) or in the special
sense in contrast with "fathers" and "young men." Perhaps by "little children" he addresses the whole group and
by "fathers" and "young men" divides them all by age into
two groups (Westcott). Findlay so understands it; he calls
these verses (2:12-14) "Religion for Age and Youth." At
any rate the items given by John suit this interpretation;
forgiveness of sin applies to all; personal and long knowledge of Christ who has been from the beginning (1:1; Jo.
1:1) is pertinent for the fathers; victory over the evil one
(masculine accusative *ton,* and so probably in Matt. 6:13)
is to the point for young men. Then he repeats his appeals
with the use of the epistolary aorist (*egrapsa* in place of
graphō present) with slight changes: *paidia* for *teknia* (both
diminutives), knowledge of the Father instead of forgiveness of sins, and for young men there is added the fact that
they are strong and that the Word of God is abiding in
them, enough (such a combination of human and divine
energy) to overcome the evil one.

Law (*Tests of Life,* p. 309) suggests that John was interrupted at the close of verse 13 and on resuming repeated
the appeal in changed form. This is ingenious, but not convincing. More probable is the view of John A. Broadus that
the solemn repetition is intended to call emphatic attention
to the command in verse 15: "Love not the world nor the
things in the world." The use of *kosmos* (world) here is
thoroughly Johannine and apparently means more than the
wicked portion of mankind, this present world apart from

God, of which Jesus said the disciples, though in it, were not to be, (Jo. 17:15f.) and into which Jesus had been sent (Jo. 17:18f.). Satan, on the mount of temptation, claimed the rule of all the world (*kosmos* in Matt. 4:8, *hē oikoumenē*, the inhabited earth in Lu. 4:5). In fact, as Westcott shows, there is a striking parallel between "all that is the world—the lust of the flesh and the lust of the eyes and the pride of life" (verse 16) and the three temptations in Matthew 4:1-11 and Luke 4:1-13. "The three false tendencies" (Westcott) in this passage "cover the whole ground of worldiness." The first temptation offered to Christ was the appeal to hunger, the most elementary lust of life; the second in Matthew's order was an appeal to personal ostentation, the pride of life, "the call to claim an open manifestation of God's protecting power"; the third (Matthew's order) with its offer of the power and glory of the world is kin to the lust of the eyes and the ambitions of life. All this is of the world, not of the Father. John feels the contrast keenly between the love of the world and the love of the Father. Brooke denies that John's terms here cover all sins and do not form an exact parallel to the mediæval *voluptas, avaritia, superbia*. But "there can be but one supreme object of moral devotion" (Westcott). There are beautiful things in the world, but they are as nothing in comparison with the Father's love, just as Jesus placed love to Him before every relation in life (Lu. 14:25f.)—even the closest and dearest ties. Worldliness means not merely the sinful extravagances of life and seductive charms of things doubtful or sinful; the whole world of sense about us must be kept subordinate and secondary to the life of fellowship with God in Christ. God's love alone satisfies and lasts.

It is pitiful to know how many Christians are powerless because they lead prayerless lives out of touch with God. "The world passes by (like a procession) and the desire for it, but the one who keeps on doing the will of God abides for ever." That is what makes a life worth while, doing the will of God. Findlay calls this love of the world "the love that perishes." The object of it (the world) passes away and the love also disappears. "The world is a bewildering paradox," but the love of God grows brighter and richer for evermore.

Westcott and Hort make a decided break in the text between 2:17 and 2:18. Westcott, indeed, thinks that in 2:18 to 4:6 we have "the central subject of the Epistle, the great conflict of life" which he subdivides into (a) the revelation of falsehood and truth (2:18-29), (b) the children of God and the children of the devil (3:1-12), (c) brotherhood in Christ and hatred of the world (3:13-24), (d) the rival spirits of truth and error (4:1-6). In a broad and general way that is true, but it is hard to confine the argument to any outline. Law *(Tests of Life)* takes up topics selected from different parts of the Epistle like the doctrine of God as life and light, the doctrine of Christ, witnesses to the doctrine of Christ, the doctrine of sin and the world, the doctrine of propitiation, eternal life, the test of Righteousness, the test of Love, the doctrine of assurance, eschatology. That, again, is all true, but not in that order or in any order. John touches each subject again and again. Likewise Hayes describes the book as the Epistle of love, of knowledge, of the incarnation, of the atonement, of personal experience, of fellowship, of purity, of victory. But these topics follow no formal analysis. Findlay takes smaller paragraphs at a time and has trouble enough even then. He calls 2:18-27 "the last hour." Certainly John begins on that line in "a natural transition from the thought of the transitoriness of the world to that of the approaching end" (Brooke). The phrase "last hour" is anarthrous and may be more qualitative of the period (Westcott) than a definite statement of the nearness of the end (Brooke).

John was now old and, like the other apostles (now all gone but him), he had hoped to see the Master's return before his death. Indeed, the Lord had said that if it was His will that the Beloved Disciple live on while He was coming, that was no concern to Peter (Jo. 21:20-23). But

Jesus did not say that John would not die. Yet there was the hope. The Master had urged them all to be ready, for He would come, when He did, like a thief in the night (suddenly and without warning). "A last hour it certainly was; and it might be (who could tell?) the last hour of all" (Findlay). But how long is this "last hour"? Who knows that? If it is the last dispensation how long will it last? They had heard that "Antichrist was coming." Who is he? Findlay thinks that no particular individual is in mind, for "history passes through great cycles, each of which has its last anticipating the absolute conclusion." "Many great and notable days of the Lord there have been, and perhaps will be—many last hours before the last of all."

Undoubtedly, but even so it is not clear as to John's meaning. One thinks of Paul's "man of sin" who has his "parousia" (II Thess. 2:3-12) and of the many signs and symbols and the certainty and nearness of the Second Coming of Christ in John's Apocalypse. For myself, I prefer the expectant attitude enjoined by Jesus with a mind alert to all the perils of the crisis in which we live without placing tags on this or that person as "antichrist." Many antichrists had already come, John claimed (2:18). Surely many more have come since John wrote. The term "antichrist" means "opposer of Christ" and also "one who seeks to supplant Christ." John alone of New Testament writers uses the word, but Jesus Himself foretold "false christs" (*pseudochristoi*) who claimed to be "the Christ" (Matt. 24:23) and that seems to be John's idea. They are rivals of Christ and there have been many. John uses the word in the singular again in verse 22, in 4:3, and in II John 7, each time with the article, though not so in 2:18. Apparently the great antichrist was still to come, but meanwhile a cleavage had come between true believers and followers of these antichrists (probably Gnostics). "They went out from us but they were not of us." Their departure from the Christian fold revealed their true character. The words of John are pertinent to-day for those who seek to spread

Christian doctrine out so thin and broad that it will include even Hinduism. Union is nothing like so important as unity and life in Christ. Schism is sometimes necessary for the life and health of the vine as Jesus so clearly taught. Dead branches must be lopped off (Jo. 15:2). Outward fellowship signifies nothing if there is no inward bond of life in Christ.

True Christians have the "anointing" (*chrisma*, from the same root *chriō* as *Christos*) of Christ by the Holy Spirit, not baptism as Brooke holds. "And you have a 'chrism' from the Holy One" (2:18) "The Holy One" is Christ. God "anointed" (*echrisen*, Acts 10:38) Christ "with the Holy Spirit and power." Christ promised the Holy Spirit to teach "the disciples the truth (Jo. 16:13-15). Hence they know the truth, in distinction from these "antichrists" and their followers. Hence also John has written them— because they understand what he is saying and know no lie comes out of the truth, which is more than some people see to-day. The gullibility of apparently reasonable people is amazing, when they listen to lies claiming to come out of God's Word. But there is antiseptic power in the life in Christ.

John terms the denial of Jesus as the Christ (the Anointed One) "the master-falsehood" (Westcott). The article here (the liar) "denotes the liar *par excellence*, in whom falsehood finds its complete expression" (Brooke). It is a picture of Cerinthus who did this very thing and in so far is "the antichrist," for he held that "the Christ" was an *aeon* that came on the man Jesus at His baptism and left Him on the Cross. But the term, "antichrist," includes more than Cerinthianism and describes to-day those who seek to rob Jesus of His deity. They deny the union of the human and the divine in the one person Jesus Christ, the Word become flesh (Jo. 1:14). The double negative in 2:22 is a true Greek idiom (denies that He is not). In so doing one "denies the Father and the Son" as Jesus Himself claimed (Jo. 5:23; 14:6). Confession of the Son is necessary for confession of the Father. Jesus is the one way to the Father. This they know. John pleads that they hold on to it. Then they will "abide in the Son and in the Father." That is to say, the only way to abide in the Father is to abide in the Son. This is Johannine, to be sure, but it is also Pauline teaching and—Petrine, too (Acts 4:12). The promise which Jesus (emphatic *he, autos*) gave is eternal life (Jo. 6:47; 8:51; 15:4). He said: "I am the resurrection and the life" (11:25), "I am the way and the truth and the life" (14:6).

John explains (2:26) why he has written "these things to you concerning those who are trying to lead you astray." He cannot remain silent when his "little children" are in dire peril from the slick-tongued sophists of his time. They ought to hold fast, for "the 'chrism' which ye received from him abides in you." As a result "ye have no need that one keep on teaching you." But all the same he lifts his voice in exhortation: "But, as his anointing (chrism) is teaching you concerning all things and is true and is not a lie (true Johannine style), and as he taught you, do ye keep on abiding in him" (2:27). Then the "antichrists" can do them no harm. "And now," says John in a tender appeal, "keep on abiding in him, in order that, if he be manifested (the second coming, as in 3:2), we may get (*schōmen*, ingressive second aorist subjunctive) boldness and not shrink in shame from him at his *parousia*." He may come at any time, so be ready to greet Him gladly. Verse 29 gives considerable trouble: "If ye know that he is righteous, know that every one who does righteousness has been begotten of him." The subject of verse 28 is Christ and He naturally is the subject of verse 29. Christ is elsewhere termed "righteous," but nowhere else is one said to be "begotten of Christ." "To be born of God" is a common Johannine phrase (Jo. 1:12f.; 1 Jo. 3:9; 4:7, 5:1, 4, 18). We are also born of the Spirit (Jo. 3: 6, 8). Certainly to be born of Christ is a possible idea.

John marvels at the quality (*potapēn*) of the Father's

love (3:1-3) "that we should be called children of God," and the wonder still is in the unique Johannine addition, "and we are," which parenthesis occurs also in John 5:25 ("and now is") and in Revelation 2:2; 3:9 ("and are not"). "This parenthetical addition is an emphatic expression of the Apostle's own faith" (Westcott). John takes up again the statement in 2:29 that "every one who does righteousness is begotten (reborn) of him." He does not here use Paul's word for "sons" (*huioi*, Rom. 8:14, etc.)—used by Christ also (in Matt. 5:9)—but the word for "children" (*tekna*), common enough in this Epistle (verses 2, 10; 5:2, besides the diminutive *teknia*, little children, 2:1, 12, 28, etc.). The world failed to recognise God as the history of the race shows (Rom. 1:20-23), though nature plainly speaks of Him. Still more, the world did not recognise God in Christ (Jo. 16:3)—nor even the Jewish people when Christ came to them (Jo. 1:11). It is small wonder that the world does not understand God's children. The world hated Christ before it hated His followers (Jo. 15:18f.). But the glory of it all is the fact that we are here and now the children of God, with unknown glories still to come, "for it has not yet been made manifest what we shall be. We do know that, if he be manifested, we shall be like him, because we shall see him as he is." The aged Apostle looks wistfully and expectantly into the face of death and sees the Master of Life and Death. He may come to him before death, but certainly at death. John is as exultant as Paul in Philippians 1:21f. It is not John's prerogative alone; it belongs to "every one who has this hope resting upon Him" (Christ).

But such a destiny of likeness to Christ with such a hope of certainty calls for constant purifying discipline (*hagnizei*, not the *katharizei* of 1:7 of the blood of Christ) on the part of those who are to appear in Christ's likeness in the presence of God, "even as he (*ekeinos*, that one, usually Christ in John's writings, when standing alone) is pure." Christlikeness includes this ideal of personal cleanness. The

BIRDVILLE
BAPTIST CHURCH
LIBRARY

blood of Christ alone cleanses us from all sin (1:7), but the individual Christian alone can consecrate himself to a life of purity after the example of Christ.

John now faces squarely the problem of sin in the life of the individual in a memorable, and often misunderstood, passage (3:4-12). The words are thoroughly Johannine (sin, lawlessness, manifest, do, abide, see, know, lead astray, righteous, righteousness, begotten, works, devil, children, hear, love, message, brother, evil). The article with both sin and lawlessness *(hē hamartia, hē anomia)* shows that the two terms are interchangeable. Sin is not simply missing the mark, but also breaking God's law. It is a lesson sadly needed especially to-day,—that *lawlessness is sin.* The tenses here call for careful and constant attention. "Every one who keeps on doing (linear, present participle) sin keeps on doing lawlessness." It is the habit of sin that John has in mind. The use of emphatic He *(ekeinos)* referring to Christ, occurs three times here (verses 3, 5, 7) as does "was manifested" *(ephanerōthē)* of Christ and us (2, 5, 8). The clause in verse 5, "that he bear the sins," reminds us of the Baptist's language in John 1:29, except that here we have the plural (sins) and the effective aorist subjunctive *(arei)* instead of the present indicative *(airei)*. John repeats the idea from various angles. The man who keeps on abiding in Christ does not keep on sinning. On the contrary, the man who keeps on sinning has not seen or known Christ (God in Christ, he means by "him").

John pleads with his "little children" that they let no one (like Cerinthus, or Mrs. Eddy to-day) lead them astray. He (Christ) is righteous and is the standard for us all. The one who keeps on doing sin (Johannine phrase) is of the devil, "for from the beginning the devil has been sinning" (progressive present). That is his nature and his habit. In simple truth, "for this purpose was the Son of God manifested that he might destroy (effective aorist subjunctive, *lusēi*) the works of the devil." "The one begotten of God (like 2:29) does not keep on sinning, because God's seed

abides in him, and he is not able to keep on sinning" (verse
9). John does not here say "is not able to commit a sin,"
for that idea requires the aorist infinitive *(hamartein* or
hamartēsai), but he uses *hamartanein* (present infinitive)
which is always linear and can only mean "keep on sinning"
(the habit of sin). With this clearly in mind, and John's
Greek is as plain as a pikestaff, there is no contradiction
with 1:8, 10 and 2:1. Denial of a sinful nature (1:8) or of
any sinful act (1:10) is a lie. But there is a world of difference between one sin in a struggle against sin (2:1) and the
habit of sin (3:9), which is what John is seeking to prevent
(2:1). The habit of sin, in fact, is what marks off the
children of the devil (verse 10. Cf. Jo. 8:44) from the children of God (the spiritual children of God, not God as
Creator of all men, but God the Father of the saved). One's
life shows whose child he is (God's or the devil's). Not
having the habit of righteousness and not loving (as a habit)
one's brother is proof enough. So John repeats his message
(2:9-11) that we keep on loving one another. The case of
Cain is to the point. He did not love his brother and so
slew him.

This subject of loving one another fascinates John
the Apostle of love. So he proceeds to point out the
reason for the world's hatred of followers of Christ (3:13-
15). There is no ground for surprise. It hated Jesus first
(Jo. 15:18). Here, alone in the Epistle, John addresses his
readers as "brothers" instead of "little children." He appeals to the common consciousness of all true believers
("we know") that they have passed from death (spiritual)
into life (spiritual and eternal), "because we love the
brethren." This notion of brotherhood in the word *adelphos*
is older than Christianity, as the papyri show, but it shines
with new lustre in the union in Christ (the blood bond in
Jesus). In truth, he who does not keep on loving the
brotherhood abides in spiritual death. The one who keeps
on hating his brother is a murderer at heart as Jesus said
(Matt. 5:22). The word here for murderer *(anthrōpo-*

ktonos, man killer) is precisely the one used by Jesus of the devil (Jo. 8:44), the father of all murderers. Eternal life does not abide in a murderer. John does not make a hero of the gangster.

The supreme example of love is found in Jesus who laid down His life for us (3:16-18) voluntarily (Jo. 10:17f.). We ought, if need be, to follow Christ's example, even though there is not the same value in our doing it. Paul (Rom. 5:7f.) shows the difference to be that Jesus gave His life for us while we were yet sinners. We may not be called on to make so great a sacrifice, but we can at least help the one that we see in need and not shut (effective aorist) tight the door of compassion. That is not loving in deed and in truth, but only in word and tongue (cf. James 2:14-26). We should "share" our goods as well as our words and emotions with those in need.

Findlay happily terms 3:19-24 "Christian heart assurance." "The fruit of love is confidence" (Westcott). These. verses "have always been recognised as touching the very heart of the Christian faith" (Brooke), though there are points of difficulty in the exegesis. We at least shall know that we are on the side of truth and not of error (like Gnosticism). And even "in the presence of God (in prayer and fellowship) we shall persuade (or still, appease) our heart as to whatsoever (probable meaning of *hoti ean* as indefinite relative, and not "that if") our heart condemn us, that God is greater than our heart and knows all things." This holy boldness of the believer is illustrated by the conduct of Simon Peter with Jesus by "the Beloved Lake": "Lord, thou knowest all things; thou knowest that I love thee" (Jo. 21:17). Peter made this appeal in the full glare of his own terrible sin. It is true that we dread for man, let alone God, to read the inner secrets of our hearts (Rothe), but the Christian looks on God as all-loving as well as all-knowing (Brooke), and that makes all the difference. The full grasp of God's love for us silences the condemnation of our own hearts, for His love is a love that knows all and still loves, a love that gave the highest for us (Jo. 3:16) and that cannot be made to cease loving us (Rom. 8:31-39). In moments, when our heart is stilled before God, we even have boldness with God, that dares and challenges us to prevailing prayer: "Whatsoever we ask we receive from him." That is the ideal of Jesus for His followers: "All things whatsoever ye pray and ask for, believe that ye did receive *(elabete)* them and it shall be so unto you" (Mk. 11:24). This assumes fellowship and acquiescence in the will of God, but it explains also our failures in prayer. The reason for this power is added by John, "because we keep on observing his commandments and doing the things pleasing before him." That is where we fail. The essence of God's commandment is that "we trust the name of his Son Jesus Christ and keep on loving one another as he gave us commandment." The blessed result of all this is that such a one "abides in him (God) and he (God) abides in him" (the keeper of God's commandments). This is what "fellowship" with God means (1:3-10). And God has given us the Holy Spirit that we may know that He is abiding in us. God's Spirit bears witness with our spirit that we are God's children. This is the confident assurance open to all of us, the witness of Christian experience of grace. Cf. 4:13 and John 14:16.

But the Holy Spirit has rivals for the control of the human spirit (4:1-6). There are other voices that clamour for a hearing and gain it with some, sirens that fascinate and lead astray those that follow. The disciples of Christ must test "the spirits whether they are from God, because many false prophets have gone forth into the world," wolves in sheep's clothing as Jesus pictured them. "Beloved, do not believe every spirit," when they cry: "Lo here, or lo there." The Master foresaw this peril which is always at hand for the gullible and the unsuspecting who are looking for the latest fad in theology or science. It is absolutely essential, in the medley of conflicting voices which we have to-day—such as atheism and materialism and pantheism and humanism and Unitarianism and Christian Science—that the disciples of Jesus be able to "recognise the Spirit of God." John tells how this can be done: "Every spirit which confesses Jesus Christ as come in the flesh is of God." The correct text here has the perfect active participle *(elēlu-thota)* and not the perfect active infinitive *(elēluthenai)*. The preëxistent, Son of God (the Word of Life) "came in the flesh" (Jo. 1:14) and the one personality is "Jesus Christ." John here rules out both kinds of Gnosticism (the unity of the person "Jesus Christ" against Cerinthianism, the actual humanity against Docetism). Both the deity and the humanity are affirmed. *Per contra,* denial of this is "the spirit of antichrist" which is already at work in the world. The followers of Christ have already "overcome them" (the false prophets of verse 1), because God, who is in them, is greater than the antichrist in the world.

The line of battle is drawn between God and antichrist and men must take sides. One is reminded of "St. Paul's confessional watchword *Kurios Iēsous,* Jesus is Lord" (Findlay) as in I Corinthians 12:3. There are those to-day, as there were in Paul's day and that of John who (Nietzsche, for instance) call Jesus Christ "anathema." One's attitude towards Jesus Christ is the test for the "Spirit of truth and the spirit of error." Jesus had already called the Holy Spirit the Spirit of truth (Jo. 14:17. Cf. I Cor. 2:12ff.). Christ is still the touchstone of the ages for the distinction between truth and error.

And now John justifies his epithet as the "Apostle of Love" in 4:7-21, a passage that is only equalled by Paul's Hymn on Love in I Corinthians 13. Paul's chapter is a perfect prose poem, while John's is like a diamond turned round and round for different angles of light to flash upon it. It is not easy to analyse as is Paul's. Westcott and Hort make three paragraphs in the Greek text (7-10, 11-16^a, 16^b-21). Brooke makes four thus: 7-10 mutual love because of the Incarnation, 11 and 12 love of the brethren a test of fellowship, 13-16^a proofs of fellowship, 16^b-21 love

and faith in relation to judgment. Westcott *(Comm.)* has
three: 7-10 the ground of love, 11-16ᵃ the inspiration of
love, 16ᵇ-21 the activity of love.

In 7-10 "the ground of love" is plainly stated: "We love
one another because love is of God." "The one who loves
God is begotten of God and knows God." God is love, not
love is God. God has manifested His love in sending His
only begotten Son (Jo. 3:16), "that we may come to live
through him." Our love for God is result, not cause, and
supreme love is seen in God's sending His Son as "a propitiation concerning our sins" (cf. 2:1).

In verses 11 to 16ᵃ John goes on with the theme of God's
love, "to him a never-ceasing wonder and enthronement—
the thought of the eternal Father's love, that flows through
Christ into human souls and draws them into blissful union
with itself and with each other" (Findlay). Here he brings
out sharply "the inspiration of love": "If God so loved us
(the very word *ēgapēsen* of Jo. 3:16), we also ought to go
on loving one another." No one, he adds, has ever beheld
God (1:18) save as Jesus has revealed Him (14:9). By such
continual love of one another, "His (God's) love is perfected in us" (verse 12, repeated in verses 17 and 18).
Only when we so love one another is God's love seen in its
full perfection (fruition). Then we know also that God is
abiding in us (14:23). John appeals to his own personal
experience of Christ (we have beheld, *tetheametha,* as in
1:1, and 1:32, 34 of the Baptist's witness) as qualifying
him for bearing witness concerning his being sent as
"Saviour of the world" as some of the Samaritans early
discovered (4:42). We need a like experience with Christ
to qualify as witnesses. By "confession" of Jesus Christ as
the Son of God John means not lip confession merely, but
that surrender of the heart which opens the door for fellowship with God. Once again (verse 16ᵃ) John reiterates his
knowledge and belief in "the love which God has in us."

In 16ᵇ to 21 John is discussing "the activity of love."
He repeats what he has said in verse 8 ("God is love") and

also his preceding argument about abiding in God by abiding in love and so gaining perfect love, thereby to express a further purpose ("that we may keep on having boldness in the day of judgment"). John has not dropped the idea of the Parousia (2:28) and Judgment (cf. "the last day" in Jo. 6:39f., 44, 54; 11:24; 12:48). But there is no occasion for fear on the part of the believer who has Christ as Propitiation and Paraclete (I Jo. 2:1f.). Our present likeness to Christ is one ground of confidence (3:1-3). Perfect love drives fear out of the house. This is true at home and with God. "Fear has (includes) punishment," but that is not true with the believer in Christ. With Christ as Propitiation and Paraclete, we have no fear from any source (Rom. 8:31-39). God "first" (*prōtos*) loved us (verse 10; Jo. 3:16). Our profession of love for God ("If any say, I love God") and continued hatred for one's brother proves one a liar, as he has already said about knowing Christ (2:4). And, what is more, "the one who keeps on hating his brother whom he has seen is not able to go on loving God whom he has not seen." Hence the command of Christ (Jo. 13:34) that we love one another is to the point.

But love with John is not mere emotion. As with Paul, who ranks it with and above faith and hope, (I Cor. 13:13), so John places love first, but it is grounded in trust (5:1-12). The word "faith" (*pistis*), so common in Paul's Epistles, occurs only once in John's Epistles (I Jo. 5:4), not at all in his Gospel, but several times in the Apocalypse (2:13, 19; 13:10; 14:12). But the verb believe (*pisteuō*) is commonly used in John's Gospel and Epistles to mean "believing in Jesus Christ." So in 5:1 John connects believing and loving with the new birth: "Every one who believes that Jesus is the Christ is begotten of God, and every one who loves the One who begat him (God) loves the one who is begotten of him." That is axiomatic—or ought to be. So then "we know experimentally that we are loving the children of God whenever we are loving God and doing His commandments." Love works both ways (4:11f., 20).

Each form of love (for God and for the brotherhood) includes the other. The supreme proof of love for God is the keeping of His commandments, which are not burdensome, when love exists.

The Christian has the conquering power of faith because he is the child of God (5:4). John heard Jesus say, "I have overcome the world" (Jo. 16:33), as He faced the Cross. His own brother James had died the victim of Jewish hate. He had seen Paul and Peter die as martyrs for Christ. Persecution and tribulation cannot rob the Christian of victory: "And this is the victory that overcame the world, our faith." Death only accents this victory. In true Johannine style, he repeats the challenging question: "Who is he that overcomes the world except he that believes that Jesus is the Son of God?" (5:5). The Deity of Jesus Christ lies at the basis of faith. John now explains the reason for such faith (5:6-9) in language that has often been misunderstood. The Baptism (water) and the Cross (blood) bear witness to the real humanity of Jesus (against the Docetic Gnostics). The Son of God existed with the Father before the Incarnation and came to earth with the Father's approval and blessing, and the Holy Spirit bears witness also. So then these three witnesses (the water or Baptism, the blood or Cross, the Holy Spirit) testify for God concerning His Son. If we accept the testimony of men, surely we are willing to receive that of God. The correct text does not have the spurious addition about the Trinity (verse 8) which Erasmus foolishly put into his second edition of the Greek Testament on the evidence of a later minuscule, apparently made to order. The Trinity is clearly presented in the New Testament, without reference to these spurious words.

The believer in the Son of God has also the witness of inward experience ("in himself"). This inner witness comes from self-surrender to Jesus Christ (5:10-12). The use of the negative form is startling enough, for refusal to believe God's witness about His Son makes God a liar. To sum it all up in one phrase, this witness consists in the eternal (spiritual) life which God gave us in His Son. To have the Son is to have life here and now. God's Son alone can give this life to men.

John is anxious that his readers shall clearly understand his message. So in an epilogue (5:13-21) he repeats succinctly the substance of it all. The aim, stated in 1:3f., is now (5:13) said to be "that ye may know that ye have eternal life." Hence "I have written to you, the ones who believe on the name of the Son of God." This knowledge brings "boldness" or confidence in prayer that is according to the will of God (5:14f.). Pray for a brother who is caught sinning, provided he is not sinning a sin unto death (5:16f.). John does not explain what this sin is. Apparently he has in mind the wilful rejection of Jesus Christ, already described in verses 9 to 12, and like in character to the blasphemous accusation concerning the works of Christ pictured in Mark 3:29 (Matt. 12:32; Lu. 12:10). The author of Hebrews (10:26-30) describes the terrible plight of those who sin wilfully after receiving the knowledge of Christ. John does not here forbid prayer for such people, but he does not command it. Surely we can pray on and leave the result with God.

John closes the Epistle with a threefold use of "we know" (*oidamen*) in verses 18, 19, 20. Findlay terms this "the Apostolic Creed" in epitome. The first item in this creed of the aged Apostle is "holiness." The child of God does not keep on sinning. The second item is the cleavage among men resultant on the new birth, the children of God as over against the children of the devil. We are on God's side, while the whole world of sin is in the grip of the evil one. The third item is the Incarnation of God's Son who has come to give us knowledge of the true God. This true God is made known to us in His Son, Jesus Christ who has brought us eternal life from the Father. The last word is a warning against idols. It was pertinent then and it is pertinent now. Even in so-called Christian lands vast multitudes place self, money, pleasure, power in the place of God in Christ.

XII

JOHN LEADING IN MISSIONARY PROPAGANDA

(SECOND AND THIRD JOHN)

1. *Authorship and date.* The author calls himself "the elder" (II Jo. 1; III Jo. 1), a claim not made in First John. This title does not prove that the Beloved Disciple of the Fourth Gospel is not the same person as the Apostle John. Peter calls himself both apostle (I Pet. 1:1) and elder (5:1). We have seen already that the so-called "Presbyter John" of Papias is really the Apostle John. The dates of these two epistles in relation to those of the First Epistle and the Gospel and Apocalypse are wholly uncertain. The same language and ideas and style that we find in the First Epistle occur in them. The kinship is too close to be mere imitation.

2. *Second John.*

(a) *If to a lady.* This is in itself entirely possible. It is the obvious and natural way to take the language. Paul wrote to Philemon, to Timothy and Titus, and sent greetings to eight women prominent in the church in Rome (16: 3-15): Prisca, Mary, Tryphena, Tryphosa, Persis, the mother of Rufus, Julia, and the sister of Nereus. He sent the Epistle by Phoebe. Peter sends the greetings of "the co-elect lady in Babylon" (I Pet. 5:13). If John is addressing this Epistle to a lady of prominence in Christian activity, it may seem strange that her name is not mentioned. It is even suggested that the name is Cyria or Electa or even Eclecta Cyria. Like names do occur in the papyri and the inscriptions. Some have suggested that it is the mother of Jesus who is meant, or Martha. This is pure hypothesis and an anachronism, besides. If a lady is meant we do not know her name. *Kurios* sometimes occurs in the New Testament for Sir (Jo. 4:15) and it is possible that this is the meaning here like our "Lady" or "Madame." It is even suggested that the use of *kuria* has a playful turn here, though the use of *eklecta* (elect) is rather against that idea. There is really no strong objection to taking "lady" here in its literal sense.

(b) *If to a Church*. According to this view, a church is personified by the use of *kuria* (lady) just as the people of God (the spiritual church) are called the bride of Christ (Eph. 5:22-33). Certainly this interpretation is possible also. In that case, the "sister" of the Elect Lady would be a church also (in Ephesus where John is). The "children" would be the members of each church. If a church is addressed, it could be Pergamos, Smyrna or some other in the region of the Province of Asia or Asia Minor. There is a frequent change from singular to plural and back again, but this is natural in either interpretation, for the "children" are included in the address (verse 1). It is not unseemly for the aged Apostle to show interest in the family life of that day nor is it inappropriate for him to exhibit keen interest in the doctrine and life of the neighbouring churches as he lingers on in Ephesus. There are, to my mind, no conclusive arguments to decide between a "lady" and a "church" as the recipient of the Epistle, though I incline to the obvious sense of "lady."

(c) *The salutation (1-3)*. There is no article with "elect lady" and, none is needed if a proper name, or even a title is meant. John expresses his love for the elect lady and her children and claims a like love for them from "all who have known the truth." It is argued by some that such language could be true only of a church of great importance, but Paul uses almost identical language ("not I alone, but also all the churches of the Gentiles") of Priscilla and Aquila (Rom. 16:4). A Christian woman like Priscilla could have called forth such love and praise from John and all the others.

John is sure that "the truth," in opposition to Gnostic error, will abide with us for ever. Christ is the Incarnate Truth. In I John 1:6 John speaks of our "doing the truth." John inserts his confidence (in a parenthesis) "and it will be with us forever," as in I John 3:1 ("and we are"). He adds also that "grace, mercy, peace will be with us" (prediction rather than mere wish), because these graces come "from God the Father and from (repetition of *para* showing the twofold personal relation of Father and Son to us) Jesus Christ the. Son of the Father" (a unique phrase), and all "in truth and love," "the two vital elements in the Christian Faith" (Brooke).

(d) *The exhortation. (4-11).* Westcott has a pertinent comment: "The rise of false teachers, who seem to have affected superior knowledge (v. 9 *proagōn*), and neglected moral duties (cf. I John 2:4), leads St. John to emphasise the duty of active love, which is the sum of the divine commandments (4-7); and then to insist upon the necessity of guarding inviolate the 'teaching of Christ,' the historic Gospel which conveys the revelation of 'the Father and the Son' (8-11)." John's joy in finding some of the children of the Elect Lady walking in truth is possibly due to his seeing them in another city than that where the "Lady" lives. This could be due either to their presence in Ephesus (as in verse 13), to John's visit to the city where they were, or to reports to John by some of the travelling preachers (Brooke). The joy is real whether the children are members of a church or of an actual family. These absent "children" reflect credit on the "mother." The request to the "Lady," John admits, is not new (cf. I Jo. 2:7f.), but still needed, "that we keep on loving one another."

This is the burden of the First Epistle as also of the Second; here, as there (I Jo. 5:1-4), John links love with walking according to God's commandments. That is walking in love, keeping God's commandments. There is need of this pointed emphasis because "many deceivers have gone forth into the world, who do not confess Jesus Christ as coming into the world" (verse 7). The Docetic Gnostics denied the Incarnation (the humanity of Christ) and the Cerinthian Gnostics distinguished between the man Jesus and the *aeon* Christ. John here refutes both heresies (as in I Jo. 4:2), only in this instance he uses the present middle participle "coming" *(erchomenon)* instead of the perfect active "come" *(elēluthota)* of I John 4:2. There he refers to the historic fact of the Incarnation (Jo. 1:14), here to the denial of the possibility of the Incarnation. He is not speaking here of the Second Coming of Christ. John warns his readers not to destroy by false teaching what he had brought, but to receive a full reward for loyalty to "the teaching of Christ" (verse 8). These Gnostics were "going beyond" the teaching of Christ (verse 9) with their wild theories. The proof that one "has the Father and the Son" is precisely this holding fast to the teaching of Christ as the norm or standard of Christian doctrine and life.

We live to-day in an age quite similar to that of John, with all sorts of fanciful theories that lead men astray from the truth as it is in Jesus. He is the truth and all else needs to be brought to book in Christ. This is the supreme issue in our day as in John's time. He saw it clearly and proclaimed it clearly. With John, Jesus is not a way of salvation and life, but *the* way, the *only* way to the Father. John is not a reactionary. He is not opposed to new truth. He welcomes all truth. But Jesus Christ, the Incarnate and Risen Son of God, is the test of all truth. He alone is the Saviour of the world, the Redeemer from sin. John is so much concerned about loyalty to the teaching of Christ that he forbids hospitality to propagandists of hostility to Jesus: "If any one comes to you and does not bring this teaching, do not receive him into your home and do not say 'welcome' to him; for the one who says 'welcome' to him shares in his evil deeds" (verses 10f.).

In a latitudinarian age these words may sound harsh and unfeeling, but a little knowledge of the situation will clear it up. It is not just a case of entertaining people who disagree with one on minor matters or an emergency case when true hospitality overrides ordinary difficulties. These propagandists of error (deceivers, antichrists) were carrying on regular campaigns to destroy loyalty to Christ as Lord and Saviour. People were called on to take sides for or against Christ. These "deceivers" were also immoral in their lives. Suppose atheistic free lovers were carrying on a campaign in your town. Hospitality to such leaders would inevitably involve endorsement of their teaching and lives. John puts the matter sharply, but not more pointedly than the situation demanded.

The conclusion (12f.) explains that the brevity of the letter is because of his desire to see the "Lady" and her "children" ("you," plural *humas*) "face to face," as we say, and as Paul has it (I Cor. 13:12 *prosōpon pros prosōpon*), but here literally "mouth to mouth" *(stoma pros stoma)* or "voice to voice." That will be in both cases with joy. Meanwhile "the children of thy Elect Sister," here where John is (in Ephesus), send their salutation. Whether family or church, they are with John when he writes.

3. *Third John.*

This little Epistle, unlike II John, deals directly with names, three persons.

(a) *Gaius.* The Epistle is addressed to him, but we do not know where he is. There was a Gaius of Macedonia, a companion of Paul, who was seized in Ephesus along with Aristarchus (Acts 19:29). Then there is a Gaius of Derbe who went with Paul to Jerusalem with the money for the poor saints there (Acts 20:4). And then Paul baptized a Gaius in Corinth (I Cor. 1:14) who may be also Paul's host later in Corinth, when he writes to Rome (Rom. 16: 23). This Gaius in III John may be a different man from either of these, nor do we know what position he held, whether that of elder or deacon, in the church where he lived. John terms him "the beloved" in the introduction and three times also in the body of the Epistle (2, 5, 11) as an endearing address. Paul often uses these words in salutation. John repeats his emphatic love for Gaius as if some one had denied it. He expresses concern about the health of Gaius (2) and wishes that his bodily health may equal that of his soul, a noble tribute. Travelling brethren coming to Ephesus, testify to the upright creed and conduct of Gaius, to the great joy of John, who has no greater joy than in learning that his "children" are walking in truth (II Jo. 4-6). It should be noted that "children" (*tekna*, like II Jo. 1, 13) can here only mean spiritual children like *teknia* and *paidia* (little children) in I John 2:1, 12, 14, 18, etc. To this extent, therefore, the word argues for spiritual children of a church in II John.

John praises Gaius in particular for his hospitality and helpfulness to the travelling preachers of the Gospel (5-8). At a meeting in Ephesus John had heard some of these missionaries tell of the kindness of Gaius. These men could receive nothing from the Gentiles without being misunderstood. It was for this reason that Paul supported himself (I Thess. 2: 6-9; I Cor. 9:14f.; II Cor. 12:14-16). Jesus had given like instructions on the special Galilean tour (Matt. 10:8). Paul did, while in Corinth, receive gifts from Macedonia (II Cor. 11:7-10; Phil. 4:15f.). These men went forth "for the sake of the Name," the absolute sense of the Name (of Jesus) as in Acts 5:41 and Romans 1:5. In I Peter 4:14 it is "in the name of Christ," "as a Christian." Hence, we Christians should entertain and support these workers for Christ "that we may keep on becoming co-workers with the truth," a powerful argument for continual support of the work of Christ at home and abroad by Christians. John urges Gaius to keep on helping these preachers on their way. The inns were abominable and travelling was difficult. Hospitality was a blessing.

(b) *Diotrephes (9-10)*. John has a word of warning to Gaius about Diotrephes (9-10). He had written something to the church already, either II John,—if that is to a church—or some epistle that we do not now have. This is a personal word to Gaius, who belongs to this church to which John had written. This brother Diotrephes who was also a member of this same church, had refused to entertain John on his last visit there, perhaps out of jealousy of John, or out of hostility to John because of sympathy with the Gnostics whom John so vigorously opposes. At any rate John is not afraid of Diotrephes, a self-appointed regulator of the church, whether pastor or deacon. When John comes, he will expose him to his face before the church for his "prating" against John with evil words. Diotrephes carried things with such a high hand that he not only refused to welcome the travelling preachers (missionaries) sent by John, but he actually hinders those who are willing to entertain them and tries to cast them out of the church. He is the typical church "boss" who is determined "to be first" at whatever cost to the cause, an ambition for personal preëminence, not for leadership in good works.

(c) *Demetrius (11-12)*. Gaius should beware of Diotrephes, a man who is doing evil. He should imitate Demetrius, a man who is doing good and so is of God. Demetrius seems to be the bearer of this letter from John to Gaius and John commends him warmly. He is commended likewise by all who know him, including Gaius himself, who apparently knows Demetrius and certainly knows John. The truth itself commends Demetrius. For Paul on letters of commendation see II Corinthians 3:1-3. See also Acts 18:28 about Apollos.

(d) *Conclusion (13-15)*. It is very much like II John 12f. save that in place of "paper and ink" we have here "ink and pen." "We shall speak mouth to mouth," John says. He asks that Gaius will salute John's friends "by name." Like Paul, John knows his friends by name, salutes them, prays for them by name. He is now an old man, but his mind lingers lovingly over the names of his friends in the distant church. He sends also the greetings of the friends with him. This little letter is a model of Christian courtesy and courage. The peril exposed in III John is the selfish ambition of Diotrephes with its rule or ruin policy. That feared in II John is the rash intellectualism of those who rule out Jesus Christ as the Lord and Master of all. Both types of peril are with us yet.

XIII

INTERPRETING CHRIST OUT OF A RICH EXPERIENCE

(THE FOURTH GOSPEL)

1. *The importance of the subject for to-day.* It is impossible to omit a discussion and interpretation of the Fourth Gospel in a book on the Apostle John and it is likewise impossible to make an adequate treatment in one chapter. There is a veritable library of books on this Gospel. Dr. W. F. Howard's recent Fernley Lecture (1931) on *The Fourth Gospel in Recent Criticism and Interpretation* lists ten pages of titles of books and articles on the subject which he has himself examined, all in this century save nine (some two hundred books and articles). The total since the year 1800 of important books would probably reach a thousand. One who wishes to go further into the long and vigorous debate concerning the Fourth Gospel will find the most important older literature discussed in Moffatt's *Introduction to the Literature of the New Testament* (1911). But, whatever view one holds as to the authorship, few deny the supreme importance of the Fourth Gospel. Many call it "the supreme literary work of the world." Origen said: "This Gospel is the consummation of the Gospels as the Gospels are of all the Scriptures." Clement of Alexandria said: "John, last of all, perceiving that what had reference to the bodily was sufficiently detailed in the Gospels, encouraged by his friends, and divinely incited by the Spirit, composed a spiritual Gospel." To come to more recent times, Tholuck says: "This Gospel speaks a language to which no parallel whatever is to be found in the whole com-

149

BIRDVILLE
BAPTIST CHURCH
LIBRARY

pass of literature." Philip Schaff terms it "the holy of
holies of the New Testament." James Drummond, the
Unitarian scholar of Oxford, expresses my own attitude
when he says: "And when we remember how it has moulded
the faith and touched the heart and calmed the sorrows of
generations of men, we must approach it with no ordinary
reverence, and with a desire to penetrate its inmost meaning
and become more thoroughly imbued with its kindling
power."

This reverent attitude must not be the excuse for a reactionary obscuration, for hiding the real facts, for refusing
to see new light concerning the Fourth Gospel. Only one
does wish to be reasonably certain that speculative theories
which overthrow the Johannine authorship of the Fourth
Gospel have actual historical foundation before one turns
away from the vast mass of historical evidence in its support. Lord Charnwood (*According to St. John,* p. 35), for
instance, ridicules the belief of some modern scholars in the
mythical Presbyter John and that the Apostle John suffered
early martyrdom like his brother James: "There could be no
better example of a vice which microscopic research seems
often to induce,—that of abnormal suspiciousness towards
the evidence which satisfies normal people, coupled with
abnormal credulity towards evidence which is trifling or
null." Lord Charnwood attributes the three Epistles to the
Apostle John and the Gospel to a pupil of the Apostle and
thus, himself, splits a very narrow hair of distinction in
style between Gospel and Epistles. We can all respect the
methods and motives of the critics of various schools concerning the Fourth Gospel. Each man can only speak for
himself in the light of all the known facts. It is a marvel
that John's Gospel contains only fifty-three pages in the
Greek text of Westcott and Hort, and only twenty-seven in
the American Standard Version in English. Hayes (*op. cit.,*
p. 81) observes that Boswell's *Life of Samuel Johnson* has
1824 pages, Allen's *Life of Phillips Brooks* 1596, Weiss's
Life of Christ 1143, Geike's 1236, Edersheim's 1524, Keim's

1904. "And yet the Fourth Gospel is worth all these other books put together."

2. *The unity of the Book.* This is disputed by those who admit only portions of it as genuinely Johannine, and by some who deny any apostolic fragments. Bacon, in his *Introduction to the New Testament* (1900), found marks of three writers: (a) The "witness" or the Beloved Disciple, apparently the Apostle John; (b) The "reporter" of the Apostle's witness, the "Elder John" of Ephesus, who wrote also the Epistles; (c) The "redactor," who compiled the Gospel from the reporter's use of the witness and added the appendix or epilogue. But in *The Fourth Gospel in Research and Debate* (1910) Bacon dismisses the Apostle John as the "witness" entirely, rejects the mythical "Presbyter John" as the reporter and suggests a nameless author (p. 453): "For convenience let us call him *Theologos.* The Elder *Theologos* will be the author of the Gospel in the form it possessed before the final revision, which aims to adapt it to general circulation and identifies its enigmatic figure of the Beloved Disciple with the Apostle John." This identification Bacon terms "a pious fraud" (p. 447). In his posthumous work, *The Gospel of the Hellenists* (1933), Bacon holds that (p. vii) "a late tradition, confessedly founded on the two closing verses of an appendix written and attached in order to secure for the document canonical authority, ascribes the work in a guarded manner to the Apostle John." But it is begging the question to call this appendix "a late tradition." It is the oldest tradition that we have and is confirmed by all the early evidence, rightly understood, as has been shown in chapter II and III of this book. Bacon insists that we must get rid of this "late tradition": "Release cannot otherwise be had from the cramping preconceptions of the past" (p. viii). But where is the "early tradition" (to take the place of the "late tradition") which will also be free from "the cramping preconceptions of the past"?

This great unknown Ephesian Elder "is worthy of the succession of Peter and Paul and Apollos," "a prominent leader of the churches in Asia," and "will at last be able to speak for himself" (p. 5). Bacon writes, as the discoverer of a diamond of rare value in "this nameless Elder": "The well-meant, but by no means disinterested, efforts to clothe his utterances with an apostolic authority he nowhere claims, are but grave-clothes which impede his movements and muffle his voice." From the days of the "pious fraud" of the closing verses of the Appendix till now, the world has had to wait for Bacon's discovery of the "prominent leader," "this nameless Elder" disclosed by Bacon's critical ingenuities; there is not a single trace of him in the second and third centuries at which time all the writers attribute this greatest of books to the Apostle John. Dr. A. E. Garvie in *The Beloved Disciple* (1922) identifies the "witness" with the Disciple whom Jesus loved, but not with the Apostle John. The Evangelist, who wrote the Prologue and the body of the book, he thinks, may be the so-called Presbyter John of Ephesus. The Redactor then wrote chapters 6 and 21. R. H. Strachan in *The Fourth Gospel* (1917) thinks that the original notes of the Apostle John have been revised and recast by a later editor. Vacher Burch in *The Structure and Message of St. John's Gospel* (1928) suggests that the Apostle John wrote the Gospel soon after the Crucifixion in Aramaic, but that a Redactor later translated it into Greek and added chapters 17, 20, 21. Bernard in his two volumes on John's Gospel in the *International and Critical Commentary* (1929) thinks that the Apostle John is the Beloved Disciple and the eye-witness, but that the Presbyter John actually wrote the book. Like variations are also found among German scholars. H. H. Wendt holds that the Apostle John wrote the Prologue and the longer discourses. It is interesting to note that Streeter, who rejects the apostolic authorship, says (*op. cit.*, p. 392): "It would seem clear that the hope that by critical analysis, sufficiently refined, we can reconstruct the sources used by John is chimerical." But against all the theories of editing and redactions lies the uniformity in language, thought, and style. There are no linguistic variations that evidence for several writers. The book is a unity from beginning to end. W. Bauer (*Handbuch zum N. T.*, Aufl. 2, p. 229) pointedly says: "One and the same man has written the whole book. Not at one stroke, but as he brought himself to his task in many an onset." This is capitally put. E. F. Scott, though denying the Johannine authorship, insists on the integrity of the book (*The First Age of Christianity*, pp. 217f.). The modern scholars who propose partition theories strike out in the dark and give no solid basis for their divergent views. The book stands or falls as a unit. There is, of course, the addition of 21:24 by the Ephesian elders, but the Beloved Disciple instantly adds his last word in 21:25. The oldest manuscripts do not contain 7:53-8:11, which passage was certainly not an original part of John's Gospel, though probably a true incident.

3. *Alleged displacements.* There is some tendency to rearrange some of the chapters in the Fourth Gospel on the ground that they originally had a different order. So Moffatt in his *New Translation* places 7:15-24 after 5:47, 10:19-29 after 9:41, 11:18f. after 11:30, 12:44-50 in the middle of 12:36, 15 and 16 in the middle of 13:31, 18:19-24 after 18:14. Spitta had already suggested rearrangement of portions of the Gospel. The Sinaitic Syriac has another rearrangement of verses 13 to 28 in chapter 18. This may be due to a scribe's blunder. Bernard (Vol. I, p. xxvf.) rejects these rearrangements in chapter 18, though he accepts several others (p. xviif.). F. Warburton Lewis in his *Disarrangements in the Fourth Gospel* (1910) argues that there was a primitive disturbance of the leaves of the manuscript. Stanton in *The Gospels as Historical Documents* (Part I 1903, Part III 1920) argued in Part I strongly that the Apostle John was connected with authorship of the Fourth Gospel, but in Part II he changed to the view that the author was a disciple of the Apostle John who incorporated John's witness in the Gospel. Stanton denies any dislocations on a large scale, but admits "that in a few instances

editorial remarks have been introduced and sayings added
in a manner inappropriate to the context" (Part III, p. 73).
He cites chapter 6 as a case where the author himself placed
the teaching of Jesus in the synagogue after the miracle of
feeding the five thousand because the author himself applied
the words of Jesus to the Lord's Supper (Part III, p. 239f.).
This instance illustrates how speculative and whimsical the
whole displacement theory is. One is moved to suggest that
before doing such violence to the text of the Fourth Gospel,
one try to see what the author's real idea may be in the
arrangement as it has come down to us.

4. *Accepting the Johannine authorship.* "He who writes
on the subject should at least know his own mind as clearly
as Lightfoot and Zahn on the one hand, or Schmiedel,
Wernle and Loisy on the other" (A. E. Brooke, *Cambridge
Biblical Essays*, p. 291). That is certainly true, even if one
has to appear dogmatic in stating it because of lack of
space. It is already plain to those who have read chapters
I, II, and III of this book that I am convinced, in the full
light of ancient testimony and modern knowledge, that the
Apostle John is the author of the Fourth Gospel. By the
Beloved Disciple of the Fourth Gospel the Apostle John is
meant, Streeter admits (*The Fourth Gospel,* p. 432) and
this "can hardly, I think, admit of serious doubt." The
claim of the author to be an eye-witness of the life and work
of Jesus Christ is a matter of grave importance. "The
Fourth Gospel professes to be the work of an eye-witness,
and of an eye-witness who enjoyed an intimacy with our
Lord allowed to none besides" (Marcus Dods, *Expositor's
Greek Testament*). The early writers accepted this claim
as true. Irenaeus, Clement of Alexandria, Tertullian,
Theophilus, Heracleon, and the Muratonian Fragment ad-
mittedly ascribe the Gospel to the Apostle John and Tatian
uses it with the Synoptics in his Harmony. Epiphanius
mentions the Alogi as rejecting the Johannine authorship.
The mention by Papias of the Elder John has been already
dismissed and shown to be in reality an allusion to the

Apostle John. George the Sinful has likewise been misunderstood about the supposed early death of John. Dr.
Maurice Jones in *The New Testament in the Twentieth
Century* (p. 388f.) says of Bacon's attacks on the Johannine authorship: "He has covered the ground so carefully
and completely that it is difficult to imagine what more can
be said in defence of his view. And yet I am not convinced.
. . . After weighing all the arguments very carefully I must
confess that the authorship of the Fourth Gospel still remains for me an open question, but what little bias I may
have is on the side of St. John."

That is my own feeling except that my "bias" is stronger
than that of Maurice Jones in favour of the Johannine authorship. I have tried to look at all the arguments advanced against the Johannine authorship since the days of
Evanson and Bretschneider, and I am persuaded that much
of it is in the nature of catching at straws and running after
will-o'-the-wisps into side issues that lead away from the
plain path as marked out in the Fourth Gospel itself, and
supported by the early testimony. Those who reject the
Johannine authorship are, beyond a doubt, sincere, but
sometimes they do not see the wood for the trees. George
Salmon, for instance, made a strong defence of the Johannine authorship in his *Introduction to the New Testament*
(1884), but in his posthumous volume, *The Human Element in the Gospels* (1907) he suggested that it was John's
hermēneutēs or assistant who wrote it, because of the story
of the raising of Lazarus in chapter 11. The evidence was
precisely the same as before, but Salmon's difficulty over
such a miracle as the raising of Lazarus from the dead made
him change his mind. A like case is that of William Sanday,
in whose book, *Authorship and Historical Character of the
Fourth Gospel* (1872), a powerful defence of the Johannine
authorship was modified to include the possibility of authorship by another member of the inner circle of Jesus on a
par with John (the view of Delff) in his *The Criticism of
the Fourth Gospel* (1905). This book was followed, in

1907, by *The Life of Christ in Recent Research* in which Dr. Sanday tries to explain "Miracles" (chapter viii) in the Fourth Gospel by the statement, "we must remember that an interval of from fifty to sixty years had passed between the events and the time at which he wrote. During all those many years he must have heard his own stories told by others besides himself; they might easily have received slight accretions, which he could not well distinguish from the original facts of his own consciousness. He was also in any case a writer of vivid imagination."

It is plain, therefore, that it is the miracles in the Fourth Gospel that, as with Salmon, are troubling Sanday. In Sanday's last book, *Divine Overruling* (1920), he goes as far as Salmon: "I'm afraid there is one important point on which I was probably wrong—the Fourth Gospel" (p. 61). But though they weakened in their previous convictions before death, as sometimes happens with old men, the arguments previously made by Salmon and Sanday remain. The authorship of the Fourth Gospel is not a matter to be settled by a majority vote or by the changes in the opinions of this or that scholar.

Surely those who, in the light of all the known facts, still adhere to the Johannine authorship have no occasion to feel lonesome when such names as the following can be listed in favour of that view: Ezra Abbott, Alexander, Alford, E. H. Askwith, Baumgarten-Crusius, Bertholdt, Beyschlag, Bleek, Bunsen, Dom Chapman, Charteris, Camerlynck, W. T. Davison, James Denney, M. Dods, De Wette, James Drummond, Ebrard, H. H. Evans, Ewald, Fisher, C. Fouard, Franke, Gloag, F. Godet, C. R. Gregory, Hase, Haussleiter, Hayes, James Iverach, M. Jones, Lagrange, Lange, Robert Law, J. J. Lias, Leathes, Lechler, Liddon, Lightfoot, Lücke, Luthardt, McClellan, McDonald, Meyer, Wm. Milligan, Neander, Nolloth, Norton, James Orr, Peake, Plummer, Pressensé, H. R. Reynolds, J. S. Riggs, Ritschl, J. Armitage Robinson, Schleiermacher, Scott-Holland, Scott-Moncrief, Tholuck, Thoma, Wace, Watkins, B. Weiss, Westcott,

Wordsworth, Zahn, and when a genuine Johannine source is held by Spitta and Wendt. Not to make the list too long, I have omitted many, including Salmon and Sanday for the reason already given above. Great names can be given on the other side of men who agree only in denying full Johannine authorship, men like E. A. Abbott, Bacon, F. C. Baur, Bernard, Bousset, Bretschneider, Brooke, Brückner, Buttmann, Burney, Carpenter, Charnwood, Cone, S. Davidson, Delff, Dibelius, Dobschütz, Evanson, Garvie, Goguel, Grill, Harnack, Heitmüller, Hilgenfeld, Holtzmann (H. J. and Oscar), W. F. Howard, H. L. Jackson, Kreyenbühl, Loisy, Martineau, McGiffert, McGregor, McNeile, Moffatt, Muirhead, Pfleiderer, Renan, Réville, Schmiedel, Scholten, Schwartz, E. F. Scott, Volkmar, Zeller, Von Hügel, J. Weiss, Weizsäcker, Wellhausen, Wendland, Wernle, Windisch, Wrede, and—in their last opinions Salmon—Sanday, Stanton, and R. H. Strachan. Clearly the decision is not unanimous, to say the least. But one should draw his conclusion, not from a list of names, but from the facts before him. There are difficulties in accepting the Johannine authorship, but many more and graver difficulties in rejecting it. Some of these points will come up for discussion as we proceed.

5. *The personal equation in the Record.* There is an undoubted similarity of style and tone in the discourses and the narrative portions of the Fourth Gospel. There are, indeed, passages where it is not possible to tell clearly where discourse ends and narrative begins as in 3:16, 31; 12:44. It is only natural that an old apostle, who has brooded long over the words of the Master, most of them spoken originally in Aramaic, should give a condensed report both of the dialogues and the discourses. The translation must inevitably be in the author's own *Koine.* This same problem confronted the author of each of the Synoptic Gospels which have more similarity in the reports of the words of Jesus, but often with numerous variations as a harmony shows. The discourses in John 14 to 17 present a special problem in the extent of the matter preserved. The Holy Spirit is

particularly mentioned as given to bring to remembrance the substance and meaning of Christ's words. But even so John's peculiar style is manifest here also. However, this point cannot be pressed unduly to prove that Jesus Himself did not use this style of teaching, since there is one Johannine aerolite preserved in the Logia of Jesus (the Q of criticism), the oldest known document of the Gospels, the non-Markan portion of Matthew and Luke, namely, Matthew 11:25-30 and Luke 10:21-24, a passage as Johannine as anything in John's Gospel.

Granted the genuineness of the Fourth Gospel, the problem finds a ready explanation in the fact that the Beloved Disciple entered into and understood certain moods of the Master better than the others. These high levels of Christ's mind are beyond literary invention, and find their only solution in their preservation in the mind and heart of the one closest to Him. "Compression involves adaptation of phraseology" (Westcott). But John's spiritual temperament did not alter the matter of the Master's teaching in his vivid reminiscences.

6. *The relation to the Synoptic Gospels.* Moffatt (*Introduction, etc.,* p. 533) agrees with Westcott (Vol. I, p. clvi) that the Fourth Gospel presupposes the Synoptic Gospels. The effort of Burney (*The Aramaic Origin of the Fourth Gospel,* 1922) to prove that it preceded the Synoptics has not succeeded. Outside of the feeding of the five thousand (Jo. 6:1-13) and the crossing over to Capernaum (6:14-21) there is very little in the Fourth Gospel, before the account of the last week in Jerusalem, that is in the Synoptic Gospels. The bulk of the material is new, additional, but not contradictory with the mention of two passovers (2:13ff.; 6:4) not in the Synoptics nor with the fact that most of the ministry presented is in Judea and Jerusalem, while that in the Synoptics is mainly in Galilee till the last journey to Jerusalem. This earlier Jerusalem ministry though not given, is implied in the Synoptic records. John also refers to an earlier ministry in various parts of Palestine (Jo. 1:35-4:

45). In the closing chapters about Jerusalem (12-20) most of the items given supplement the Synoptic accounts and give many evidences of an eye-witness like 19:35. Chapters 12 to 17 are entirely new except the Triumphal Entry (12:12-19), the anointing of Jesus by Mary of Bethany (12:2-8), the pointing out of Judas and the warning to Peter (13:21-38). Chapter 11 is so new and startling that it has led Salmon to give up the Johannine authorship on the ground that, if true, the Synoptic Gospels would have told it also. There is a like omission in the Synoptics of the name of Malchus as the name of the servant of the high priest whose head Peter tried to cut off, but John, writing after Peter and Malchus are both dead and Peter is out of harm's way, gives it (18:10). Precisely so we know that the chief priests took counsel to put Lazarus to death as well as Jesus (Jo. 12:9f.), ample reason for silence on the part of the Synoptics concerning Lazarus while he still lived.

All these facts indicate clearly that the Fourth Gospel was written to give matter that supplemented the accounts in the Synoptics. Some scholars argue that John's account of the last supper flatly contradicts the Synoptic statement that Jesus ate the regular passover meal on the evening of the 14th Nisan, that it shows that He ate it the day before and, as the Paschal Lamb, was crucified at the time the lamb was ordinarily slain. I do not believe that this is the true interpretation of John (13:1f., 27; 18:28; 19:14, 31). I think that these passages, rightly understood, agree with the statements in Matthew 26:2 (Mk. 14:1; Lu. 22:1). See for discussion my *Harmony of the Gospels* (pp. 279-281). The portrait of Christ in the Fourth Gospel is, in all essentials, the same as that in the Synoptic Gospels and in the Logia of Jesus (Q), as I have shown in *The Christ of the Logia*.

John has the advantage of a longer perspective for seeing the proper proportions of the Master. His intimate knowledge of Him has been tested by a long and blessed experience. Also, he writes in Ephesus, a great Greek city, and with an outlook on the Greek world and so is able to give the world not merely "The Gospel of the Hellenists" (Bacon), but the Gospel for the whole world and for all time. He is himself a Jew, with intimate knowledge of Palestine and especially Jerusalem, but he is now, though originally a mere Galilean fisherman, a great Christian theologian of supreme genius, familiar with Jewish theology (including Philo of Alexandria), knowing also the views of the Gnostics, with their subtle perversion of Christ's person and teaching. Ripened into full maturity of his marvellous powers, he is moved to tell the story of Jesus Christ as he knows Him. This he does with no reflection on the Synoptics, but with the steady purpose to add what he can to their wondrous narratives. Only John can rise to this stature. M. Jones feels keenly the predicament of those who reject the Johannine authorship: "But greatest of all the difficulties in the way of accepting the opposite conclusion is that no satisfactory answer is given to the question, 'If St. John did not write the Fourth Gospel, *who* wrote it?'" (*op. cit.*, p. 388). With John as the author the path is plain. Nolloth *(The Fourth Evangelist)* has a full and fair treatment of the Fourth Gospel and the Synoptic Gospels (pp. 111-171).

7. *Relation to the Epistles.* There are a few scholars, Moffatt among them, who deny the same authorship for the three Johannine Epistles. Moffatt credits the Apocalypse and Second and Third John to the so-called Presbyter John, but holds that the First Epistle and the Gospel come from the same author, who is neither the Apostle John nor the so-called Presbyter John. But there is the same identity of style in First John and Second and Third John that we find in the Gospel. The arguments for identity of authorship of Gospel and Epistles is conclusive, as stated by Brooke in his volume on the Epistles of John (pp. i-xxvii), Westcott in his volume on the Epistles of John (pp. xliii-xlvi), and by W. F. Howard in his *Fourth Gospel in Recent Criticism and Interpretation* (pp. 252-257). It is by no means certain whether the Gospel was written before or after First John.

It is even possible (see chapter XI), as some hold, that First John was sent forth at the same time as the Gospel. This identity of authorship is held by those who attribute the books to the so-called Elder John or to a "great unknown," as well as by those who hold to the actual Johannine authorship. The same writer who wrote the Gospel wrote the Epistles.

9. *Relation to the Apocalypse.* Here we confront a far more serious problem. Dionysius of Alexandria, in the third century, felt that the diction of the Apocalypse differed so radically from that of the Gospel and the Epistles that a different author was necessary for it. He held the Johannine authorship of the Gospel to be beyond dispute, but denied it for the Apocalypse. He said that some ascribed the Apocalypse to Cerinthus, as the Alogi (according to Epiphanius) made Cerinthus the author of both Gospel and Apocalypse. James Drummond, who accepts the Johannine authorship of the Gospel, argues that "the question of the Apocalypse is far from settled; and while it is still *sub judice* we must judge of the Gospel upon its own merits" (*op. cit.*, p. 443). That is certainly true, but also meanwhile "we must accept it as genuine, at least till some new evidence, whether arising from the Apocalypse or from any other source, demands a reversal of our judgment." Howard (*op. cit.*, p. 123) holds that "the opinion of the majority of modern scholars endorses the judgment of that remarkable higher critic of the third century, Dionysius of Alexandria" against the Johannine authorship of the Apocalypse.

The modern commentators on the Apocalypse are divided on the point. Moffatt *(Expositor's Greek Testament)* assigns the Apocalypse to the Presbyter John, as suiting "better than any other contemporary figure." Charles *(Int. and Crit. Comm.)* finds two or more authors named,—John (the Elder, the prophet, etc.) who wrote parts and edited it, but not the Apostle John. Charles has a "Short Grammar of the Apocalypse" (pp. cxvii-clix). Swete in his great commentary, "while inclining to the traditional view which holds that the author of the Apocalypse was the Apostle John," "desires to keep an open mind upon the question." Beckwith in his Commentary (p. 353) holds to the Apostolic authorship in view "of the exceptional force of the external evidence" and the proof of "John's activity in Asia at the end of the century." There are linguistic differences between the Gospel and the Apocalypse that call for discussion. These will receive treatment in chapter XIV. For the present we may simply say that the facts do not render it impossible for the John of the Apocalypse to be the Apostle John. But it should also be understood that, if the John of the Apocalypse should finally be shown to be not the Apostle John, that conclusion would in no way disprove the Johannine authorship of the Gospel. The nature of the Apocalypse and the excitement of the visions and the isolation of the author in the Isle of Patmos have some bearing on the grammatical aspects of the book.

9. *The historical worth of the Gospel.* It is this aspect of the problem that distresses many who fear or favour the non-Johannine theories of the Fourth Gospel and even of some who accept it. Marcus Dods (*Expositor's Greek Testament,* pp. 655, 657) feels it very keenly: "If this claim (of being an eye-witness) be true, and if the Gospel be indeed the work of the Apostle John, then we have not only the narrative of one who saw and was a part of what he records, but we have a picture of our Lord by one who knew Him better than any one else did. . . . But if it is not historically reliable and if the utterances attributed to our Lord were not really uttered by Him but are merely the creation of the writer, . . . ascribed to the Founder of the Church to account for and to justify some of its developments, plainly its value is widely different from that which attaches to a reliable record of the words and actions of Jesus." That does not overstate the situation. The Fourth Gospel claims "to be historically reliable" and, if untrue, "the Church has been throughout its history gravely in error regarding the claim of its Founder, and this lies at the

door of the Gospel." So keenly does R. H. Strachan feel this point that, after writing in Hastings' *Dictionary of Christ and the Gospels* that "the Gospel is a genuine Johannine work from the pen of the Apostle, who wrote from Ephesus," in 1925 he wrote *The Fourth Evangelist: Dramatist or Historian*. Having given up the Johannine authorship, he sees the alternative before him, and labours to prove that "historicity" is more than mere accuracy in facts, turning more on "the assurance brought by the Fourth Evangelist's work that the Christ of Paul and of the Christian Faith is congruous with belief in an historic personality" (p. 26[n]). Fine phrases, indeed, but poor consolation in place of the personal testimony of the last eye-witness. A. E. Brooke in *The Historical Value of the Fourth Gospel* (*Cambridge Biblical Essays,* p. 292f.) says bluntly: "And who would reconstruct the history of the ministry of Jesus Christ on earth must make his choice between the Synoptic record and the Johannine narrative. The time for compromise is past. One or other of the alternatives must be taken."

That sounds like the death-knell of the harmonies, like my own, that still use all four Gospels. We now have harmonies that use only the Synoptic Gospels and leave to one side as unhistorical the Fourth Gospel. And yet E. A. Abbott dares to say in the Preface to his series called *The Fourfold Gospel* (1913-17): "Comparing the present volume with my article on the Gospels in the *Encyclopaedia Biblica* (1901) and in the *Encyclopaedia Britannica* (1880) and with earliest parts of *Diatessarica*, I find the Fourth Gospel, in spite of its poetic nature, is closer to history than I had supposed. The study of it, and especially of those passages wherein it intervenes to explain expressions in Mark altered or omitted by Luke, appears to me to throw new light on the work, acts, and purposes of Christ, and to give increased weight to His claims on our faith and worship." That is an honest confession and goes far to explain some of the prejudice against the Fourth Gospel. The best

BIRDVILLE
BAPTIST CHURCH
LIBRARY

answer is the careful reading of the Gospel itself. "But the question really is whether the claim of Jesus is true or not. One may be forgiven for suspecting that some of the opposition to the Fourth Gospel arises from a belief that it was not" (E. H. Askwith, *The Historical Value of the Fourth Gospel*, p. 315). After careful study of each item in the Fourth Gospel, Askwith does not hesitate to credit the Fourth Gospel with the highest historical worth "in opposition to much of the criticism of our day, which denies to this Gospel serious historical value" (p. 4). Westcott sharply asks (p. cxi): "Does the Evangelist forfeit his claims to be a truthful historian, because he turns his eye steadily to the signs of the central laws of being?" He answers (p. cxiv): "It is then no disparagement of the strict historical character of the Fourth Gospel that the writer has fulfilled the design which he set before himself, of recording such 'signs' out of the whole number of Christ's works as he considered likely to produce a specific effect." Streeter is content to find satisfaction in the author as "mystic and prophet" rather than historian, as poet and dreamer, "perhaps the greatest of all mystics" (p. 366), combining Plato and Isaiah, in von Hügel's phrase, "striving to contemplate history *sub specie aeternitatis* and to englobe the successiveness of man in the simultaneity of God" *(Encyclopaedia Britannica).* But such fine phrases do not make up for the loss of an actual eye-witness who used the simplest language in expressing the deepest and the highest ideas about the Son of God and the Son of man, "the Word made flesh and dwelling among men" whose glory John claimed to behold. There is small comfort in Bacon's pretentious claim to have discovered a great unknown as the author of the Fourth Gospel, least of all in his depreciation of the Apostle John: "The real John had no more to give him prominence during his lifetime than we should expect from his Galilean antecedents" (*Gospel of the Hellenists,* p. 33). Even Wrede (*Charakter und Tendenz des Joh. Evang.,* p. 25) considers the accuracy in detail a mark of the historical trustworthiness of the Fourth Gospel. Lightfoot's judgment of the Fourth Gospel accords with my own experience: "We cannot rise from the perusal of the characters as they appear in the Fourth Gospel without the assurance that we have been introduced to real, living persons, described by some one who knew them well. Individuality is seen to be stamped on every face. Exactly in the same way, as we mark the progress of events gradually unfolded before us in the narrative, our conviction becomes more and more settled that the guide who conducts us has been an eye-witness of the incidents which he records. In order to get the full effect of the extreme naturalness of the description, we have only to read the historical portions successively, and to remark how vivid is the sequence of the narrative as it opens out from point to point."

There is a story told of a famous novelist who was held back by doubts about the deity of Jesus. One night she read the Fourth Gospel through at one reading. The next morning she gladly confessed her faith in Jesus Christ as her Saviour. The power of this greatest of all books lies precisely in this: that John, one of the most gifted of men, after long years of growth, practice, and reflection, wrote about the Son of God Incarnate (whom he knew more intimately than any one else), in the simplest manner possible, telling in the briefest space only the things that he himself knew. The picture drawn is true to life and immortal with the reality of fact and truth. It is imperishable and will withstand all the peckings of critics, from Bretschneider to Bacon. A. E. Brooke (*Cambridge Biblical Essays*, p. 328) feels hopeful that "the time will come for gathering up the fragments of the Fourth Gospel which are of historical value for the story of the ministry of Jesus Christ in Palestine and His teaching during His earthly life." He thinks "that the broken pieces which remain are neither so few nor so fragmentary as the literature of the last few years has left us to suppose." The hostile critics will be "the fragments," not John's Gospel. John has told what he saw and as he saw it. "And he that has seen has borne witness and his witness is true" (Jo. 19:35).

10. *The purpose of the Gospel.* This is made plain in John 19:35 in the second clause of the sentence: "And he knows that he is speaking true things that you also may keep on believing." It is possible that the "he" *(ekeinos)* before "knows" may refer to Christ, to God, or to the Holy Spirit, but Bernard rejects all these possibilities in favour of the natural reference to the "his" *(autou)* just before, that is to the author (the witness), John in fact. "Here we hold it to refer emphatically to the Beloved Disciple, whom we identify with the son of Zebedee" (Bernard). That is for Bernard the "witness" as distinct from the "evangelist" (the writer of the Gospel). But, as we have seen, there is no such divided authorship in the book. The one mind of the Apostle John dominates the whole. Once again the author makes plain his purpose: "But these have been written that you may keep on believing that Jesus is the Christ the Son of God, and that, believing, you may keep on having life in his name." The purpose is precisely the same as that stated in John 9:35 with further explanation. The use of the present subjunctive in both instances *(pisteuēte* instead of *pisteusēte* ingressive aorist subjunctive, and also *echēte* instead of *schēte)* suggests that John's immediate concern in his Gospel is to hold believers to simple and loyal trust in Jesus as Messiah, that they may continue to possess eternal life, which is only possible by Christ's power (in His name). At once there arises the background of Gnostic propaganda (both Cerinthian and Docetic) with the lowering of the place of Jesus either as a mere man (Cerinthus) in distinction from the *aeon* Christ, or as only an *aeon,* far below the status of God, but not a man at all. Just as Paul in Colossians drove full tilt against the beginnings of this subtle heresy by presenting Christ as preëminent in nature and grace, as the very Image of God, so John in this Gospel feels the call to give a full length portrait of Christ as the Son of God in His preincarnate state (the Logos), in His

life on earth (the Logos made flesh), and in His resurrection from the dead in proof of His claim to deity.

The humanity of Jesus Christ is genuine, as John makes clear, but it is not an ordinary human life that John discloses. It is that of one who before His incarnation existed with God, as very God (Jo. 1:1, 14, 18), and who came to earth to reveal the Father to men. There were those who, under the influence of Stoicism, found refuge in pantheism. John's Gospel gives the picture of God in Christ as a person. "The Fourth Evangelist proclaimed to the Christian world of his time that the eternal Logos, the living and active Word of God, had become incarnate in Jesus. The Christian religion, the perfect revelation of God, was rooted in history" (Howard, *op. cit.*, p. 237). Burkitt (*The Gospel History and Its Transmission*, p. 256) goes that far, but denies historicity to the narrative: "The Fourth Gospel is written to prove the reality of Jesus Christ. But the Evangelist was no historian; ideas, not events, were to him the true realities, and if we go to his work to learn the cause of events we shall only be disappointed in our search." But John uses both *alēthinē* (genuine) and *alēthē* (true) concerning his message in John 19:35. That claim cannot be satisfied with "ideas, in place of events," as "the true realities." The unwillingness to take John's purpose in his own words reaches its climax in Loisy (*Le Quatrième Évangile*, pp. 128f.) who holds that "the loved disciple is the young church to which is entrusted the heritage of Judaism and Judaic Christianity." And that in the name and guise of scientific historical criticism!

The Apostle John was the greatest of mystics in the highest sense of that word, but he at least used language in a way that people can understand. His Gospel is a "spiritual" one, but it is also "historical" in the ordinary sense of that word. He tells actual facts. The prejudice against John's Gospel because of its sustained pictures of the deity of Christ applies to the Synoptic Gospels also, as J. Weiss says (*Das älteste Evangelium*, p. 97): "The Christology of

Mark stands far nearer to that of John than people usually admit." It is undoubtedly true "that the structure of the Fourth Gospel corresponds with the fulfilment of a profound purpose" (Westcott, Vol. I, p. cviii). But it is not vitiated as history by reason of that fact. That is true of each of the Gospels and should be true of any history worth reading. John wrote with a purpose, and that the highest that ever moved any writer, and on the noblest theme possible to man. Surely he is not to be discredited because of this fact.

11. *The method employed in the Book.* Here again John tells us and does not leave it to speculation. At the end of chapter 20 he adds in verses 30 and 31: "Many other signs therefore did Jesus do in the presence of his disciples which are not written in this book; but these have been written that you may keep on believing that Jesus is the Christ the Son of God and that, believing, you may keep on having life in his name." He has made a selection out of the vast material at hand, so vast that he adds in 21:25: "There are many other things which Jesus did, which if written in detail, I do not think that the world itself would contain the books written" (from time to time). That is hyperbole, to be sure, but on the basis of the Four Gospels that we do possess, the volumes produced through the centuries stagger the mind. The presses were never so busy as now in publishing new interpretations of Jesus of Nazareth. John wrote his Gospel long after the Synoptics had appeared, in order to give his personal and supplementary contribution to the story of Jesus Christ. He, as a rule, assumes what the other Gospels tell, and fills in here and there out of his own rare and rich experience. He selects a few out of the vast number (cf. "the signs" in Jerusalem, 2:24; 3:2; 11:47; 12:37) to prove his point concerning the exalted claims of Jesus.

There is not in John the "reduced" Christ of much modern criticism. John presents the actual deity of Jesus Christ as we find it in the Logia (Q), the Synoptics, the Acts,

Paul's Epistles, Hebrews, and even in James (1:1; 2:1). We have a right to insist that John has not perverted or distorted the picture of Christ by what he has given and by what he has not used. He claims that the examples are representative. Some modern critics balk at the raising of Lazarus in chapter 11 as beyond belief. But there are raisings from the dead in Luke (7:11-17), in the Synoptics (Mk. 5:21-43; Matt. 9:18-26; Luke 8:40-56), and even in the Logia of Jesus, our earliest Gospel document (Matt. 11:5; Lu. 7:22). If Jesus raised the dead at all, the case of Lazarus is no whit more incredible than the others. The fact that John, alone, tells it is easily intelligible in view of the threat of the chief priests to kill Lazarus (Jo. 12:9-11). Two of John's miracles—the feeding of the five thousand (6:1-13) and the walking on the water (6:16-21)—are given by the Synoptics. The discourse in the synagogue in Capernaum is significant, coming, as it does, after these miracles, just as is the discussion which comes in chapter 5 after the healing of the lame man and that in chapter 9 after the healing of the man born blind. The turning of the water into wine in chapter 2 is a nature miracle, as is the draught of fishes in chapter 21. The only other miracle is the healing of the son of the ruler of Capernaum (chapter 4). The healing of the ear of Malchus is not told by John in 18:10. These signs, with the discourses following them, occupy a large portion of the Gospel, but by no means all. There are other discourses or dialogues not connected with specific miracles of great importance like those in chapters 3, 4, 7, 8, 10, 12, 13-17. John has purposely selected representative details, incidents, dialogues, and discourses to fill out his picture of Christ.

Surely this method "is then no disparagement of the strict historical character of the Fourth Gospel" (Westcott, Vol. I, p. cxiv). It is precisely what every serious historian has to do. He is compelled to interpret the mass of material which he has already accumulated and digested. It is the method announced by Luke in his Gospel (1:1-4) in his

dedication to Theophilus, "that thou mayest know fully the
certainty concerning the matters about which thou wast in-
structed."   It is the method of the true historian that in-
duces confidence, not distrust, provided the writer is competent to handle his material. This requirement is fully met
in the case of the Apostle John, the Beloved Disciple, who
knew best his exalted subject and was best qualified by
temperament, genius, and grace, to discuss it in brief compass.

12. *The Prologue (1:1-18).* The introduction to John's
Gospel is different from the genealogical one in Matthew 1:
1-17 and the historical one in Luke 1:1-4. The Gospel of
Mark has no introduction, but plunges at once into the ministry of the Baptist and, after the baptism and temptation of
Jesus, passes on at once to the Galilean ministry.   John
also, after the introduction, begins with the ministry of the
Baptist. Matthew and Luke give two separate accounts of
the birth and childhood of Jesus before the baptism and
temptation, while John fills out the blank between the baptism and temptation, on the one hand, and the Galilean
ministry of the Synoptics, with a brief account of the early
ministry in various parts of Palestine (1:19-4:42). John in
the Prologue has an apparent allusion to the birth narratives
of Matthew and Luke in 1:14 (the Word became flesh), but
with no details. John's introduction at once lifts his narrative out of mere biography and shows the eternal relations of
that *Logos* (the Son of God, Jesus Christ). He does this by
the use of a Greek word (*Logos*-Word) which has philosophical affinities from Plato and the Stoics to Philo, who
uses it constantly. But John's *Logos* is personal, not a
mere Platonic idea, nor a Philonic abstraction (at times
pantheistic). John employs some of the terms of Philo,
which he could easily have learned in Ephesus, but when he
"goes on to identify Him (the *Logos*) with a man whom he
had seen and with whom he had lived on terms of friendship, he parts company with the Alexandrian writer" (Nolloth, *The Fourth Evangelist,* p. 187). There is certainly

much kinship in John's use of *Logos* with the Hebrew *Dabhar* in the Old Testament and the Aramaic *Mēmra* or Targum *Mēmra*. Indeed, J. Randel Harris (*The Origin of the Prologue to St. John's Gospel*, 1917) finds more striking similarities of language with the wisdom books of the Old Testament and the Apocrypha than with Philo and Heraclitus. Nolloth holds that "there is no question that the author of the Fourth Gospel was a profound thinker" (*op. cit.*, p. 172) and he devotes a chapter to "The Philosophy of St. John." Streeter (*op. cit.*, p. 367) says: "The author of the Fourth Gospel stands between two worlds, the Hebrew and the Greek, at the confluence of the two greatest spiritual and intellectual traditions of our race. In him Plato and Isaiah meet." Yes, but they meet in one who is not just "mystic and prophet" and philosopher. He is also biographer, historian, and theologian. Heraclitus, Plato, and Philo by the use of Logos "desired a theory of the universe; John sought to set forth the significance of a personal historical life" (Iverach, in *Intern. St. Bible Encycl.*). He used the term in "an endeavour to describe what John had grown to recognise as the essential meaning of the person of Jesus." Baldensperger (*Der Prolog des vierten Evangeliums*, 1898) rightly sees that the Prologue is an essential part of the Gospel and not a mere addendum (Harnack) perhaps by another hand.

It is true that in the Gospel the term *Logos* is not applied to Christ outside of the Prologue, though we find it again of Christ in I John 1:1 and Revelation 19:14. But the bold and great picture drawn in the Prologue dominates the entire Gospel. Bernard (Vol. I, p. cxliv) has ventured to arrange the Prologue in strophic form as "The *Logos* Hymn." "The Prologue is a philosophical *rationale* of the main thesis of the Gospel." By the use of the term *Logos* (both reason and word) John is able to show that Jesus is God's Expression (*exēgēsato*, interpreted, verse 18) of Himself. God is like Jesus. If we wish to know God, look at Jesus Who has revealed Him in personal bodily form, in human personality, the actual combination or union of God with man. The line of thought in the Prologue is plain, though profound. In verse 1 comes the direct statement of the eternity of the *Logos*, the fellowship (*pros* with the accusative) of the *Logos* with God on a plane of equality, the actual deity of the *Logos*. It is this verse that has prejudiced the minds of Unitarians against the Johannine authorship and the historical worth of the book. Yet two of the staunchest defenders of the Johannine authorship are Ezra Abbot, the great American scholar, and James Drummond, the English Unitarian of Manchester College.

John never steps down from this lofty plane. There is no "reduced" Christ for him. In verses 2 to 5 he repeats his previous statement and adds the creative activity of the *Logos* as the agent *(dia)* through whom God made the universe—precisely the position of Paul concerning Christ in Colossians 1:15-17, and that of the author of Hebrews in 1:2 and 3. He explains that the *Logos* is both the Life and the Light of men, two great Johannine words (I Jo. 1:2, 5) claimed by Jesus for Himself (Jo. 8:12; 9:5; 11:25; 14:6). He concludes this section with a graphic picture of pagan darkness in which the *Logos* as Light not put out by it has been shining all the while. In John 12:35, the only other example of the word in John, the word *(katalambanō)* means to "overtake." Here before the Incarnation "overcome," or "put out," suits better than "comprehend," or "grasp." The Light shone on, though dimly, in the thick darkness.

In verses 6 to 8 John explains how there came a witness, sent of God, "to bear witness concerning the Light, that all might believe by means of him." This was the mission of the Baptist and he was true to it. He was not the Light, and he knew it. Baldensperger needlessly suggests that the purpose of this Gospel is to depreciate the Baptist in relation to Christ.

Verses 9 to 13 give the varying ways in which the Light has been received in the world. He was all along the perfect (*alēthinon,* genuine, not just true, *alēthes*) light, that was to come into the world (thus taking *erchomenon,* coming, with *phōs,* Light, as is done of Christ in 6:14; 11:27; 16:28; 18:37), the Light that enlightens every man with what light he may have. Christ, as the Creator, has a cosmic connection with every man, though not as Saviour. All that is true (the Truth) comes from Christ, as every lie comes from the devil (the father of lies). It was an anomalous situation, for all the time the *Logos* (the Life, the Light) was in the world that He had made, but the world did not recognise or acknowledge Him.

In due time He came to His own home, but His own people (kin, so to speak, *hoi idioi,* the Jews, for Jesus' was a Jew on His human side) refused to accept Him. This "Hebrew Tragedy" (Condor) saddened John's heart, Jew himself, as he wrote in his old age in Ephesus, long after the destruction of Jerusalem. There were some who did receive the *Logos* but they were those specially prepared by divine power (*exousia,* right, privilege) to become "children of God" in the spiritual, not merely creative, sense, those who believe on the name (power) of this *Logos.* These children of God were "begotten of God," a fundamental idea in this Gospel (3:3-7; 8:42) and in First John (3:9; 5:1). It is spiritual generation in contrast with physical birth. There is some western evidence (b, Irenaeus, Tertullian), adopted by Blass and Resch, for the singular as a direct reference to the Virgin Birth of Christ, but the plural is correct.

Verse 14 states the Incarnation plainly: "And the Logos became flesh." Here "became" *(egeneto)* is in sharp contrast to the eternal preëxistence "was" *(ēn)* in verse 1. It is the definite entrance into His human existence of the eternal *Logos.* There is here no description of the Virgin Birth as given in Matthew and Luke, but that account seems clearly implied, because the Incarnation by the *Logos* is no ordinary birth after human fashion, nor is it the indwelling of God in a man. It is God "become flesh." The only adequate, even possible, explanation of this language and that

of Paul (II Cor. 8:9; Phil. 2:5-11) is the Virgin Birth,
unless one accepts the Gnostic interpretation that Jesus was
all *aeon* and not man at all, or all man with the *aeon* Christ
on Him from His baptism to His death (Cerinthus). But
John's Gospel and Epistles vigorously oppose and expose
Gnosticism. It was no phantom Christ of whom John says:
"We beheld his glory" (repeated in detail in I Jo. 1:1-3).
"He tabernacled among us" in an actual human body, called
a "tent" also by Paul (II Cor. 5:1). But though a real
human body (the incarnate *Logos*), it was also a glory as of
"the Only Begotten from the Father, full of grace and truth,"
a reminiscence of John's experience on the Mount of Transfiguration (Lu. 9:28-31), an unforgettable experience
described by Peter also (II Pet. 1:16-18), a glory that rests
upon the whole life of Jesus as John contemplates it.

Verse 15 is a parenthesis. The testimony of the witness
to the superior glory of Jesus is cited at this point as well as
later (1:19-27; 3:26-30). Jesus is *after* John in His Incarnation, but *before* John in His pre-incarnate existence and
above him in all things. This verse is a repetition of the
previous statement in verses 6 to 8.

In verses 16 and 17 the idea in verse 14 is resumed and
explained. "We all (John and all believers) received of his
fulness" (a Gnostic word here used of the fulness of Christ's
divine attributes as by Paul in Col. 1:19; 2:9), and with an
endless supply of grace ("grace answering to grace," John's
only use of *anti*), new grace for the new day, coming in
for ever like the waves of the sea on the shore. "Grace"
(charis) is John's distinctive word for the Gospel (as it is
Paul's) while "law" *(nomos)* sums up the Old Testament
(Moses). Christ is the giver of grace. Truth also comes by
Jesus Christ. Verse 18 presents succinctly the incarnate
Logos (verses 1 and 14) as the revealer of God who is unseen by man, save as "God Only Begotten" (correct text)
"interpreted" *(exegēsato,* like our exegesis) God. He is
both Idea and Word. We can now tell what God is like,

since we know Jesus. John is now ready to proceed with the book.

13. *The argument (1:19-20:31)*. Without attempting a formal analysis we can follow the unfolding of John's line of thought in a series of paragraphs that flow in rapid movement. There is no effort to give all that Jesus did and said. With the Synoptics before him, he supplements items here and there that in a marvellous way light up the life story of Jesus and show that He is what He claimed to be, the Son of God. Moreover nowhere is the human side of Christ's life more vividly presented. There will not in this chapter be room for detailed exposition, even on the scale just done with the Prologue. We can only touch the turning points and keep a true perspective as we go on with John as our guide.

The Baptist's Witness about the Messiah (1:19-36)

John had said (1:7) that the Baptist was sent to witness concerning the Light and that he witnessed that the *Logos* was far above him (1:15). Now he proceeds to show precisely how the Baptist bore his witness. He refused to pass himself off to a committee of Sadducees, sent by the Pharisees in the Sanhedrin, as the Christ (the Messiah). He was only a voice crying in the wilderness to make ready the way for the Lord. The Messiah was already at hand, standing all unknown, in the midst of them. John had indeed baptized him, and had seen the proof of his Messiahship in the sign given by God. John felt unworthy to unloose the latchet of the Christ's shoes. This was at Bethany beyond Jordan. The next day the Baptist sees Jesus coming towards him and in ecstasy hails Him in the words of Isaiah as "the Lamb of God that bears away the sin of the world." He bears emphatic witness as he identifies Jesus as the Messiah: "And I have seen and I have borne witness that this is the Son of God." The next day again he repeats his witness about His being the Lamb of God. He gave Jesus a last longing look as He passed out of his sight, but not out of his mind.

Jesus Winning His First Disciples (1:35-51)

As is natural these first disciples come from the disciples (learners) of John the Baptist. Two of them heard his witness to Jesus and took him at his word and followed Jesus. One of these was Andrew, the other clearly John the author of the book. They were invited by Jesus to His abode (probably a tent) in Bethany. They spent that first glorious day (from ten A. M., Roman time, till afternoon) with Jesus, a day that lingered always in John's mind. They were convinced that the Baptist was right. Andrew went at once to tell his brother Simon. John probably told his brother James the great and glad good news about Jesus the Messiah. They had made the greatest discovery of the ages. John tells the story of the interview of Jesus with Simon and the prophecy that he would become a rock (Cephas, Petros). Here are four followers of Jesus. The next day—glorious days these—Jesus finds Philip of Bethsaida—the same city of Andrew and Simon—and bids him follow Him. Then Philip finds Nathanael (Bartholomew) and manages to bring him to Jesus, who quickly dispels his doubt, so that Nathanael proclaims Him as "the Son of God, the King of Israel." It was a glorious beginning. One wins one. If only it had kept up through the ages! Now it takes a hundred to win one, so slow are we.

The First Miracle (2:1-11)

It was in Cana in Galilee, at a wedding to which Jesus with His six disciples and His mother were invited, apparently also the brothers (and sisters?), for they are with Him immediately afterwards (2:12). Probably the Baptist would not have gone to a wedding with its joyous feasting (Lu. 7:33f.). One thinks of this contact of the Jesus with His mother, the first since he began His messianic work. It was an auspicious occasion for her in view of her long cherished hopes about Him. It is not surprising that she should tell Jesus about the failure of the supply of wine in the hope that He would do something about it. Jesus made a gentle protest to His mother about this apparent interference in His messianic task, but then He did change the water into wine. "The conscious water saw its Lord and blushed" (Crashaw). This first manifestation of His glory was a nature miracle, the hardest of all for modern men to believe. But, if Jesus really is the Son of God, is anything "hard" for Him to do that is in accord with the will of His Father? We are challenged here with our real idea of God;—whether we conceive of Him as slave of His own laws (the laws of nature) or as the supreme personal force over all through His own will. The six disciples believed more firmly than ever.

The First Visit to Capernaum (2:12)

It was a happy family gathering (the mother, the brothers and possibly sisters, the six disciples and with Jesus) in this chief commercial centre by the Sea of Galilee. There is no indication of the attitude of the brothers towards Jesus at this stage. Later they will manifest their disbelief in His claims (7:5). Perhaps as yet their jealousy had not been aroused; they may even have enjoyed the novelty of the sensations created by the miracle in Cana.

The First Visit to Jerusalem (2:13-3:21)

The ministry of Jesus had been going on some months (perhaps six) and now the passover was at hand. Jesus, like other pious Jews, went up to Jerusalem. Here He is confronted with the traffic in the court of the Gentiles in the temple where money-changers had their tables, and where sheep and cattle and doves for the sacrifices were bought.

BIRDVILLE
BAPTIST CHURCH
LIBRARY

Jesus was fully conscious of being the Messiah the Son of God: "Take these things hence and stop making my Father's house a house of merchandise." It was a messianic claim and act. He had a whip of cords in His hand, but was unknown to those who fled as guilty cowards before this stern command. Outside they rallied and demanded proof (sign) of His right to do what He had done. He gave them a sign which neither they nor the astonished disciples then understood, namely the promise of the raising of His body (temple) in three days after they should destroy it. The Synoptics (Mk. 11:15-18; Matt. 21:12f.; Lu. 19:45f.) tell of another cleansing of the temple three years hence, just after the Triumphal Entry. Many scholars are unable to see that such an act could be repeated and argue about which is the more suitable date (at the beginning or the close of the Master's ministry). Why not on both occasions? One's experience with reforms in city life to-day does not argue for permanency, but the reverse!

John adds a paragraph (2:23-25) about the tremendous impression made in Jerusalem by Jesus through His teaching and the signs wrought, none of which are described. But Jesus knew the hollowness of this enthusiasm and did not believe in His acclaimers half as much as they proposed to believe in Him. But there was one man, a Pharisee and member of the Sanhedrin, Nicodemus by name, who was really impressed by the deeds of Jesus as being proof that God was with Him. He was anxious to learn more and yet he did not wish to compromise himself with his colleagues who were already hostile to Jesus, as an interloper and a disturber of the established order. So he slipped over to the lodging place (probably a tent) of Jesus by night. Apparently John, the author of the book, was present, since he gives the dialogue in detail. Jesus could, of course, have told it to John, as well as the details of the interview with the woman of Samaria (Jo. 4). At any rate, here we see Jesus dealing with a Jewish scholar with all his theological prejudices and opinions. Nicodemus is kindly received, but

is thrown on the defensive at once by the strange utterance
of Jesus about being born again, which he takes to refer to
a second physical birth. Jesus explained it as a birth of the
water and the Spirit, not of the flesh, putting water as the
symbol of the spiritual birth, a figure of speech which Nicodemus, as a Pharisee, should have understood. But he was
no better off than when Jesus called it simply being born of
the Spirit (spiritual birth, regeneration). The scholar was
dense, as often such are, and Jesus could only lament his
ignorance. He illustrated once more the necessity of the
Cross as illustrated by the lifting up of the serpent in the
wilderness by Moses. John adds (3:16), the wonderful
saying about God's purpose in giving His Son for our sins,
that we may believe and live. Already men were choosing
darkness rather than light because their deeds were evil.

The Early Judean Ministry (3:22-4:3)

Jesus withdrew from Jerusalem into the land of Judea.
The conflict with the Pharisees in Jerusalem was already
keen. The Baptist was carrying on his work higher up the
Jordan Valley, in Aenon near to Salim. He had already
fulfilled the purpose of his ministry in pointing out Jesus
as the Messiah. These two men of destiny had met and
parted. The work of Jesus was linked with that of John,
but there was no rivalry between them, save in the minds
of some jealous disciples of John, who blamed him for having baptized and given his approval to Jesus. Once John
was the hero of Palestine. Now the crowds went with Jesus,
and John was a fading light. But this utterly failed to stir
jealousy in the heart of "John the Loyal." It was precisely
as it should be. "He must increase, while I must decrease."
He is the Bridegroom, while John is only His friend. In
that he has his joy. Jesus found out ere long that the
Pharisees were scheming to seize Him. They had already
succeeded in getting John into the clutches of Herod Antipas (Lu. 3:19f.), in the prison of Machaerus. The Phari-

sees perceived that Jesus was baptizing (through His disciples) more disciples than John. They foresaw more trouble from Jesus than from John, who before the crowds had dared to their very faces to call them broods of vipers. So Jesus left Judea and went towards Galilee.

A Samaritan Ministry (4:4-42)

The direct path led through Samaria. It was a stiff day's walk to Sychar near Schechem and Jesus and His six disciples reached it at six in the evening (Roman time). They were hungry, and Jesus sent the disciples into town to buy food. He Himself, weary from the long tramp, sat on the curbstone of the well that Jacob had dug here. Meanwhile a woman of Samaria came with her skin bag to get water for her family, as they do yet. John gives a graphic picture of how Jesus, tired as He was, overcame race and sex prejudice, took the initiative, began with the common topic of water, led her on to the subject of the living water, excited her curiosity, exposed her sinful life, held her to the point when she wished to change the subject to a theological dispute, declared to her the true nature of God as Spirit, and of worship irrespective of place, and finally revealed Himself to her as the Messiah. It is a masterpiece of dramatic narrative, but more than a masterpiece of pedagogic skill, the way this searcher of hearts won this poor sinful woman to eternal life. Her joy overflowed to her neighbours whom she brought to see and hear Jesus. The disciples on their return stood aghast at seeing Jesus talking with a woman in public and they wondered at the strange joy in His soul. He had meat to eat that they did not understand, doing His Father's will and finding joy for Himself and for them. There was a brief revival in Sychar itself, when the Samaritans rose to full confession of their faith in Jesus as "the Saviour of the world"—not of Jews only, but of Samaritans, of Gentiles, of all races.

Back in Galilee (4:43-54)

Jesus left Judea because He was so popular there that He had aroused the envy of the Pharisees. He went on into Galilee, where was His home (Nazareth), but little affected, as yet, by His ministry. There was only a brief stay in Cana and Capernaum. Jesus Himself quoted the proverb that a prophet has no honour in his own country. But His fame had preceded Him into Galilee, carried thither by people from Galilee who had seen His wondrous deeds at the passover in Jerusalem. Once again Jesus is at Cana, where He had wrought His first miracle. A courtier in Capernaum had a son sick unto death. He had heard of Jesus and so came to Him in Cana, begging Him to come to Capernaum to heal his son: "Sir, come down before my son die." Jesus was touched by the plea of this officer and granted his petition. The man believed and his son was healed at once. He and his household believed in Jesus at once. This was a second miracle in Cana—fortunate town.

Renewed Hostility in Jerusalem (Chapter 5)

This feast that drew Jesus back to Jerusalem may have been that of the passover, pentecost or tabernacles. There is absolutely no way to decide. If not a passover, there may still be an unnamed passover before or after. The healing of the lame man (lame for thirty-eight years) at the pool of Bethesda who was waiting for the water to be disturbed created a stir among the Pharisees, since it was done on the Sabbath. When blamed for carrying his pallet on the Sabbath, he laid the responsibility for it on the man who had healed him, not knowing who it was. Later Jesus rebuked the man for his sins, the cause of his lameness apparently, whereupon he told the Pharisees that it was Jesus. This information gave the hostile Jewish leaders ("the Jews" as often in John) ample ground for persecuting Christ, which they did with great violence. The defence of Jesus, "My

Father works up till now and I work," angered them still more. They now "sought to kill him, because, not only was he breaking the Sabbath, but was speaking of God as his own Father, making himself equal with God." Here already we see the line of attack by the Jewish ecclesiastics. Jesus was tearing down their cherished customs and He was guilty of blasphemy in claiming to be equal with God. His assumption of deity was the inflaming torch for their anger. It will blaze hotter and hotter till the crucifixion.

Jesus, fully aware of the issues involved, stood His ground and, in a marvellous speech in defence of His claim of equality with the Father as the Son of God, expounded that relationship and claimed that whoever refused to honour Him failed to honour the Father. He has the power of life and death from the Father: He bears the witness of the Baptist, of the Father, of the Scriptures, and in particular of Moses, who wrote of Him. The issue is now squarely joined for all time.

The Climax of the Galilean Ministry (6:1-7:9)

Once again we see Jesus in the north, but just "beyond the Sea of Galilee, *that is* of Tiberias." It was again the time of the passover (6:4) and, if the feast in 5:1 is a passover, then by John's Gospel a skip of a whole year has intervened. But Jesus did not attend this passover because they sought His life in Jerusalem (5:18; 7:1). He is on the mountain side, east of the Sea of Galilee near Bethsaida Julias (Lu. 9:10), whither He had gone with the Apostles, for rest, after their return from their preaching tour of Galilee. But the crowds called for more teaching and in the mid-afternoon Jesus fed the five thousand in the wonderful miracle. This is the only miracle recorded by all the Four Gospels. It created so much excitement that the crowd wanted to take Jesus by force to Jerusalem and proclaim Him king (6:14f.)—as the long-looked-for political Messiah. They meant under Jesus to start a revolution and throw off the hated Roman yoke, as the Zealots attempted later, to the ruin of the city and nation in A.D. 70. Jesus seeing the peril of the situation hurried the apostles off to go in the boat back to Capernaum and sent the crowds away to spend the night in the hills and fields. But He Himself "went up into the mountain apart to pray" (Matt. 14:23).

The disciples, too, evidently felt the impulse of the excited crowds. No one understood that Jesus was a spiritual, not a political, Messiah. Alone with His Father, Jesus found sympathy and help. It was the same temptation of the devil to win the power and glory of the kingdoms of the world by compromise. About the fourth watch (3 A.M.) of the night Jesus came walking on the water (another nature miracle) to the amazement of the disciples, who were still struggling with a storm on the sea. "They were afraid," John says, but finally were willing to receive Him into the boat (6:21).

The crowds next morning perceived that Jesus, as well as the disciples, was gone and followed in some boats from Tiberias. They found Jesus in the synagogue and blandly suggested another feast (breakfast) at His hands. The remarkable dialogue, by which Jesus led this motley crowd from the thought of the bread desired by them to that of Himself as the bread of eternal life—the spiritual appropriation of Himself,—has been woefully misunderstood. Some scholars frankly take it as an invention of the author to make Jesus teach His own sacramental views about the Lord's Supper. Others take it as Jesus predicting by anticipation the Lord's Supper. Why not understand it in the obvious and natural way, as Jesus using the miracle of the loaves and fishes to try to lift the crowd to some appreciation of what He really is; not a political Messiah, not even like to Moses with his daily manna, but one who was going to give His life for them, to be made their sustaining life by trust in Him? It was, to be sure, too high a teaching for the hungry crowds—this notion of a spiritual Messiah with His spiritual bread embodied in Himself—and so they quickly left Him alone with the apostles who, themselves, were staggered and, for a moment, faltered. The reply of Peter to the question of Jesus shows that they had decided to remain, after having considered leaving with the crowd of deserters. But there is treachery even among them, as Jesus saw, for Judas had it in his heart to betray Him. It was a crisis in the work in Galilee and in the life of Jesus.

John now in the narrative, again skips a period of time—six months. The feast of tabernacles was approaching and Jesus meant to go. But He would not go up with the caravan through Perea, the usual way, with a grand procession, as His brothers in derision of his messianic claims, proposed to Him (7:3-5). They probably knew of the desertion of the crowds in Galilee. Jesus rejected the scoffing advice of His brothers. He did go up a few days later, but in precisely the opposite manner—privately, not publicly (7:10).

A Crisis in Jerusalem (7:10-10:39)

In this long section about the Jerusalem ministry we see the forces working rapidly to the inevitable culmination. Jesus had apparently remained away from Jerusalem for a year and a half, but there has been no relaxation in the hostility of "the rulers of the Jews" in Jerusalem. It is a live question in secret, among the crowds at the feast of tabernacles, whether in view of the known purpose of the leaders to kill Him (7:11-13) Jesus will dare to come to the feast. Some take up for Jesus, some ridicule Him. Suddenly in the midst of the feast Jesus is seen teaching in the open court in the temple. He answers the sneer of the rulers that He is not a schoolman with a claim that He and His teaching come from God and with a sharp query why they seek to kill Him (7:11-19). Some of the multitude from Galilee, who do not know of the previous attempt to kill Him in Jerusalem (5:18), retort that Jesus has a demon, whereupon Jesus explains His charge (7:20-24). A group of people in the city, who know the plots of the rulers, sneer at the weakness of the rulers in not executing their purpose, and refer to a piece of popular theology concerning the sudden appearance of the Messiah as if from heaven (7:25-27), in the same way as the devil proposed to Jesus to let the people see Him come down from the pinnacle of the temple. The repetition of Christ's claim of divine origin enraged some of the Jerusalem crowd who, however, dared not to seize him, while others of the crowd from Galilee championed Him as being the Messiah (7:28-31).

The Pharisees in their rage sent officers (temple police) to arrest Him, but Jesus proceeded to show His superiority to their plots and schemes by going where they could not come (7:32-36). On the last day of the feast, the eighth day, when the ritual comprised an offering of water, Jesus stood (as if watching the people) and used the water as a picture of the living water (cf. 4:14 to the woman of Samaria) which the believer in Him received. The punctuation in verse 38 is uncertain and difficult. Westcott, for instance, once held the "his" (*autou*) used with the word belly to refer to the believer (so Bernard), but changed to the view that it refers to Christ. Either makes sense.

The multitudes from Galilee are again divided, some openly saying that Jesus is the Messiah, others sneering that the Messiah comes from Bethlehem, not Galilee, and wanting to kill Him (7:37-44). The report of the temple police to the Sanhedrin group angers them greatly: they have come back without Jesus and their excuse, the marvellous talk of Jesus, only makes the matter worse. Here Nicodemus puts in a word for justice to Jesus and receives a scowl of rage for his daring. He, too, is branded as a Galilean, this one-time secret enquirer (3:2). There is action of the most dramatic sort, pictures drawn from life by this skilful writer who was himself present. John knows how to tell it.

The story of the woman taken in adultery (7:53-8:11) does not occur in the oldest documents. It is not a part of the Fourth Gospel, but is, apparently, a true incident.

Some manuscripts put it at the end of the Gospel, and some even in Luke's Gospel.

In 8:12 to 50, apparently after the feast, when the crowds from Galilee, some of whom were friendly toward Jesus, have gone, Jesus has a fierce conflict with the Pharisees. It started with the abrupt claim of Jesus in the temple: "I am the light of the world" (8:12). This language startled and angered them. It can only be justified by us to-day by the acceptance of Jesus as the incarnate *Logos*, the life, the light of the world, as claimed in 1:1-18. On that assumption the claim falls in with ease. Otherwise, like many modern critics and the ancient Pharisees, one is in opposition. The one who believes in Jesus on this plane "will have the light of life."

No wonder the Pharisees challenged this claim and demanded proof. Jesus gave them "the Father" as the proof. Whereupon they ridiculed Him for His uncertain paternity (called a bastard in the Talmud) and the tension became acute (8:12-20). But Jesus repeated His claim. He explained that He was from above while they were from beneath, but refused to call Himself "Messiah" because He realised they would give a political meaning to the title and charge Him before Pilate with treason against Caesar. He does refer to their lifting up the Son of man as the proof to them that He is the Messiah. Many of the Pharisees were convinced and believed in Jesus (8:21-30).

But Jesus was not sure of these sudden believers and, as on the occasion of the first visit to Jerusalem (2:23-25), He tested their alleged faith by a series of thrusts that revealed their shallowness and real hostility, till infuriated they tried to kill Him on the spot (8:31-59). One can understand Christ's motives here, with care to see the rapid turn taken by these Pharisees. They resent the charge that they are in bondage to sin, and that Jesus terms them children of the devil. They accuse Him of being a Samaritan and having a demon—the two meanest things they could think of on the spur of the moment. His claim to Abraham's knowing Him and to eternal existence is the limit with their patience.

Chapter 9 gives a vivid picture of the healing of a man born blind. Jesus saw him as he passed out of the temple, and healed him by telling him to go to the pool of Siloam and wash his eyes. This miracle was also done on the Sabbath. The people who used to give alms to the blind beggar were amazed and they took him to the Pharisees to explain it. These, on their part, were confronted with the quandary of such a deed being done on the Sabbath by God. They appealed to the man's parents, who passed it back to their son. With fine raillery the beggar chided the Pharisees for their hypocritical hair splitting. In the end he was cast out by the Pharisees. On seeing Jesus again he was led to believe in Him and to worship Him as his Saviour. This remarkable incident opened the way for Jesus to picture the Pharisees as thieves, robbers and hirelings who when the wolves come, desert the sheep to save themselves. He is Himself the Good Shepherd who lays down His life for His sheep, with power to take it again. "I came that ye might keep on having life and may have it in abundance." The Pharisees themselves were divided over the claims of Jesus.

At the feast of dedication Jesus is in Jerusalem again. The Pharisees crowd around Him with a demand that He tell plainly who He is. To apply to Himself the term "Christ" (Messiah) would be to precipitate the end. They knew well enough that He did so claim, but His hour had not yet come. When He repeated His claim that God was His Father, they took up stones to stone Him. Jesus defied them and went forth out of their hand. It was plain what the end would be.

In Bethany Beyond Jordan Once More (10:40-42)

So Jesus withdrew from Jerusalem to Perea to the place where the Baptist had borne witness to Him (1:28-36). John was long since dead, but the people in Bethany remembered his words about Jesus as the Messiah, and when now they saw, they recognised Him for themselves (a striking witness to the power of John's preaching).

The Raising of Lazarus (11:1-53)

This great miracle, so graphically described, is the one that led Salmon to renounce his belief in the Johannine authorship of the Fourth Gospel, after proving it conclusively on other grounds. But that is pure prejudice against the supernatural in Jesus Christ. That prejudice applies also to His preëxistence, His birth, His deity, His resurrection, and to all His other miracles. The other Gospels do not tell of this miracle, probably because Lazarus was still alive when they wrote. John makes it the crucial event that prompted the Sanhedrin, led by Caiaphas, to the decision to put Jesus to death at the earliest possible moment (11: 47-53). This was no new purpose on their part, but a call for immediate action, in order if possible, to keep the people from flocking to Christ's standard. The narrative in John has all the earmarks of truth. The delay of Jesus was deliberate. The two sisters act in perfect part, according to the picture of them in Luke 10:38-42. The emotions of Jesus, as He stood by the grave of His friend, are natural and profound. He knew that the Father had already granted His request. There is no objection to this miracle that does not equally apply to the other raisings from the dead. To Martha, Jesus said: "I am the resurrection and the life" (11:25).

The Retreat to Ephraim (11:54-57)

It was inevitable that Jesus should now leave the vicinity of Jerusalem. It was probably only some three weeks before the passover. Here Jesus was on the edge of the desert where the devil after His baptism had tempted Him, offering Him the rule of the kingdoms of the world if only He

would bow down and worship him. It is a reasonable conjecture that the devil made Jesus another visit at this juncture. He could remind Jesus of the enmity of the ecclesiastics, and how He was in hiding from them instead of being
king of all, as the devil had once proposed.

An Incident in Bethany near Jerusalem (12:1-8)

It was six days (Friday afternoon) before the passover.
Jesus had come by way of Galilee and was again in Bethany,
near Jerusalem. John tells the story of the feast in honour
of Jesus given by Simon the leper and of the beautiful act
of Mary of Bethany who anointed the feet of Jesus in
preparation for His burial. She, alone, grasped the truth
in Christ's predictions of His death. Mark (14:39) and
Matthew (26:6-13) place this incident on the following
Tuesday evening. Perhaps John mentions it here because
it is his last mention of Bethany. He relates that it was
Judas Iscariot, already a thief, who raised objection to
Mary's waste of so much money, a criticism endorsed by the
other apostles. But Jesus rebuked them all and praised
Mary for her loving insight. It is a tragedy to see this
incident confounded with the somewhat similar incident in
Luke 7:36-50 and, worst of all to have Mary Magdalene
and even Mary of Bethany identified with the sinful woman
of that occasion.

Just Before the Passover (12:9-11)

The common pilgrims from Galilee and from the region
of Jerusalem, learned that Jesus was at Bethany at the home
of Martha and Mary, together with Lazarus, whom the
Master had recently raised from the dead. So they came to
see Lazarus as well as Jesus. This excitement made the
Sanhedrin decide to kill Lazarus as well as Jesus. With
both of them dead, perhaps Lazarus would remain dead.
So they argued, not in the least convinced by the raising of

Lazarus that Jesus was the Messiah. It is not credible that the Apostle John should make up this story in order to prove that Jesus is the Messiah. The fraud in such a deception would cry to heaven. To deny the actuality of this miracle is to discredit the Gospel completely.

The Challenge to Jerusalem (12:12-19)

John gives no details of the preparation for this decisive event, but simply speaks of the conduct of the crowds who hailed Jesus as the king of Israel. At last Jesus by this act is proclaiming Himself as the Messiah of prophecy, promise and hope. He is not the political Messiah of their hope, but He is so received by the surging masses, and Jesus lets it go at that for the moment, knowing full well that this act would be the occasion of His trial and condemnation. His hour had now come. The people who were present when Lazarus was raised from the dead took special pride in that fact. The Pharisees looked on in dismay and blamed one another for what looked like complete collapse of the campaign against Jesus: "Ye see how ye are not helping at all; lo, the world is gone after him." But Jesus knows how fleeting this victory would be.

The Request of the Greeks (12:20-50)

Among the throngs at this passover were some Greeks, proselytes of the gate who had come up to worship, and had heard all the talk about Jesus. These men, naturally, were eager to meet Jesus. They came to Philip with a polite request: "Sir, we desire to see Jesus." But Philip, though he had a Greek name himself, was embarrassed by the request, for the middle wall of partition between Jews and Greeks (Eph. 2:14) had not yet been broken down by the Cross of Christ. He left the Greeks and consulted Andrew, who also bore a Greek name. They brought the puzzling problem of race prejudice to Jesus, who took it so seriously that He had

INTERPRETING CHRIST   191

an agony of heart like that which He underwent a few days
later in Gethsemane. It was the same problem, to be solved
only by the lifting up of Jesus on the Cross (12:32). Thus
will He draw men of all races to Himself and to each other.
So in a solemn soliloquy Jesus agonises over dying to live,
as the true philosophy of life.

The disciples listened in awe and without understanding.
The crowds wonder how the Christ (the Son of man) could
die when they understood that the Messiah was to abide
for ever. The Father comforted the heart of Christ with an
audible voice, as at His baptism and on the Mount of
Transfiguration. No one else understood the Father's message. John adds that many of the rulers actually believed
on Jesus, with all the evidence in His favour, but they hesitated to confess Him because of the Pharisees who would
turn them out of the synagogue. Joseph of Arimathea and
Nicodemus, members of the Sanhedrin, will later come forward to bury Jesus. Were they among those who had held
back from fear? Cowardice before one's set plays its part
in keeping people from becoming Christians.

Rivalry Among the Twelve and the Exposure of Judas
(13:1-30)

The breaking out of jealousy over the seats at table at
this last passover is told by Luke (22:24-30). John takes
up the story of how the jealousy keeps up till, during the
midst of the meal, Jesus arises, girds Himself with a towel
and, with a bowl of water, begins to wash the feet of the
disciples. His purpose was not to make a new church
ordinance but to give the disciples an object lesson in
humility. The lesson was sadly needed, especially by Simon
Peter. Jesus applied the lesson of service as showing the
path to greatness and suddenly, disturbed in spirit, said:
"One of you will betray me." It was a bolt from the blue;
each looked at the others. John had gotten the post of
honour in front of Jesus, so that his head could rest on the

bosom of Christ, as they reclined on their left sides. Peter beckoned to John to ask Jesus who was to be the guilty one. They were so excited that few, save John and Judas, noticed Peter's gesture. But Judas saw it and knew now that Jesus knew and that John knew. In his resentment at his exposure he listened to the impulse of the devil and went out at once to carry out the bargain of hell, already made with the Sanhedrin, to betray Jesus that night. It was indeed, though the time of the full moon, the blackest of all nights.

Jesus Preparing the Eleven for His Death (13:31-17:26)

Barnas Sears termed this section of John's Gospel the Heart of Christ. So it is. Judas has gone and the Master turns to the eleven with deep concern as to how they will bear His death and departure from them. He speaks of His death as being glorified, but they will not see it so at first. He urges that they love one another in this crisis. In particular, He warns Peter, so full of confident boasting, and predicts that he will deny Him thrice before the cock crows for day.

It is a sad hour and Jesus offers consolation to the disciples who will be bereft of His presence (chapters 14-16). He will come back for them and take them to be with Him and the Father (14:1-7). He answers the doubt of Thomas by saying: "I am the way, and the truth, and the life." Meanwhile (answering the perplexity of Philip in 14:8-11) He has revealed the Father to them. Because of His going they will do works even greater in extent and He will answer their petitions to the Father in His name (14:12-15). Besides, (in answer to the wonder of Judas—"not Iscariot") they will have another paraclete, the Holy Spirit, who will be their teacher and guide and will enable the Father and the Son to dwell in their hearts (14:16-26). As a parting legacy Jesus leaves them His peace, richer than any that the world can offer (14:27-31). Apparently they arose and started out of the wondrous upper room, but as they went

out Jesus continued His talk. He gave them the parable
of the vine and the branches and urged abundant fruit-
bearing to prevent the necessity for lopping off of dead
branches at pruning time (15:1-16). They will need to
love one another and may expect the world's hate, as He has
had it (15:17-25). They will have the help of the Holy
Spirit in special measure after His departure. His task will
be to convict the world and to enlighten the disciples, to
take of the things of Christ and make them plain (15:26-16:
15). Jesus will go, but He will come back soon (His resurrection on the third day). The apostles were puzzled (16:
16-24). He, therefore, drops proverbs and tells the apostles plainly that He is going back to the Father from whom
He came, but that He is victorious even in death (16:25-
33). Somewhere, probably in the shadow of a wall on the
way to Gethsemane, Jesus stopped and prayed His intercessory prayer (ch. 17). He first thanks the Father that
He is going back to the glory that He left before His Incarnation (1-5). Then He makes a plea for these eleven
men on whom so much responsibility will rest (6-19).
Finally Jesus pleads for the spirit of unity and power upon
all believers through the ages, that the world by their witness may be won (20-26).

In Gethsemane (18:1-12)

John tells nothing of the agony in Gethsemane (already
fully told in the Synoptics). He takes up the story at the
point where Judas arrives, with the band of soldiers and
temple police, armed with lanterns and torches and weapons.
Judas will take no chances, for he knows the strange power
of Jesus, and also that Jesus knows of this plot to betray
Him. John tells also how Judas took advantage of his
knowledge of Jesus's habit of going to the Garden of
Gethsemane to pray. He knew that he was sure to find
Jesus there. He also tells how, when Jesus confessed to being the one wanted by the officers and soldiers, they all fell

back upon the ground. This Jesus did to show His power and to make clear that His surrender was voluntary. John alone mentions the name (Malchus) of the servant of the high priest whose head Peter tried to cut off. Christ's rebuke to Peter includes also the statement of His purpose to drink the cup from His Father. Then without warrant or charge the officers arrested Jesus and bound Him.

The Trial of Jesus and the Denials of Peter (18:13-19:16)

John alone tells of the preliminary examination by Annas, the ex-high priest and father-in-law of Caiaphas (18:12-23), while the Sanhedrin was assembling, and of the protest of Jesus to the sneer of Annas and the blow from the officer. John places the denials by Peter, partly while Jesus was before Annas (18:15-18) and partly while He was before Caiaphas (18:25-27). He alone tells how Peter was brought into the court by the Beloved Disciple who was known to the high priest. The story is a sad one and is sharpened in the third denial by the question of a kinsman of Malchus, who saw Peter trying to kill Malchus. John gives no details of the other two stages of the Jewish trial before Caiaphas and the Sanhedrin—the condemnation of Jesus just before dawn and the ratification of the verdict in the early morning hours. He does say, however, that Jesus was sent by Annas to Caiaphas (18:24). His account is merely supplementary to the Synoptic record.

John passes by the remorse and suicide of Judas Iscariot also, but he gives more details of the Roman trial by Pilate than do either of the Synoptics. He says that it was "early" when Jesus was brought before Caiaphas (18:28) and "about the sixth hour" when the condemnation took place (19:14), six o'clock A.M., Roman time. He shows how the members of the Sanhedrin refused to enter Pilate's palace because they wished to go on with the passover festival ("eat the passover," 18:28) and how Pilate wanted to turn the case back to the Sanhedrin who did not report their

condemnation, but explained that they wanted the death of
Jesus, the right to decree which was no longer in their hands.
Then Pilate took Jesus from the portico overlooking the
pavement inside and faced Him with a straight question as
to whether He was "the king of the Jews." The answer of
Jesus convinced Pilate that Jesus was no rival of Caesar,
but, as king of the kingdom of truth, only a harmless en-
thusiast, at most. So Pilate went out and proclaimed the
innocence of Jesus. John tells also about the effort of
Pilate to have Jesus released by popular demand, and the
outcry for Barabbas. Then Pilate had Jesus scourged, and
introduced him arrayed in purple with a crown of thorns
upon his head, as the innocent mock king with the half
humorous words: "Behold the man!" But the Sanhedrin
roused the mob to cry: "Crucify him." In a fret Pilate
said: "Take him yourselves, and crucify him for I find no
crime in him" (19:6), the strangest verdict ever rendered
by a judge. Then the Jews tell why they want Him put to
death—"because he made himself the Son of God." In
fear Pilate sought once more to find out from Jesus who He
really was. Rebuffed by Jesus, once again he sought to release Him, whereupon the Jews threatened to tell Caesar
that he had released a rival king to Caesar. In angry des-
peration Pilate said: "Behold your king" and surrendered to
the Jews. It is a graphic story.

The Crucifixion and Burial (19:17-42)

John was an eyewitness of the crucifixion (19:35), as of
the trial, and gives items not as a rule in the Synoptics.
He notes that Jesus "went out bearing the Cross for himself" (19:17). He tells about the casting of lots by the four
soldiers for the seamless garment of Christ, as He hung on
the Cross (19:23-24). He alone notes that the inscription
on the Cross was in Hebrew, Latin, and Greek (19:20) and
he speaks of the stubborn refusal of Pilate to change his
language. John alone gives the picture of the small group

of women with the mother of Jesus standing by the Cross, and the message of Jesus to His mother and the Beloved Disciple to take each other as mother and son (19:25-27). John alone gives the cry of physical anguish, "I thirst" (19:28) and the cry of victory as He died, "It is finished" (19:30). It is John who tells of the piercing of the side of Jesus and the coming out of water and blood (19:31-42). Once more John, alone, tells of the part that Nicodemus played in helping Joseph of Arimathea bury the body of Jesus with spices (myrrh and aloes) and that Joseph's new tomb was in a garden.

The Resurrection (chapter 20)

John gives the story of Mary Magdalene coming early in the dawn and finding the empty tomb and running, in turn, to tell Peter and John (together again) who run a race to the tomb and find it empty, but orderly; (evidence that convinced John before seeing Him that Jesus was risen, 1-10). When Mary Magdalene came back, after Peter and John had left, she is astonished by seeing Jesus, unrecognised at first, but revealed as He called her name. He commissions her to go tell His disciples the glad news. She had the most wondrous story ever heard: "I have seen the Lord." But the disciples would not at first believe her or the other women (Lu. 24:10f., 24). They no longer remembered the promise of Jesus to rise on the third day from the dead.

That Sunday evening the disciples (men and women) gathered with closed doors and listened to the story of the women and Simon Peter who had, himself, seen Jesus. They were all jubilant over the confirmation from the two disciples from Emmaus, when to the amazement and confusion of all (20:19-23), Jesus, Himself, stepped into their midst. Slowly Jesus convinced them that it was He (Lu. 24:38-43) and gave them a new commission for evangelization. Thomas was absent and the disciples flatly failed to convince him that Jesus was risen till, on the next Sunday, Jesus appeared again and challenged him to believe (20:24-29). Thomas rose to the occasion with words of noble faith: "My Lord and my God." But even so Thomas by not believing the witness of the others had missed the highest faith.

Apparently John closed the book with verses 30 and 31 which give the method and the purpose of the book. It is not likely that the book was published without the Epilogue (chapter 21). But, even if it was, the Epilogue must have been added shortly afterwards.

14. *The Epilogue (chapter 21).* There is no proof that this appendix was added by another author, for it is in the same style. John may at first have thought of closing with chapter 20, but we are glad that he did not. The apparent reason for adding this Epilogue seems to be to correct the erroneous idea, circulated because of John's extreme old age, that he was not going to die at all, but would live on till Jesus came again. John tells this story in its true setting, leading up to it by the wonderful account of the fishing scene by the "beloved lake." Seven of the apostles, including the sons of Zebedee (here alone so named in this Gospel), acting on the proposal of Simon Peter, go on a fishing excursion. They fish all night and catch nothing (an experience not uncommon with them, Lu. 5:1-11). Next morning Jesus appears on the shore. John recognises Him but Peter leaps out to go to Him. That was a wonderful breakfast as guest of Jesus on the shore, and Jesus searched Peter's heart by three pointed questions concerning his former boast of love and the three tragic denials. Peter was duly humbled but trusted Christ's knowledge of the heart to understand him now. The Beloved Disciple had heard about the prophecy of a martyr's death for Peter, and the command for Peter to keep on following Jesus. Peter turned, as they started on, and saw John following them. With irresistible curiosity Peter wanted to know what was to be the fate of the Beloved Disciple. Then it

was that Jesus rebuked Peter's idle curiosity by saying: "If I wish him to remain while I am coming, what is that to thee? Do thou keep on following me" (21:22). John is careful to correct the misinterpretation of this language of Jesus.

Verse 24 seems to have been added by the friends of John in Ephesus. They identify the Beloved Disciple (the Apostle John) as the author of the book and affirm that they know the witness to be true. This is the earliest testimony concerning the authorship of the book. It is possible, as was true of Paul, that John dictated the book and had his friends in Ephesus read it over, and that verse 24 is their endorsement. Men who deny the Johannine authorship nevertheless admit that it is in accord with the claim of the book. For myself I prefer the claim of the book, the confirmation of these Ephesian elders or friends of John, the testimony of Polycarp, Irenaeus, and all the rest, to the modern guesses of men who have entangled themselves in their own ratiocinations. Admit the deity of Jesus Christ and the reality of His miracles, and the difficulties disappear. Verse 25, of course, is hyperbole, but a natural one.

XIV

SEEING VISIONS IN THE ISLE OF PATMOS

(The Apocalypse)

1. *The author.* He, himself, claims to be John (1:1, 4, 9; 22:8). So then it is not anonymous. It cannot be called pseudonymous, for he does not say that he is the Apostle John. That, however, is the natural meaning, because the Apostle John was the outstanding John in Christian circles. There is a late legend in George Hamartolus (ninth century) that John was put to death by the Jews, with an alleged quotation from Papias which does not say that he was put to death at the same time as James in A.D. 44, but which does speak of his living in Ephesus. Dionysius of Alexandria (third century) doubted that the Apostle John was the author of the Apocalypse because of the differences in style. He suggested some other John, possibly the so-called Elder John, certainly not John Mark. Westcott held to the early date of the Apocalypse as the easiest way to agree to the Johannine authorship. Swete sums it up thus: "While inclining to the traditional view which holds that the author of the Apocalypse was the Apostle John, the present writer desires to keep an open mind upon the question." Peake (*Revelation of John,* p. 69) is "unable to accept any view as to the authorship of the Apocalypse." Moffatt thinks that the data suggests Presbyter John more than any other possibility. My own feeling is that the case here is not as strong for the Apostle John as in the Fourth Gospel, but that the balance of probability is on that side. He appears here as the son of thunder of the Synoptics and of

I John, mightily moved by the persecutions and by the visions that hold out final triumph.

2. *Relation to the fourth Gospel.* There are many unquestionable similarities, unlike as the two books appear on the surface. "The main idea of both is the same. Both present a view of a supreme conflict between the powers of good and evil. In the Gospel this is delineated mainly in moral conceptions; in the Apocalypse mainly in images and visions. In the Gospel the opposing forces are treated under abstract and absolute forms, as light and darkness, love and hatred; in the Apocalypse under concrete and definite forms, God, Christ, and the Church warring with the devil, the false prophet, and the beast. But in both books alike Christ is the central figure. His victory is the end to which history and vision lead as their consummation. His Person and Work are the ground of triumph, and of triumph through apparent failure" (Westcott, *Comm. on John,* Vol. I, p. clxxi). That in broad outline is true.

There are many likenesses in detail of language and thought. One of the most striking is the use of *Logos* (Word) for Jesus Christ in John 1:1, 14 and Revelation 19:14, nowhere else employed in the New Testament save I John 1:1. But there are pronounced differences in style; the historical being used in the Gospel, the apocalyptic in Revelation, somewhat like the difference between I Thessalonians 4 and II Thessalonians 2 and the rest of these two epistles, as Lightfoot has argued. More than this, as numerous lapses show, there are in the apocalypse variations in strict grammar so great that Charles in his commentary makes a special grammar for them, of which more later. Westcott on the basis of these differences argued for an early date for the Apocalypse before John learned his *Koine* well. Some, like Dionysius of Alexandria, urge that the same writer for both Gospel and Apocalypse is impossible. Some credit one to the Apostle John, some the other, and some neither. If both are by the Apostle John and both are late, one is at liberty to suggest that, though John, like

Peter, was not a schoolman (Acts 4:13), yet in the Gospel and the epistles which were written from Ephesus with the possible use of an amanuensis—certainly of competent help (John 21:24)—the Apocalypse was written while alone in Patmos, in apparent haste, in great excitement due to the visions, in involved apocalyptic style, and possibly without careful revision in linguistic details. These facts go far toward explaining the differences in smoothness of style. There are probably other reasons beyond our knowledge. As a result of these considerations one hesitates to affirm that John, if also the author of the Fourth Gospel, could not also have written the Apocalypse and even have done it last of all.

3. *The place.* John says: "I John, your brother and co-partner in the tribulation and kingdom and patience in Jesus, came to be in the island that is called Patmos because of the word of God and the witness to Jesus." This looks like banishment from Ephesus to this small island in the Sporades group, "in the Icarian Sea between Icaria and Leros, about 40 miles S.W. by W. from Miletus" (Swete), "the first or last stopping-place for the traveller on his way from Ephesus to Rome or from Rome to Ephesus." It is some ten miles long and half a mile wide, rocky and mountainous and the environment here "doubtless shaped to some extent the scenery of the Apocalypse into which the mountains and the sea enter largely" (Swete). For a modern picture of the island to-day see Geil's *The Isle that Is Called Patmos* (1905). It has a good harbour, but is sparsely settled. It is a weird and suitable place for apocalyptic visions.

4. *The readers.* The Apocalypse is addressed "to the seven churches of Asia" (1:4) which are named in 1:11 as Ephesus, Smyrna, Pergamum, Thyatira, Sardis, Philadelphia, and Laodicea. These seven form a sort of loose circle on the Roman road from Ephesus and back. There were other churches in the Province of Asia like Colossae (Col. 1:2), Hierapolis (Col. 4:13), Miletus (Acts 20:17), Troas (Acts

20:5; 2 Cor. 2:12), and later, if not already, at Magnesia and Tralles (see Epistles of Ignatius). John chose these seven either because of his fondness for the number seven in this book or because he was well-known to them and had special relations to them. Ephesus had been his headquarters before his exile to Patmos. From Ephesus he had carried on missionary work (III John 3, 5-8, 10) and it was the most important city in the province.

The entire book was designed for public reading in each church (Rev. 1:3). It was probably copied by each church and a copy passed on to the neighbouring churches, as was done between Colossae and Laodicea with Paul's Epistles (Col. 4:16). Thus the Apocalypse would spread rapidly throughout the province and into adjoining provinces. It is certain that John meant to reach with this message "all churches throughout the world" (Beckwith). These seven churches merely represented the whole, as Ezekiel selected seven nations to represent all the Gentiles (Ezek. 25-32). The severe persecutions of the time would give keen poignancy to the book as it was eagerly read. In Ramsay's *Letters to the Seven Churches* (1904) we have an admirable picture of the seven cities to which the Apocalypse was sent and of the bearing of the known facts about them on the interpretation of the messages to each of them.

5. *The date.* The arguments for the last years of the reign of Domitian are quite conclusive. Irenaeus says (Adv. Haer. iii. 18. 3) of the Apocalypse of John: "It was seen not long ago, but almost in our own generation, at the end of the reign of Domitian." Eusebius himself (*Church History* iii. 23. 1) adds: "At that time (after the Apocalypse) the apostle and evangelist John, the one whom Jesus loved, was still living in Asia, and governing the churches of that region." Victorinus (*Apoc.* x. 11) confirms it: "When John saw these things he was in the Island of Patmos, having been condemned to the mines by the emperor Domitian." Swete concludes: "Early Christian tradition is practically unanimous in assigning the Apocalypse to the last years of

Domitian." And yet Hort, Lightfoot, and Hort, the great Cambridge trio of the last century, held that John wrote the Apocalypse in the early years of Vespasian's reign, just after Nero's death. This position they held chiefly because of the grammatical lapses in the Apocalypse which were due, they said, to John's lack of knowledge of Greek at this early period. The allusion in 17:10f. to the eighth who is one of the seven was applied to Vespasian and to the expectation of the return of Nero. But Domitian is himself called by the Christians, Nero *redivivus,* because he persecuted the Christians as Nero had done. The spiritual decline in the churches of Ephesus, Laodicea, and Sardis suits the time of Domitian far better than that of Vespasian, so close to the time of Paul. There are other ways of explaining the differences in language besides the theory of the early date of the Apocalypse. Apart from that element, the argument is conclusive for the time of Domitian.

6. *The linguistic peculiarities of the Apocalypse.* There are two extreme views on this subject. Charles in his great Commentary on the Apocalypse gives in Vol I "A Short Grammar of the Apocalypse" (pp. cxvii-clix) in which he says (p. cxliii): "The linguistic character of the Apocalypse is absolutely unique." On the other hand, Archbishop Benson in his *Apocalypse* (Essay V pp. 131ff.) has a chapter headed "A Grammar of Ungrammar" in which he holds that every lapse in grammar in John's Apocalypse is intentional for a definite reason. I agree, rather, with Swete (*op. cit.,* p. cxx) that "his eccentricities of syntax are probably due to more than one cause." Charles insists that the author thought in Hebrew and wrote in Greek, and that is probably true. The Fourth Gospel has a Semitic mould, though comparatively free from Semiticisms which are frequent in the Apocalypse. Some of the lapses from concord are undoubtedly intentional like the use of the nominative case after *apo* in 1:4 and the use of *ho* as both article and relative (also 11:17) to emphasise the unchangeable character of God. Others, like the failure of concord in case in

BIRDVILLE
BAPTIST CHURCH
LIBRARY

apposition, particularly in participles, as in 2:20, occur in so careful a writer as Luke (Acts 15:22f.) and also in ancient Greek writers, only they are far more frequent in the Apocalypse.

At this point several things should be considered. One is whether in the Apocalypse John is not writing without an amanuensis—or at least with a different one from the one employed in the Gospel and Epistles. Another question to consider is whether John himself was able in Patmos to give the book a careful revision such as he and his friends did for the Gospel. We know from Acts 4:13 that John was not a man of technical literary training like Paul, Luke, or Apollos. Another thing to bear in mind is the exciting effect of the visions on John's mind unless they are assumed to be purely literary devices, not actual visions. Even so, the composition would be a far more complicated thing than a historical narrative and the use of material so long familiar to John as was the life of Jesus. Many of the peculiar Greek forms and constructions appear constantly in the papyri of the first century A.D. They are marks of the vernacular in contrast with the literary *Koine*. There are, however, many linguistic similarities between the Apocalypse and the Fourth Gospel like the use of parallelisms, antithesis, parenthetic explanations, repetition of the article, coincidences in the use of words and phrases. These argue for identity of authorship. Of the 913 separate words in the Apocalypse, 416 (Swete) occur also in the Gospel. Both attach special meanings to a number of characteristic words. The wide difference in subject matter justifies much of the difference in vocabulary. On the whole Swete properly concludes "that it creates a strong presumption of affinity between the Fourth Gospel and the Apocalypse, notwithstanding this great diversity both in language and in thought."

7. *The unity of the book.* The book in its present form claims to be by one author named John (1:1, 4, 9; 22:8). "The book creates the *prima facie* impression that it is by

one author or editor" (Swete). Traces of literary unity in language, thought and style run all through the book. The same symbolisms reappear in all phases of the book. And yet, no book of the New Testament has been the victim of such violent dissection. These critical analyses fall into three general lines. (1) Revision of previous apocalypses either Jewish or Christian, each, complete in itself, worked over by an editor or editors. Voelter and Vischer argue this view. (2) The compilation theory. The idea here is that a redactor loosely put together separate Jewish or Christian apocalypses, making a jumble of the whole. Spitta advocated this view, as does also Briggs. (3) The incorporation or interpolation theory, according to which a single writer carried out his plan by the use of fragments of former apocalypses. He makes original use of previous material. Weizsäcker suggested that the occasional lack of cohesion was due to the interpolation of fragments not from the author's pen. Gunkel sought the explanation in the climax of a long course of apocalyptic traditions going back to the creation myths of Babylonia. Many scholars have argued for this view with modifications like Baljon, W. Bauer, Bousset, Calmes, H. J. Holtzmann, Jülicher, Moffatt, Sabatier, Schoen. According to J. Weiss, John wrote the original Apocalypse before A.D. 70 and an editor issued it in its present form in the reign of Domitian. Charles makes a sharp distinction between the author and the editor, especially in 20:4-22:21. He calls this editor "very unintelligent" (Vol. I, p. li), and worse: "By this and other like unwarrantable devices this shallow-brained fanatic and celibate, whose dogmatism varies directly with the narrowness of his understanding, has often stood between John and his readers for nearly 2000 years. But such obscurantism cannot outlive the limits assigned to it" (Vol. I, p. lv). It is respectfully submitted that Charles's own "dogmatism" here is "obscurantism" enough for ordinary purposes. He feels endowed with a sudden intuition to clear up this wonderful book hidden by the "editor" (Charles's man of straw) for two thousand years. There are still scholars who hold to the unity of this greatest of all apocalypses, men like Beckwith, Beyschlag, Düsterdieck, Hilgenfeld, Swete, Warfield, B. Weiss, Zahn. When the critics differ so radically in their partition theories, one may be pardoned for holding to the unity of the book. The difficulties are greatly lessened if one does not come to the book with preconceived theories of its plan and purpose.

8. *The use of the Old Testament.* In the appendix to the second volume of Wescott and Hort's Greek New Testament it is shown that of the 404 verses in John's Apocalypse, 278 contain references to the Old Testament. No other book of the New Testament shows such constant use of the Old Testament. And yet there is not a single formal quotation in them all. The instances consist of the use of Old Testament words and phrases (the vocabulary of the Old Testament) without any regard to the context or, on the other hand, of clear and definite use of the context, but always in an original and independent application of the particular history or prophecy or symbol cited to the matter in hand. This is done from memory and not by copying a manuscript. The author is steeped in the Old Testament language and thought. As a rule he uses the words found in the Septuagint, rather than his own translation from the Hebrew. A few words, like Abaddon (9:11) and Har Magedon (16:16), seem to come directly from the Hebrew. In the case of Daniel the text used by John is more like the translation of Theodotin than the Septuagint. The Old Testament colouring of the language of the Apocalypse comes from the books of the law, Judges, Kings and Chronicles, the Psalms, Proverbs, the Song of Solomon, Job, all the major prophets and seven of the minor prophets. Half of the references are to the Psalms, Isaiah, Ezekiel, Daniel. "They are those which abound in mystical and apocalyptic elements" (Swete). There are instances which show knowledge of the sayings of Christ like Revelation 21:6 (cf. John 4:10). In Revelation 1:5 the language reminds us of

Colossians 1:18. We know that John was familiar with the Synoptic Gospels and wrote the Fourth. He probably was acquainted with Paul's epistles. There are many scholars who think that the Apocalypse of John makes abundant use of the Jewish Apocalypses of which we have many still preserved, but so careful and open-minded a scholar as Swete (p. cliii) says: "Here it is enough to say that while they shew the writer of the Christian Apocalypse to have been familiar with the apocalyptic ideas of his age, they afford little or no clear evidence of his dependence on Jewish sources other than the books of the Old Testament."

9. *The apocalyptic method.* "The Revelation of John is the only written apocalypse, as it is the only written prophecy of the Apostolic age" (Swete, *op. cit.,* p. xix). Prophecy was revived by the Baptist, who was a prophet and more than a prophet. There were other prophets in New Testament times (Acts 11:27; 13:1; Eph. 4:12, etc.). Paul speaks of revelations (apocalypses) in I Corinthians 14:6, 26, 30; II Corinthians 12:1 and uses this method in II Thessalonians 2. People rightly regarded Jesus as a prophet (Matt. 16:14), though he was far more, the Son of God and the Son of man, the Messiah, Lord and Saviour. In Matthew 11:25 Jesus thanked the Father that "Thou didst reveal *(apekalupsas)* them unto babes." That is *apocalypse,* God revealing hidden things unto men. Jesus used the apocalyptic method at length in the great discourse on the Mount of Olives (Mark 13; Matt. 24 and 25; Lu. 21:5-36) and occasionally at other times. Indeed, there is a school of modern critics (Albert Schweitzer, for instance) who treat Jesus as apocalyptic and eschatological always, and ethical only at rare intervals *(ad interim)*—a gross misapprehension of the Kingdom of God as taught by Christ as being spiritual, individual, present, eternal, with culminating growth, climacteric. There is a great deal of eschatological prophecy about last things in Isaiah, Ezekiel, Zechariah, Daniel and the Psalms. This great Christian Apocalypse of John is greater than all others, though using

language from all of them. There are preserved many other non-canonical Jewish apocalypses (Second Esdras, Testaments of the Twelve Patriarchs, Sybilline Oracles, Book of Enoch, Apocalypse of Baruch, Assumption of Moses, Book of Jubilees, etc.). These are all pseudonymous and attributed to authors of an age long past, but this is not true of John's Apocalypse nor of the Christian Shepherd of Hermas.

10. *The use of symbols*. It is characteristic of apocalyptic literature to use symbols of various kinds, and especially to employ numbers in a symbolic sense. Teaching by symbols runs all through the Old Testament and appears particularly in the later prophecies like Daniel and Ezekiel. These images (word pictures) are drawn from all forms of nature (animal, vegetable, humanity, earth, sky, heaven, hell), much of it from the Old Testament, but always adapted to the present occasion. Much of the imagery is "merely designed to heighten the colouring of the great picture and to add vividness and movement to its scenes" (Swete). Sometimes John interprets the symbol, as in 1:20; 4:5; 5:6; 12:9; 17:9f.; 12:5. At other times the meaning is plain in spite of the symbol, as in 1:13ff.; 4:2. But in some cases we are left wholly in the dark, as in 6:2; 7:4; 11:8. About numbers "it is not to be supposed that specific meaning attaches invariably to a given numerical symbol" (Beckwith, *op. cit.*, p. 251). Beckwith pointedly adds: "An essential thing is that we should neither take the number literally, nor seek to find in it a recondite, mystical meaning." Simon Peter can be quoted against interpreting the number "one thousand" literally in God's way of counting time (II Pet. 3:8). And yet we continually find the changes rung on the precise meaning of 3, 3½ (time, times, half a time, 42 months, 1260 days), 4, 7, 10, 12, 1000.

We are not to say that the use of these numbers is accidental in the Apocalypse. "The writer's partiality for them is due, in some measure, to his Semitic habits of thought.

To the Hebrew mind *seven* denotes completion, as we gather
from countless passages of the Old Testament" (Swete).
So the Holy Spirit is symbolised. The selection of seven
churches out of the many in Asia serves as a sort of keynote
in the Apocalypse for the lampstands, the angels, the stars,
the seals, the trumpets, the bowls, etc. But sometimes, even
when emphasis is laid on the number that occurs only once,
as in 13:18, we are unable to explain it, for the manuscripts
differ between 666 and 616 and it remains for us more
cryptogram than symbol. There is surely little place for
dogmatism in the interpretation of numbers in this book of
symbols and the other figures. As these words are written
there is a really pitiful attempt going on to make "the mark
of the beast" in 13:16f. symbolise the N. R. A. of the
present United States government. Revelation is a series
of pictures, partly kaleidoscopic, partly like moving pictures,
a powerful panorama. The important thing is to see the
pictures, to get the impact of the whole. Then handle the
details as one is able to do.

11. *Emperor worship.* That began early, even in the
reign of Julius Caesar. Octavius was called Augustus
(*Sebastos*, Revered). Caligula wanted to set up a statue of
himself in the temple in Jerusalem. Nero posed as a god.
In time the worship of the emperor became the national
religion and the occasion of the persecution of the Christians who refused to subscribe to it. In the case of Polycarp the issue was put squarely up to him (*Kurios Kaisar*
or *Kurios Iēsous*) and he was burned because he would not
say *Kurios Kaisar*. Paul saw it coming and foretold in
Thessalonica the conflict between the Kingdom of Jesus and
the Kingdom of Rome (Acts 17:7). In writing to the
Thessalonians he predicted the coming of the Man of Sin
(II Thess. 2:3-12). John called the great adversary of
Christ Antichrist (I Jo. 2:18, 22; 4:3), though he also spoke
of "many antichrists" as Jesus did of "false christs." Certainly we know that Domitian made even stronger claims to
divinity than did Nero and that he carried on a far more

severe persecution of the Christians because they would not worship him. John wrote his Apocalypse in the fierce light of these persecutions by Domitian and he employs the apocalyptic imagery and symbolism in order to reveal his message in a form as free as possible from grounds for imperial attack. So he calls Rome, "Babylon," and Nero and Domitian, possibly, the beast (first and second?). At any rate, John is picturing the titanic struggle between the kingdom of Christ and the world power of Rome. Under different forms through the ages this conflict is repeated. It was placed squarely before Jesus on the mount of temptation by the devil, for Jesus refused the devil's compromise.

12. *The purpose of the book.* It is an apocalyptic prophecy in the form of an epistle addressed to seven churches in the Province of Asia (1:4, 11), with a special message to each church (chs. 2 and 3) to be read in public to the church (1:3) and is designed to meet the immediate crisis confronting them because of the persecutions under Domitian, who has become a second Nero. This is the immediate purpose of John. These seven churches in these great cities are representative of those all over the world and they were now in peril from the world spirit of commercial and material prosperity. John had probably laboured in all these cites during his residence in Ephesus and now in exile his heart turned to them. In fact, he was commanded to write (1:11; 2:1, 8, etc.), except once when he was forbidden to write (10:4). The Emperor Domitian was assassinated September 18, A.D. 96, so that the book was written shortly before that date. He was succeeded by Nerva, who apparently did not persecute; but Trajan came to the throne A.D. 98, and in A.D. 112 began to persecute Christians, as we know from the correspondence between the younger Pliny and Trajan. After that persecution raged, off and on, with great fierceness for more than two centuries. These churches were strengthened by John's messages, as we can see from the Epistle of Ignatius early in the second century.

BIRDVILLE
BAPTIST CHURCH
LIBRARY

It is plain however that John had a wider purpose than the immediate and practical one in respect to the seven churches. John foresees a dreadful conflict between Christ and Apollyon (Satan), between the kingdom of God and the world power as represented by the Roman emperors, between Christ and antichrist. This conflict will go on till the climax of all comes, till Christ comes again in triumph. At the close (22:18f.) John adds a warning against any one who tampers with the prophecy in his book, as if conscious that the book would have a wider and more permanent mission than just to the seven churches. There is no reason to doubt the reality of the visions any more than those in Isaiah, Peter, Paul, but we do not have to suppose that John wrote down these ecstatic experiences at once on having them. He may have taken a little time for reflection, but, even so, we do not have to regard them as mere literary inventions like Milton's *Paradise Lost* or Bunyan's *Pilgrim's Progress*. The dominant note in the book is the certainty of the final triumph of Christ over all His foes (Satan, together with the two beasts—the one from the sea and the one on land). Those who fall as martyrs in the conflict will receive special honour and glory. There are frequent glimpses of heaven that cheer those in the stress and strain of the struggle on earth. The Risen Christ directs the conflict from heaven and guides it through its varied phases to complete victory at last, when the redeemed, represented as the bride of Christ or the city of God, dwell with God for ever. The book presents in bold and powerful outline a picture of conflict and final triumph. Children love to hear the book read aloud, for they enjoy the panorama without bothering over the meaning of each symbol.

13. *Theories of interpretation.* These are manifold, and new ones are continually advanced. The old English divine, Dr. Robert South, said that the Apocalypse either found one insane or left him so. That is one extreme, far from the truth, though one must admit that the book does have a strange fascination. The other extreme may be illustrated

by the great German scholar, Adolph Harnack, who regarded the book as one of the simplest to understand in the entire New Testament, that is, if one uses Harnack's key to the symbols. Each age has had its own fad or fads in interpreting this wonderful book. It can be assumed that most, if not all, the symbols were intelligible to the hearers and readers in the seven churches. The word apocalypse means revelation. The book was meant to reveal, not to conceal, "things which must shortly come to pass" (1:1), and the word of Jesus to each church is: "He that has an ear, let him hear what the Spirit says to the churches" (2:7, etc.). Sir W. M. Ramsay (*Letters to the Seven Churches*) has thrown a good deal of light on the original significance of the symbolism of the messages to the churches from the archaeological discoveries in the history and geography of each city. But the interpretation of some of them is wholly lost to us, even in a case where the mark of the beast is the number of a man and wisdom is said to lie in seeing it (13: 17f.). It is not plain to us now at any rate.

One of the first abuses in exegesis of the book is what is termed Chiliasm. Cerinthus, the great adversary of the Apostle John in Ephesus, took a grossly sensual view of the millennial promises (Eusebius, *Hist.* iii. 28) and Papias is said by Eusebius (*Hist.* iii. 39) apparently to have interpreted John's Apocalypse as a picture of sensuous bliss. Justin Martyr was familiar with this view as was Tertullian. Irenaeus (*Haer.* v. 35.2) on the basis of Revelation 21 looked for a terrestrial kingdom of Christ for a literal 1000 years and a restored Jerusalem, as indeed many do to-day. With the conversion of Constantine in A.D. 325 many began to date the millennium from that year, with the end of the world to come one thousand years from that year. As the first thousand years of the Christian era drew on, many expected the end to come then and some made their wills in view of that event as certain. As time went on and 1325 drew near there was a like anticipation. As protests grew against Roman Catholicism, from the time of Luther on, the era of almost universal Roman sway over Christendom was regarded as the dark ages (the time of intellectual and spiritual darkness before the renaissance). The two beasts were often interpreted as Pagan Rome and Papal Rome. To offset this view Roman Catholic scholars proposed two views. One is the preterist view which interprets everything as fulfilled in the past, either in Nero's time (Neronian Preterist) or in Domitian's time (Domitianic Preterist). But the impossibility of identifying the events with the symbols renders both preterist views unconvincing. The other view proposed by Roman Catholic scholars is the futurist interpretation, putting all the events in the future, a view that can neither be proved nor disproved. Some Protestant scholars have accepted these Roman suggestions. But the great majority of Protestant scholars answer the Romanists with either the continuous historical theory or the synchronous historical theory. Both of these views take the Apocalypse as a picture of Christian history in broad outline. Manifold identifications of men and events are proposed, but none are satisfying. The continuous theory takes each series of sevens (seals, trumpets, bowls) as succeeding each other in chronological order. The synchronous theory, on the other hand, considers the series as, in a general sense, parallel—each leading up to the end. Something can be said for both of these views, but they do not satisfy one in any single interpretation. Others go to the other extreme and see only pictures of spiritual events with no historical basis at all. So then, the world to-day is largely at sea in the interpretation of this greatest of all apocalypses. One can only give his own personal reaction to it all. Mine is that the book was written in the Domitianic persecution, to put cheer and courage in the hearts of the Christians of that time. Rome was pictured as Babylon and the conflict with Satan's world-power was presented in bold outline, with the certainty of the final triumph of Christ. Actual historical struggles were pictured, but these were meant to serve as a type of such conflicts in every age. They

will continue in varied forms till Jesus comes again to claim
His own. We can and should gain comfort and strength
from the promise of Christ's presence during our own struggles in the great world conflict with Satan.

14. *The Contents of the Apocalypse.* No formal outline
will be attempted, but an interpretation of the successive
paragraphs. We should always remember that there were
no chapter or verse divisions in the original manuscript.

The Prologue (1:1-3) comes before the Salutation (1:
4-6). Both are brief. The Prologue gives the title of the
book, Revelation of Jesus Christ. The word *apokalupsis*
occurs only here in the book, though it is common in the
epistles for the revelation of God (Rom. 2:5), of Christ
(I Cor. 1:7), of the saints at the Parousia (Rom. 8:19), or
any revelation made to a church (I Cor. 14:6). The genitive case (of Jesus Christ) can be either objective (about
Jesus Christ), as Hort takes it, or subjective (which Christ
gives), as Westcott holds, and as the next words say, "which
God gave to him (Christ) to show to his servants." The
revelation thus comes ultimately from the Father through
the Son (cf. Jo. 3:35; 5:20ff., etc.). Christ made it known
to John by an angel and John bore his witness to what he
saw at the hands of the angel. The contents of the book
are summed up in "things must shortly come to pass," how
"shortly" we are not told. But the immediate future is pictured and the final consummation, with glimpses of inter-
vening events without definite and complete data. In verse
3 the writer "claims for his book that it shall take rank with
the prophetic books of the O. T." (Swete). He repeats this
claim in 22:7, 10, 18f. He pronounces a beatitude on the
reader and the hearers and keepers (observers) of the
prophecy in the book.

In the Salutation (1:4-6) the author gives his name again
as in 1:1 and later in 1:9; 22:8. He does not call himself
apostle, just as Paul did not in I and II Thessalonians,
Philippians and Philemon. He speaks more as prophet than
as apostle or elder (I and II John), though he does not here

apply either word to himself. But clearly he thinks that
the hearers and readers will know what John he is. The
whole book is in the form of a letter and closes as one also
(22:21). The entire epistle is thus addressed to the seven
selected churches (1:11), here simply termed "churches of
Asia" (province), though named in 1:11 and afterwards
(chs. 2 and 3), each receiving a special letter. But it is a
letter of a peculiar kind bearing the prophetic apocalypse
mentioned in 1:1 and 11. The usual greeting (grace and
peace) comes here and "grace" also at the close (22:21).
The salutation comes from the Trinity, though described in
an unusual way. God the Father is called "the One who is
and who was and who is to come," presenting the unchangeable eternity of God. This idea is emphasised by the use of
the nominative case, instead of the ablative, after *apo*
(from). This idiom for the Eternal God occurs also in 1:8;
4:8, with the omission of "who is to come" *(erchomenos)* in
11:17; 16:5. The use of "the Seven Spirits which are
before his throne" for the Holy Spirit (also in 3:1; 4:5;
5:6) has given a deal of trouble. Some have tried to make
the phrase refer to the seven angels in God's presence (8:2),
but 3:1 can hardly refer to angels, and the symbols of seven
lamps (4:5) and seven eyes of the Lamb (5:6) can be for
the Holy Spirit, as is necessary here between God the Father
and Jesus Christ. Perhaps Swete is correct in thinking that
"seven" is used of the Holy Spirit because of his work in the
seven churches like I Cor. 12:10; 14:32; Heb. 2:4. Jesus
Christ is further pictured as "the faithful witness" (1:2;
3:14), "the first-born of the dead" (Col. 1:18; Ps. 88:28;
I Cor. 15:20), "and the ruler of the kings of the earth"
(17:14; 19:16). All these phrases are retained in the
nominative, though in apposition with Jesus Christ (in the
ablative), a common idiom in this book (2:13, 20; 3:12,
etc.). All this gives added dignity to the source of the
message. The salutation concludes with a doxology: "To
the one who loves (not 'loved,' as in King James version)
and loosed (not 'washed') us out of our sins by (in) his

blood, to him (to Christ) be the glory and the power for the ages. Amen." This doxology is to Christ as to God like those in 5:12, 13; 7:10. "The adoration of Christ which vibrates in this doxology is one of the most impressive features of the book" (Moffatt). But a parenthesis occurs in the midst of this doxology, just after "by his blood": "And he made us a kingdom (not 'kings') and priests (each of us a priest) unto his God and Father." Each of us has direct access to our God and Father without the need of a human priest (Eph. 2:18; Heb. 4:16; 10:19-22), blessed and glorious truth.

Verses 7 and 8, Beckwith considers, give the motto of the book. Verse 7 presents the proclamation of Christ's Second Coming as certain. The language used is a combination of Daniel 7:13 and Zechariah 12:10 and 12 as also in Matthew 24:30. Swete thinks that both Matthew and John used a collection of prophetic testimonies concerning the Messiah, a favourite idea with J. Rendel Harris also *(Testimonia)*. Romans and Jews shared in the piercing of Jesus and all tribes of the earth will mourn because of the woe that will come upon them when Jesus comes again. There is no "Christian nation," in the full sense of that term. Verse 8 gives the solemn assurance of the Lord God that verse 7 is true (cf. Ps. 46:10; 89:3f.), the Eternal God made plain by the same phrase in 1:4 and by the use of the first and last letters of the Greek alphabet (Alpha, Omega) as in 21:6 and 22:13 (here plainly of Jesus Christ, the deity of the Son) and the adjective "Almighty" *(pantokrator)*.

The opening vision of the Risen and Ascended Lord Jesus (1:9-20) dominates the imagery in each of the messages to the seven churches (2 and 3) and to a considerable extent that of the entire book. The apocalyptic element prevails from now on. John begins (verse 9) by telling who he is and how he is the brother and co-partner with the readers in the tribulation and kingdom and patience in Jesus and how he "came to be" *(egenomēn)* in Patmos because of his proclaiming the word of God and his witness to Jesus. Then he explains how he came to be in the Spirit on the Lord's Day (Sunday) when he had his first ecstatic experience on hearing the voice behind him: "What thou seest write in a book and send to the seven churches" (1:11). He turned to see the voice (by metonymy for the person speaking) and he saw first seven golden lampstands, symbols of the seven churches (1:20), like the lampstand of Zechariah (4:2) with seven lamps. In the midst of the seven lampstands he sees the glorified Christ pictured in wonderful symbolism (13-16). He is like a Son of man (Dan. 7:13) as again in 14:14, where, though glorified, He still appears as human, as Jesus (Phil. 2:11), the Lord Jesus Christ. He is clad with a garment reaching to His feet and gathered about at the breast with a golden girdle. His head and His hair are white as white wool, as snow. His eyes are like a flame of fire. His feet are like burnished brass as when refined in a furnace. His voice is the voice of many waters. He holds in His right hand seven stars. Out of His mouth proceeds a sharp two-edged sword. His countenance radiates His power like the sun. No wonder that before this wonderful vision John fell as one dead (1:17). In gentle understanding the Lord Jesus places His right hand on John, saying: "Stop being afraid; I am the First and the Last and the Living One. And I became dead and behold I am alive for the ages of the ages and I hold the keys of life and death." This much in explanation of this vision. Then Jesus renews the command of 1:11: "Write what things thou didst see and what things are and what things are going to come to pass after these things." That is a large contract. The Master gives His first explanation of "the mystery" of the seven stars (the "angels" of the seven churches) and of the seven candlesticks (the seven churches). But who are these "angels"? Each church here has its "angel." The word literally means "messenger" and can be the pastor of the church, as is probable, or a heavenly angel, or even the spirit of the church.

The special messages to each church now begin (2 and 3). In each case, except that of Philadelphia and that of Laodicea, one of the items in 1:9-20 is used of Jesus. In each instance the message is addressed to the "angel" or pastor of the church. In each instance it is the message of the Glorified Lord Jesus. In each instance attention is called to what the Holy Spirit says to the churches. In each instance the particular and actual condition of the church is pictured with a warning or a promise or both.

The church at Ephesus is addressed first (2:1-7), as was proper, since Ephesus was the chief city in the province and John's home before his exile. Before John came, this church once had Priscilla and Aquila, Apollos for a brief space, Paul for three years, and Timothy for some years. It was the seat of the worship of Artemis enthroned in her magnificent temple. Jesus describes Himself as the one who holds the seven stars in His right hand, Who walks in the midst of the seven golden candlesticks as in 1:13, 16. He claims full knowledge of the actual conditions in the church and commends the church for testing the false claimants to be apostles, like Cerinthus, for example. But there is the serious charge made of leaving their first love and their first works. They have fallen from the great height once reached. They still hate the Nicolaitans, who are described again in 2:15 as being immoral in doctrine and life, like Balaam of old. Some think that this sect were followers of Nicolaus of Antioch (Acts 6:5) who went astray, but that is uncertain. The once great church in Ephesus, however, had become mere heresy hunters without love and life and was in peril of losing the candlestick. Still there is hope that any one in Ephesus who will gain the victory may eat of the tree of life in the Paradise of God, the state of the blessed dead with God and Christ (Lu. 23:43; II Cor. 12:2f.).

In the letter to Smyrna (2:8-11) Jesus is pictured with the language from 1:17f. It was a great city—the seat of emperor worship—and the Christians were in special peril. It is a rich poor church (poor in money, rich in grace).

There were some hypocrites there who call themselves Jews (spiritual Israel like Gal. 6:16; Rom. 2:28f.). They were a synagogue of Satan. They were facing persecution and prison from the devil. The crown of life is assured to the faithful. These will escape the second death (20:6, 14; 21:8), the eternal death of the damned.

Pergamum (2:12-17) was a rival of Ephesus in political and religious importance, though not in commerce. Asklepios, the god of healing, had here a great shrine, with a college of medical priests. Here first was erected a temple to the worship of the "divine Augustus and the goddess Roma." It was a seat of Satan's throne. Jesus is described in the language of 1:16 with a "two-edged sword out of his mouth." One of the members, Antipas, had fallen a victim to persecution. The Nicolaitans, with the teaching of Balaam, had a foothold here. They are urged to repent. The victor in the struggle with evil forces will partake of the hidden manna, the life with Christ in God (Col. 3:3), and a white stone will bear his mystic name (cf. 19:12 of Christ), a pledge of the favour of God and fellowship in Christ. It is useless to press the symbolism of the white stone or pebble too far, but this much is true. See Ephesians 6:11ff. for Paul's panoply of God and Isaiah 62:2; 65:15.

Thyatira (2:18-29) was an industrial city, important especially for the manufacture of fine woollen goods with the famous purple dyes. Lydia, a seller of purple in Philippi (Acts 16:14f.), came from Thyatira. Inscriptions here reveal a guild of dyers and of other industries. Jesus (here called the Son of God) is described after the words in 1:14 about His eyes and His feet. The church is commended for its steadfastness and growth, but it had given harbour to a powerful woman (wife of the bishop, Grotius holds) who apparently posed as a prophetess of the Nicolaitans (cf. Ephesus and Pergamum) and, like Jezebel of old, taught and practised lewdness and free love. The amazing influence for evil of this woman marks off Thyatira from the other churches. She taught them "the deep things of Satan," as only a wicked woman can. Christ's judgment will come on her and her dupes that the churches may learn the way of God. Meanwhile there is hope for any one who will persevere even in Thyatira.

The church in Sardis (3:1-6) had difficulties of its own, due to the wealth and luxury of the place rather than to persecution. This city had a temple for emperor worship. It was once the seat of kings and famed for its wealth. The Holy Spirit is here referred to by "the seven spirits of God," as in 1:4 and 5:6 and the "seven stars," mentioned again (1:16, 20; 2:1). The church is at the point of death, but with a spark of life. Hence they are urged to keep awake and fight off death by holding on to Christ and repenting at once, else Christ will come in judgment like a thief, as He often foretold (Matt. 24:43; Lu. 12:39), a fact mentioned also by Paul (I Th. 5:2) and Peter (II Pet. 3:10). There are still a few faithful ones even in Sardis. These victors will be clothed in white and Christ will confess them as His before the Father and the angels.

Philadelphia (3:7-13) was a small city in a volcanic region in an open plain on one of the great trade routes. The church was small in numbers and wealth, but faithful and with an open door, already unlocked by the key of David which Jesus holds (Matt. 28:18; Heb. 3:6). There are hypocrites here and Jews who call themselves Jews (as in 2:9 in Smyrna) and are not—a synagogue of Satan. The opposition to the church here comes mainly from the Jews. But Jesus is coming "quickly" and no one will take their crown. There are a thousand Christians in this "white city" (Ala Shehr). No word of censure is spoken against this small and faithful church. On the one who conquers Jesus will write the name of God and of the new Jerusalem (21:2).

Laodicea (3:14-22) is in the Lycus valley, near to Colossae and Hierapolis (Col. 2:1; 4:13, 15, 16) and received two of Paul's epistles. It was famous for its manufacture of woollen carpets and clothing and for the worship of Asklepios who had here a school of medical priests. It was so wealthy that it could rebuild without help after the great earthquake in A.D. 60. Jesus is called the Faithful and True Witness (cf. 1:5). But the church is lukewarm, neither hot nor cold, to such an extent as to produce nausea in Christ. It is a self-satisfied church, rich in money and poor in grace, thinking that wealth makes up for spiritual dearth and death—a picture of too many dying and dead churches to-day, with outward show and pretence and no spiritual vitality! Jesus pleads with this church and pictures Himself dramatically as standing on the outside at the door and knocking for entrance. He promises joy and blessing to any one in this church that will open his heart and let Him in.

The heavenly panorama proceeds and now rapidly unfolds: "After these things I looked, and lo, a door, opened in heaven, and the first voice which I heard" (4:1), the voice heard in 1:10. Chapter 4 presents a picture of the worship of God in heaven. There is a throne and One sitting on the throne like in appearance to a jasper stone and sardius, and a rainbow round about the throne like emerald. This is the noble picture, but at once we should understand that John does not mean this imagery to be interpreted literally. He gives no image of the Lord God, but wishes us to get some conception of the glory of the Almighty which surpasses all speech, even the language of symbolism. We confront the same problem concerning the twenty-four elders clad in white and sitting on thrones and the four living creatures, one on each of the four sides of the throne of God (like respectively to a lion, an ox, a man, an eagle). The four living creatures lead off in praise and adoration of God and the twenty-four elders join in. They worship God as Creator and Preserver of the universe. It is better to contemplate this noble picture of the worship of God in heaven than to dissipate its charm by speculation over the meaning of the elders and the living creatures.

Chapter 5 gives a wonderful picture of the worship of

Jesus in heaven. John of necessity uses anthropomorphic imagery in writing of God. In God's right hand there is a book sealed with seven seals and written on both sides, probably a papyrus roll, though some scholars consider it a codex. But no one could open it, this book full of the secrets of God about things to come to pass. John wept from eager curiosity till one of the elders tells him to cease weeping, because the Lion of the tribe of Judah has prevailed to open this book. Satan is a lion (I Pet. 5:8), but he is conquered at last by Jesus, a greater Lion. But John sees further mysteries. This Lion is a Lamb, that was slain and now stands in triumph, having seven horns and seven eyes (the seven spirits of God). He came and has taken the book (so John says in his eagerness). This dramatic act by Jesus, the Lion and Lamb of God, is the occasion for worship by the living creatures and the twenty-four elders, who together sing a new song, the song of redemption by the blood of the Lamb on the Cross, making the redeemed out of every land a kingdom and priests (1:6). This new song of salvation in praise of the Lamb that was slain is taken up, first, by myriads of angels (antiphonal singing) and then, in widening sweep, by every creature in heaven and upon the earth and under the earth and upon the sea, in adoration to "the one that sits upon the throne and the. Lamb." The four living creatures said "Amen" and the twenty-four elders bowed and worshipped. Jesus Christ, the Son of God, is here worshipped in heaven precisely as the Father. And the redeemed are purchased by the blood of the Lamb. There is no side-tracking the Cross in this worship of Christ.

It is not easy to make a sharp division in the succeeding visions. The opening of the seven seals comes next (6:1-8:1), but the seven trumpets (8:2-11:19) seem to come out of the opening of the seventh seal, either parallel or successive to the seals. There is silence (8:1) on the opening of the seventh seal. And various other things come between the first six seals (chapter 6) and the opening of the seventh seal (8:1). We may first look at the events revealed by opening the six seals (ch. 6). The Lamb opens the seals one by one. The first four seals (6:1-8) are alike in that a horse comes forth in response to the call of one of the four living creatures, each horse of a different colour (white, red, black, pale). Some identify the rider of the white horse here with Christ on a white horse in 19:11f., but apparently wrongly. Conquest is the mark of the first horse, slaughter of the second, famine by the third, death by the fourth, all four plagues. Then comes the opening of the fifth seal, which is the story of the martyrs for Christ (6:9-11), who died for their witness to Christ "against polytheism and Caesarism" (Swete) or emperor worship, the very grounds on which John is in exile (1:9). The sixth seal (6:12-17) brings a great earthquake while the sun becomes black and the moon red, portents like those of the day of judgment. The great of earth hide themselves in dens and caves and call on the rocks to fall on them and hide them from the face of God and the wrath of the Lamb, "because the great day of their wrath is come, and who is able to stand"? This looks like the picture of the end of the ages, but who really knows? The panorama proceeds.

Chapter 7 is a kind of prelude or preparation to the opening of the seventh seal. There are two phases, one the sealing of the 144,000 (7:1-8), the other the victory of the redeemed hosts (7:9-17). Four angels at the four corners of the earth hold back the winds of destruction till the 144,-000 from the tribes of Israel are sealed. Apparently John employs this language for the spiritual Israel (both Jews and Gentiles), the redeemed of one generation (Swete), but some take it for martyrs only. The number (144,000) is merely a round number (12,000 to each tribe) for completeness, as again in 14:1. In this list Levi is counted and Dan left out. Here the redeemed have the seal of God (9:4; 14:1; 22:4), a mark *(charagma)* the opposite of the mark of the beast (13:16; 14:9; 20:4).

The second vision (7:9-17) pictures the triumph of the

redeemed of all the ages (Swete), the chief difference being the countless number of these and the universality of the source in land and race. They are clad in white and they sing a song of salvation to God and to the Lamb while the angels, the elders and the four living creatures add their praise. One of the elders asks John who they are, but John passes the query back to the elder who says: "These are they who come out of the great tribulation and they washed their robes and made them white in the blood of the Lamb." And yet to-day there are some who are ashamed of a "bloody Gospel" and refuse to sing hymns like "There is a fountain filled with blood." What a beautiful picture of worship in heaven do we have in 7:15-17!

The seventh seal is opened by the Lamb (8:1) whereupon there was silence for a half hour in heaven (in the panorama, of course). It is a pause in the unfolding picture, a long interval in the drama.

Then comes the giving of seven trumpets to the seven angels who stand before God (8:2). The blowing of the seven trumpets continues, with the preparations and the interlude, from 8:2 to 11:19. There is first the offering of incense upon the golden altar before the throne (8:3-5). This angel is not of the seven of verse 2. The smoke of the incense is a symbol of the prayers of the saints. The angel had laid aside the censer, but he now takes it again and pours it out for judgment on the earth.

The seven angels with the seven trumpets make ready to sound (8:6) and the first six sound in succession (8:7-9: 21). The first trumpet brought hail and fire and blood and destruction (8:7) to one third of the earth. The second trumpet foretold ruin to one third of the sea, as if a burning mountain had fallen into it (8:8f.).

The third trumpet was followed by the star, "Absinthus" or "Wormwood" which fell as a burning torch on a third part of the rivers (8:10-11).

The fourth trumpet brought darkness on a third part of the sun, the moon, the stars (8:12).

Then John hears another angel flying in mid-heaven and crying three more woes, besides the four already come, to those left on earth (8:13).

The fifth trumpet (9:1-12) is followed by a star fallen upon the earth, as already on the sea (8:8, 10). Apparently this fallen star is Satan (12:9), who has the key of the abyss (9:1). He opens the pit and lets loose demons like locusts with power of scorpions, equipped like horses for war, with faces like men, hair like women and teeth like lions with iron breastplates and with wings that roar and tails like the stings of scorpions. What a picture of monsters (veritable dragons from hell) let loose from hell by their king, the angel of the abyss, Abaddon, Apollyon in Greek, Destroyer in English. The only consolation is that they have no power to harm those who have the seal of God on their foreheads. Two more woes follow (9:12).

The sixth trumpet (9:13-21) is followed by a voice out of the horns of the golden altar before the throne calling to loose the four angels bound by the great river Euphrates, angels made ready to execute the judgment of God on the third part of men. The numbers of the cavalry are put as twice ten thousand times ten thousand (two hundred million), certainly a vast enough number! These horses are a terror, for their power was in their mouth and in their tails, with heads like lions, and fire and smoke and brimstone coming out of their mouths. The tails of these horses were like serpents with heads. But even so, the rest of men who did not perish, do not repent. They are simply hardened in their sins. They keep on worshipping demons and dumb idols and keep on, also, in their sins of fornication and thievery.

Before the third woe or seventh trumpet (11:14-19) comes, there is an interlude by way of preparation for it (10:1-11:13), two interludes, in fact. There comes, first, a special angel from God (10:1-11) clad in a cloud, with a rainbow on his head, his face like the sun and his feet like pillars of flame, and holding a little opened book in his hand.

He placed his right foot on the sea and his left on the land and cries with a voice like a lion roaring. Seven thunders follow and John is about to write, but a voice out of heaven says: "Seal what the seven thunders said and do not write them." Then the great angel, already described, lifts his right hand to heaven and swears by the Living God that time shall be no more and that the mystery of God will be finished when the seventh angel blows his trumpet. John is commanded to take that little book out of the angel's hand and to eat it. This he did and found it sweet in his mouth, but bitter in his belly.

Before the seventh trumpet is sounded comes the second interlude (11:1-13). This interlude consists in the chastisement of Jerusalem (Israel) or the measurement of the temple (11:1f.), the time set for the suffering of God's people and the triumph of the heathen as in Daniel 7:25 (Theodotion); 12:7. This time-calendar occurs several times in Revelation and in three ways; as forty-two months (11:2; 13:5); as 1260 days (11:3; 12:6); as a time and times and half a time or three and a half years (12:14). The period is the same, though we do not know how to reckon it.

Christ is the speaker in 11:3, but we do not know who the Two Witnesses are who during this period will testify for Christ (11:3-12). The two candlesticks are like those in Zechariah 4:2f., 14, but we have no means of identifying the names of these Two Witnesses. Swete sees Moses and Elijah as prototypes of the Two. Jerusalem, now destroyed by the Romans, is pictured in 11:8 as "spiritually Sodom and Egypt, where their Lord also was crucified." It almost reads like a picture of Titus' destruction of the city, though written long after that took place. A small remnant gave glory to God (11:13).

The seventh trumpet (11:14-19) is the third of these last woes. Here great voices are heard, not silence as on the opening of the seventh seal (8:1). This trumpet is called a woe, and so it is on the nations that refuse to worship God (11:18), but the outcome is victory for Christ with the

cry: "The kingdom of the world has become the kingdom of
our Lord and of his Christ, and he will reign for ages of
ages." This will be the glorious consummation of Christ's
conflict with Satan. There were reverberations of glory in
heaven and on earth.

Swete observes that if the Apocalypse had ended at 11:19,
"it is conceivable that such loss might never have been suspected." But John did not close, but went on for eleven
more chapters. There is undoubtedly a break at this point,
for a climax to the world conflict of Christ with Satan is
reached in 11:15, as glorious in a way, as anything in the
book. In 10:11 new prophecies are indicated as coming,
the "little book" which John took and ate. In a sense the
same story starts over again with a clearer vision of the
unseen forces of the underworld in conflict with Christ.
"These forces are revealed under monstrous forms, the
Great Red Dragon, the Beast from the Sea, the Beast from
the Land, and they continue to operate until their final
overthrow" (Swete). But from chapters 13 to 19 we see
repeated struggles on earth with the dragon, the Two Beasts,
the Seven Bowls, the Fall of Babylon. The book closes
with a grand picture of the redeemed as the Bride of Christ,
the New Jerusalem. Benson called the book "chaos" and
scholars do differ greatly in their interpretations. But some
order and progress can be discerned if we do not expect too
much continuity in details.

Chapter 12 seems to be a retrospective view of Satan's
effort to destroy the Messiah when He appeared on earth.
Here John employs a woman (12:1-6) to represent the
spiritual Israel, out of whom, on the human side, Christ had
come, and who is persecuted as He was (12:13, 17). No
doubt John has Isaiah 7:14 in mind, as did Matthew (1:23)
and Luke (1:31). It is the picture of the Pre-incarnate
Son of God coming to earth as a child, born of woman (Gal.
4:4), and the effort of Satan to destroy the child Jesus, as
Herod the Great under Satan's impulse attempted to do
(Matt. 2:1-23). John is not giving historical details about

Mary, the Virgin Birth, the visit of the wise men, the slaughter of the male children in Bethlehem. He denies none of these events, but simply pictures the conflict of Satan with Christ as inevitable (cf. the Temptations of Jesus by Satan). The Great Red Dragon with seven heads and ten horns (12:3) is explained in verse 9 as being the Serpent of Genesis 3:1ff., the Devil, Satan. He has seven diadems on his heads and his tail sweeps the third part of the stars of heaven. These images picture vividly the world power of Satan, who claimed to be able to give to Jesus the kingdoms of the world and the glory of them. Who to-day can gainsay Satan's claim to world power? The Dragon stands ready to devour the Child at birth. The woman flees to the wilderness for 1260 days. This imagery repeats in time much already covered by the seals and the trumpets, but one hesitates to say how long a period is meant by the numbers given. The devil fails to destroy Christ or His people.

In 12:7-12 we have a battle in the sky, in the lower heavens where dwells "the prince of the power of the air" (Eph. 2:2). We are familiar to-day with battles in the air with airplanes. Jesus spoke of His glory in seeing Satan fall as lightning out of heaven (Lu. 10:18), not heaven as the abode of God, but the air above us. In this battle Michael and his angels war with Satan who, together with his angels (demons), is hurled in defeat to the earth. It is a glorious victory because of the blood of the Lamb and the courage of the martyrs for God.

Defeated in his effort to destroy the Messiah at His birth and in the battle in the air with Michael, Satan persecutes the saints (the woman) vehemently (12:13-18). With the wings of the eagle the woman flees to the wilderness and the Serpent pours a flood after her to drown her. Probably the metaphor pictures the rivers of blood under Nero and Domitian and, later, under Decius and Diocletian. Defeated again, Satan stood on the sand of the sea.

But Satan has helpers in his fight with Christ's people on

earth in the Two Beasts (ch. 13). One Swete calls the "Wild Beast from the Sea" (13:1-10), the other the "Wild Beast from the Land" (13:11-18). This first terrible beast comes out of the sea, but also out of the abyss (11:7; 17:8), that is, hell. There is no conflict, for this beast is worshipped (12:4) as we know the Roman emperors were. Undoubtedly the Roman world power is pictured by this symbol, the agent of Satan in persecuting the Christians. The second beast (13:11-18) is like the first and endeavours to promote the worship of the first beast (12:12), as the provincial priests did in their various temples. The first beast is imperial Rome and the second beast provincial Rome, both guilty of emperor worship. The second beast has two horns like a lamb, but speaks like a dragon (the devil). Some have seen pagan and papal Rome in these two beasts and there is some verisimilitude in that view, but it is probably not correct. Deissmann (*Bible Studies*, p. 242) has shown that the word "mark" *(charagma)* in verses 16 and 17 is the technical term for the imperial stamp in official documents, with the emperor's name and the date. The servants of the beast bear the stamp of the beast, as the servants of God have the seal of God (7:3). This "mark" of the beast was a sign of loyalty in the worship of the emperor. Paul, in Galatians 6:17 speaks of his bearing in his body the "marks" *(stigmata)* of his belonging to Christ, as a slave was branded by his master. It is foolish for people to-day to find the mark of the beast in modern trade signs or symbols. The language in 13:18 is usually interpreted as referring to Nero, reappearing, in a sense, in Domitian (17:11).

Chapter 14 forms a sort of prelude to the bowls or vials (15 and 16). There is, first, the picture of the 144,000 in heaven (14:1-5. Cf. 7:1-8). It is not clear whether this number, as in 7:1-8, is a select number of martyrs or particularly saintly ones; at any rate, it symbolises a kind of firstfruits of the redeemed (14:4) and representatives of the whole number. They have the seal of God and Christ on their foreheads (cf. 3:12; 7:4f.; 22:4) in contrast with the mark of the beast (13:16 and 17; 14:9, 11). The new song of salvation (cf. 5:9) only the redeemed can sing.

There follow proclamations by three angels (14:6-11). The first angel proclaims the fulfilment of God's judgment, with a call to worship God (verses 6 and 7). The second angel announces God's judgment on Rome, called Babylon (verse 8). The third angel proclaims the awful punishment on those who worship the beast (verses 9 to 11). Verses 12 and 13 contain encouragement and comfort for the saints in the future bliss of heaven, with rest from toil and weariness.

These interludes close with a vision of One like a Son of man on a white cloud, with a sharp sickle in His right hand (14:14-20). This picture of the Parousia is like that in Daniel 7:13; Matthew 24:34; 26:64; Acts 1:9, 11; Rev. 1:7, 13; 19:11f. Three angels have already appeared in this chapter (6, 8, 9) and now a fourth comes (15) out of the sanctuary with the command to the Messiah for immediate execution of God's commands for judgment. He is the angel of the harvest (Joel 3:13; Mk. 4:29; Matt. 13:39). A fifth angel comes out of the sanctuary with a sharp sickle like the Son of man (17). Then a sixth angel comes out of the altar, where he is in charge of the fire (16:6f.). He brings to the fifth angel a message to use the sickle for the vintage, to gather in the grapes, the angel of the vintage of the ripe grapes (18-20). He may be associated with the altar of burnt offering (6:9; 11:1) like the blood of the martyrs or the altar of incense (8:3, 5; 9:13) like the prayers of the saints. It is a bold picture of God's final punishment of the wicked. Not the picture of the Victorious Christ in 19:13-15 with his garments dipped in the blood of His enemies.

The seven bowls (15 and 16) complete the series of sevens, seven seals ch. 6, seven trumpets (8-11). They are termed (15:1) "the seven last plagues." Verse 1 (ch. 15) after the author's habit, is a summary statement of the two chapters (8:2; 12:6; 21:2). There comes first an anticipatory hymn of praise (15:2-4), the song of Moses and of the Lamb by those who have triumphed over the beast. The song is from the standpoint of the close of chapter 16, after the last bowl.

From 15:5 to 16:1 preparation is made for pouring out the seven bowls. These seven angels in gorgeous apparel are given the seven bowls of the wrath of God by one of the four living creatures. They are commanded to pour them out.

The seven plagues are poured out one after the other (16:2-21). These plagues resemble the plagues in Egypt and the trumpet-blasts (Rev. 8-11). The first one (2) is like the plague of boils (Ex. 9:10); the second (3) like the second trumpet (8:8f.) and the first Egyptian plague on the Nile (Ex. 7:14f.); the third turning water into blood (4-7) to the third trumpet (8:10f.) and the Egyptian plague in Exodus 7:20-24; the fourth (8 and 9), making the sun so hot, seems entirely new; the fifth (10 and 11) causes supernatural darkness (cf. Ex. 10:22) all over the Roman empire, but people do not repent any more than they did under the fourth bowl; the sixth bowl (12-16) dries up the Euphrates (cf. the sixth trumpet, 9:14) and prepares for the coming of the kings from the east for the battle of Har Magedon. Three demons like frogs come out of the mouth of the dragon to go into the great battle between Christ and Antichrist. The name, Har Magedon, is an imaginary one. Jesus proclaims His own sudden appearance in the great conflict: "Behold I come as a thief" (16:15). The seventh bowl (17:17-21) is poured out with convulsions in the air and on the earth, an earthquake such as the world had never known. Babylon was at last remembered by God's wrath.

The panorama proceeds with new imagery. The great world power, hostile to Christ, is pictured as Babylon, the great Harlot, and her downfall is foretold (17:1-19:10). Here woman is used as the symbol of the evil forces, as in chapter 12 woman is employed to represent the people of God. Woman is the symbol of the highest and of the lowest.

In 17:1-6 the harlot, Babylon, is seen seated on the beast. One of the seven angels who has the seven bowls, the seventh, who had already announced the doom of Babylon, (16:19) leads John into a desert place and shows him a woman seated on a scarlet colored beast with seven heads and ten horns. She was gorgeously adorned with her trade as courtesan branded on her forehead, she herself the mother of harlots and drunk with the blood of the saints.

Then comes the angel's introductory interpolation of the beast on which the woman is seated (17:7-18), preparatory to the discussion of the woman herself (18:1-19:5). This beast that here comes out of the abyss is the one that in 13:1 comes out of the sea (cf. 13:3, 8 with 17:7 and 8). The two passages throw light on each other. But some of this "mystery" remains. The ten horns are ten kings (17: 12). The seven heads are seven hills and seven kings also (17:9). The one that was and is not is an eighth—apparently a reference to Domitian as Nero *redivivus*, though it is hard to count the Roman emperors, since some of them (Otho, Galba) ruled so short a time. But they carry on war with the Lamb. Some of the new kings from the ten horses will turn against the harlot and rend her. Such destruction did come about when Rome was sacked by the barbarous hordes led by Alaric, Genseric, Ricimer, Totila. The woman is Rome (17:18).

Then another angel from heaven repeats one doom of Babylon (14:8) and enlarges upon it (18:1-3). The earth was illuminated by his glory, as he pictured Babylon as the abode of demons and unclean birds.

Another voice from heaven called for God's people to flee from the doomed city (18:4f.), called on the spirits of vengeance to exact full toll of Babylon for her evil deeds (18:6-8), and pronounced solemn dirges over the ruin of so much power and wealth (18:9-19). These dirges are to be chanted over the city by the kings (9 and 10), by the merchants (11-17), by the sailors and shipowners of the world (17-19).

The saints (living and dead), including apostles, are called upon by the voice from heaven to rejoice at the downfall of Babylon (18:20). See 11:10 for previous joy on the part of the Dragon and his followers.

Another angel by a dramatic and symbolic act (the hurling of a great stone into the sea) announces the final doom of Babylon with a chant of doom, or dirge, over the damned (18:21-24).

John now hears an anticipatory chorus of joy from all the heavenly hosts, praising the victory of Christ over Antichrist, over the dragon (Satan) and his world power (19:1-10). There are four great hallelujahs (1 and 2, 3, 4, 6-8). The angels, the twenty-four elders, the four living creatures, —all the redeemed—join in this hymn of victory and salvation. It is the marriage of the Lamb with his bride (the saved of all time), Paul's church without spot or wrinkle (Eph. 5:23-33). The vision is prophetic of the final triumph of Christ and the bliss of those redeemed by His blood. John was told by the angel to write again and not to worship him as, in his ecstasy, he had started to do.

The crowning of the Messiah, the Triumphant Warrior, comes in 19:11-16. He is riding a white horse. He has many diadems on His head, His name is the Word of God (cf. Jo. 1:1), His garment is dipped in the blood of His enemies, and on His raiment is written "King of kings and Lord of lords." His victorious army clad in pure white, follow Him on white horses.

An angel now proclaims the overthrow of the beast and the false prophet (19:17-21). This angel stands in the sun and delivers a message to the birds of prey in the air, to feast on the carcases of the enemies of God after the great battle—apparently of Har Magedon (16:16) and of Gog and Magog (20:8ff.). The bold imagery is that of a battlefield and is not pleasant to dwell upon. Both the beast and the false prophet are cast into the lake of fire and brimstone, "a pool of blazing sulphur, where they will be consumed" (Swete).

The temporary binding of Satan and the martyrs' reign (20:1-6) are the occasion of endless controversy to-day. Those who take the thousand years literally overlook the fact that the Apocalypse is a book of symbols and that it is perilous to insist on that point, either in favour of the post- or the pre-millennial view. Peter's comment (II Pet. 3:8) is pertinent. It is also uncertain how the first and the second resurrection are to be understood. Certainly the second death (20:6, 14; 21:8) is the lake of fire and brimstone (hell), spiritual death. First resurrection can be spiritual, not of the body. But in any case, it seems confined to the martyrs in verse 4 and has nothing in common with Paul's language in I Thess. 4:16 or I Cor. 15:23. Special honour is to be given to the martyrs. The general resurrection for all the rest comes later (20:5, 12). "To infer from this statement, as many expositors have done, that the *ezēsan* of verse 4 must be understood of bodily resurrection, is to interpret apocalyptic prophecy by methods of exegesis which are proper to ordinary narrative" (Swete).

After the release of Satan comes the battle of Gog and Magog (7-10). Satan finds many who follow his lead in surrounding the camp of the saints, but fire comes down from heaven and the devil, with the beast and the dragon, is cast into the lake of fire.

Now comes a picture of the general resurrection and the final judgment (20:11-15). The books of life and death are opened and sentence is passed upon all. Those condemned are cast into the lake of fire and brimstone with Satan, the beast, and the false prophet.

John sees a vision of a new heaven and a new earth (21:1-8). The new Jerusalem comes down out of heaven, prepared like a bride adorned for her husband. The tabernacle of God is with men (the redeemed). Death is gone, and tears. In verses 5 and 6 God, Himself, speaks and announces the fulfilment of all His purposes. He calls Himself "the Alpha and the Omega," as in 1:8 and as Jesus does in 22:13. God promises to the thirsty a drink of the water of life.

Once more one of the angels who has the seven bowls speaks to John and taking him in spirit to a great and high mountain and the holy Jerusalem (21:10), offers to show him the Bride, the wife of the Lamb (21:9). Then follows a wondrous picture of the New Jerusalem (21:11-22:5), its light, its walls and twelve gates, its twelve foundations with the names of the apostles, the size and shape of the city, the twelve foundations likened to precious stones, the twelve pearls on each gate, God and the Lamb being the temple and the light, with no night and no abominable thing, with the river of the water of life flowing through it, with the tree of life and its fruits, and with the glory of God in all and unceasing worship of God and Christ. That is heaven at last and for ever.

The close of the book (22:6-21) is an epilogue. God is the author of the book, as was stated at the start (1:1), and so is Jesus (1:1; 22:16) to John (1:1, 4, 9; 22:8) through angelic agency (1:1; 22:6, 16). John is a prophet of God (1:9-11; 22:8-10). The book is meant to be read to the churches (1:3, 11; 22:16, 18). An angel now endorses the whole book (22:6).

Christ promises to come quickly (22:7) and promises a beatitude for the one who keeps the words of this prophecy.

John speaks again and, in awe, starts to worship the angel, but is forbidden (8 and 9).

The angel tells John to leave the book open for all to read and says that there is little hope for change now (10 and 11).

Jesus speaks again, (verse 7) and announces His speedy coming (as God counts time, II Pet. 3:8), with a beatitude for the blessed and woe for the wicked on the outside with the dogs, the sorcerers, the fornicators, the murderers, the idolators, and the liars (12-15).

Once again Jesus speaks in His own name and endorses the message to the churches (16).

The Spirit (speaking through the prophet John) and the Bride (the redeemed) make a joyful response to Christ's promise to come (17) and every one is urged to join in the plea and every thirsty one is urged to take freely of the water of life (17).

Charles holds that verses 18 and 19 were not in the original book. Beckwith is certain that it is John who is speaking, while Swete thinks that the speaker is still Jesus. Luther considered the curse in these verses an unfortunate ending to the book, as does Porter. Moffatt treats it as an editorial note claiming a canonicity on a par with the Old Testament, and considers it "a nervous eagerness to safeguard Christian teaching." But the text of the Apocalypse has suffered much at the hands of careless or perverse copyists.

Jesus makes a last response (20): "Yea, I come quickly." John answers in noble temper, "Amen. Come on, Lord Jesus." Only here do we have "Lord Jesus" in this book. Cf. I Corinthians 12:3.

The Benediction (21) is unusual in an apocalypse, but this is also a letter and ends as it begins. "An apocalypse in its inner character, a prophecy in its purpose, the book is in its literary form an epistle" (Swete).

14. *The meaning of the Apocalypse for to-day.* This wonderful book has a place for Christians who have to meet public or private trials, particularly persecutions, at the hands of the state or even from fellow Christians. Without any theory as to its interpretation, and leaving the symbols unexplained, we can get the practical value of the book in its certainty of Christ's leadership and final triumph. The book served a noble purpose for those persecuted by Domitian and later emperors. It can help us preserve a vivid sense of God and of the Risen Christ, as living and leading

and guiding His people in conflict with Satan and all the forces of evil in the world about us. God is on the side of right and righteousness. Christ has not died and risen in vain. He will come again in His own good time. It is ours to carry on for Him and with Him till He come.

XV

RIVALLING PAUL AND PETER IN HIS INFLUENCE
ON CHRISTIANITY

1. *A backward look.* One who has read this book thus
far will hardly need to wonder at my own estimate of the
Apostle John, whether he agrees with it or not. There is
no need to repeat the discussion in chapters I and X. Assuming as in the light of the evidence, I feel compelled to do,
the identity of the Apostle John, with the Beloved Disciple
of the fourth Gospel, the Elder of II and III John, and the
John of the Apocalypse, we are confronted with one of the
outstanding personalities of all time.

2. *A man of real genius.* That plus his history, environment and, most of all, his close contact with Jesus Christ,
his Lord and Master, is the explanation of the Johannine
books. Genius is a term hard to explain. Carlyle considered it simply hard work. That is an essential element in
it, without doubt, but there is something else in it also, a
subtle gift that gives one true insight, the right word, the
grasp of reality, the sure touch. Bacon in his last book,
The Gospel of the Hellenists (p. 33), brushes John aside as
the author of any of the Johannine books with exasperating
and chilling condescension in a passage that will bear repetition: "The real John had no more to give him prominence
during his life-time than we should expect from his Galilean
antecedents. Only the fact that he had been among the first
of the disciples of the Lord, had remained with James a
'pillar' of the church in Jerusalem, and had shared with him
the fate of martyrdom, serves to bring him dimly within our
view." That is the view of Bacon, but "the real John"

looms large in early Christian history, filling a larger place
than any follower of Jesus save the Apostle Paul. Bacon
accepts the legend of the early death of John and rejects the
huge mass of early testimony to the Ephesian ministry of
John and to the authorship of the Johannine books. Bacon's
belittling of the Apostle John appears to derive from the
criticism of the Sanhedrin concerning Peter and John in
Acts 4:13 "as unlearned and ignorant men" because they
were not Pharisaic schoolmen. One is tempted to agree with
James Denney (*Letters of Principal James Denney,* p. 158)
"that, if 'John' is anything like what Bacon thinks, the less
we trouble ourselves about him the better." But the judgment of the Christian world, scholars and those unlearned in
books, alike, places John on a pedestal far above the attacks
of Bacon.

3. *Responding to fellowship with Jesus.* Personality is
one of the wonders of nature. The twelve apostles all had
fellowship with Jesus. Judas betrayed Jesus, Peter denied
Him, John the Beloved Disciple entered into the most intimate understanding of the mind and heart of his Lord. It
was this mystic union with Christ that qualified John, after
long years of maturity and reflection, to rise to the heights
of the fourth Gospel. He became the eagle who could soar
in the calm empyrean above the clouds and see the eternal
glory of Christ.

4. *In touch with the world of culture.* He began as a
fisherman, and was without school training, but the contact
with Jesus awakened his gifted nature. In Ephesus he was
in contact with the Graeco-Roman world of culture. Philosophers came and went in Ephesus. John lived on to old
age in an atmosphere of literary activity. Philo, the Jew
of Alexandria, was read in Ephesus as well as Plato, the
Greek. Cerinthus, the Gnostic, lived in Ephesus and offered
his subtle sophistries about Christ. Ephesus was the home
of the worship of Artemis. Magical books were accumulated
here by sophists and soothsayers. John felt the call to interpret Jesus Christ in terms that would be understood by

men of culture as well as by the man in the street, in full
harmony with the facts as he knew them in Christ's life in
Palestine, and presenting Jesus Christ as the Son of God
(the *Logos*) and the Son of man. His language is simple
and his ideas are profound.

5. *An appeal to the deepest and the highest in man.* John
has written the eternal Gospel which touches the heart of the
man in trouble, in sin, in sorrow. What can take the place
of John 14 for the one who is in the valley of the shadow of
death? Hayes thinks that "John is the greatest theologian
and the most profound philosopher of the early Christian
church. The church Fathers rightly called him, *Ho Theologos,* The Theologian" (*op. cit.,* p. 68). It is not easy to
decide on the relative rank of Paul and John. Sheldon in
his *Early Church* (p. 104) says: "The church in its most
advanced stage will not put aside Peter or Paul in favour of
John, but acknowledge the truth taught by each." Hayes
(*op. cit.,* p. 70) thinks that "faith is all-important in Paul's
theology, hope is the keynote of Peter's preaching and of
Peter's Epistles, love is characteristic of John." Sheldon
(*op. cit.,* p. 104) voices the view of some when he says:
"The Petrine standpoint, it is claimed, affiliates with the
Roman Catholic theology, the Pauline with the Protestant,
while the Johannine represents the reconciliation and higher
union of the two. As the church has passed through a
Petrine and a Pauline stage, it has arrived now at the border
of a Johannine era." Such a distinction, however, does not
lie in Peter, Paul, or John, but in the use that others have
made of them. Peter himself was not an ecclesiastical
protagonist. No one has put this aspect of John in contrast
with Peter and Paul so well as James Stalker (*The Two St.
Johns,* p. 21): "Some have regarded this late development
of St. John's influence as a prophecy. St. Peter first stamped
himself on the Church, then St. Paul, last St. John. And, as
it was in that first period of Christianity, so was it to be in
the subsequent ages. For fourteen centuries St. Peter ruled
Christendom, as was symbolised by the church inscribed

with his name in the city which was, for most of that period, the centre of the Christian world; then, at the Reformation, St. Paul's influence took the place of St. Peter's, St. Paul's doctrine being the soul of Protestantism. But the turn of St. John has still to come: his spirit will dominate the millennial age. Perhaps in the individual Christian three such stages may also be distinguished—the period of zeal to begin with, when we resemble St. Peter; the period of steady work and reasoned conviction, when we follow in the steps of St. Paul; the period of tolerance and love, when we are acquiring the spirit of St. John." That is superbly said and there is truth in it. We have not reached the age of tolerance and love, not in full. But, beyond all controversy, the Apostle John has a message for our age. Let his voice be heard. Let not the angry clamour of critics silence the voice of the Son of Thunder against wrong in creed and conduct, or the plea of the Beloved Disciple that Christians love one another and walk in the footsteps of Jesus our Lord and Saviour. The picture of the eternal Christ given by John is that seen in the rest of the New Testament, but presented in clearer outline and in bolder relief by the one who was closest to the Master in His earthly life. Those who best know Christ in their own hearts treasure most the Christ of John and thank God for leading the Beloved Disciple to give it to the world.

BIBLIOGRAPHY

A Brief Selected Bibliography out of the Vast Literature on the Johannine Books (apart from introductions to the New Testament, lives of Christ, books on the Four Gospels, encyclopaedia articles and review articles):

The Life of the Apostle John

Benham, *St. John and His Work* (1902).
Culross, J., *John Whom Jesus Loved* (1878).
Dallmann, Wm., *John: Disciple, Evangelist, Apostle* (1932).
Fouard, S., *Jean et la fin de l'age apostolique* (1904).
Gloag, P. J., *Life of St. John* (1891).
Griffith-Thomas, W. H., *The Apostle John* (1923).
Hayes, D. A., *John and His Writings* (1917).
Krenkel, Max, *Apostel Johannes* (1871).
Larfield, W., *Die beiden Johannes von Ephesus* (1914).
Llwyd, J. P. D., *The Son of Thunder* (1932).
McDonald, J. M., *The Life and Writings of St. John* (1880).
Niese, B., *Das Leben des heiligen Johannes* (1878).
Schwartz, E., *Über den Tod der Söhne Zehedaei* (1904).
Scott-Moncrieff, C. E., *St. John: Apostle, Evangelist and Prophet* (1909).
Stalker, James, *The Two St. Johns of the New Testament* (1895).

The Johannine Literature (as a whole) and Teaching

Abbott, E. A., *Johannine Vocabulary* (1905).
Abbott, E. A., *Johannine Grammar* (1906).
Alford, H., *Greek Testament, Vol. 14* (1861).
Beyschlag, W., *Zur Johanneischen Frage* (1875).
Buchsel, F., *Johannes und der hellenistische Synkretismus* (1928).

Carpenter, J. Estlin, *The Knowledge of God in the Johannine Writings* (1925).

Ewald, H., *Die Johanneischen Schriften* (1862).

Gloag, P. J., *Introduction to the Johannine Writings* (1891).

Goebel, S., *Die Reden des Herrn nach Johannes* (2 vols., 1906, 1910).

Green, A. V., *The Ephesian Canonical Writings* (1910).

Holtzmann, H. J., *Evangelium, Briefe, und Offenbarung des Johannes* (besorgt von W. Bauer, 1905). 3 Aufl. 1908.

Kreyenbuhl, J., *Neue Lösung der Johanneischen Frage* (1905).

Leathers, Stanley, *The Witness of St. John to Christ* (1870).

Lias, J. J., *The Doctrinal System of St. John* (1875).

Lowrie, W., *The Doctrine of St. John* (1895).

Lutgert, W., *Johannes Christologie* (1905).

Matheson, George, *St. John's Portrait of Christ* (1910).

Monse, *Johannes und Paulus* (1915).

Purchas, H. T., *Johannine Problems and Modern Needs* (1901)

Schmiedel, P. W., *The Johannine Writings* (1915).

Stange, *Die Eigenart des Johanneischen Produktion* (1914).

Stevens, G. B., *Johannine Theology* (1894).

Titius, Arthur, *Die Johanneische Anschauung unter dem Gesichtspunkt der Seligkeit* (1900).

Vedder, H. C., *The Johannine Writings and the Johannine Problem* (1917).

Weiss, B., *Der Johanneische Lehrbegriff* (1862).

The Fourth Gospel

Abbot, Ezra, *On the Authorship of the Fourth Gospel* (1880).

Abbot, Peabody and Lightfoot, *The Fourth Gospel* (1891).

Appel, H., *Die Echtheit des Johannesevangeliums* (1915).

Askwith, E. H., *The Historical Value of the Fourth Gospel* (1910).

Bacon, B. W., *The Fourth Gospel in Research and Debate* (1910, 2 ed. 1918).

Bacon, B. W., *The Gospel of the Hellenists* (1933).

Baldensperger, W., *Der Prolog des vierten Evangeliums* (1898).

Barth, F., *Die Bedeutung des Johannesevangeliums für das Geistesleben der Gegenwart* (1912).

Barth, F., *Das Johannesevangelium und die synoptischen Evangelien* (1912).

Bauer, W., *Das Johannesevangelium.* 2 Aufl. (1925).

Belzer, *Das Evangelium des heiligen Johannes* (1905).

Bernard, J. H., *The Gospel According to St. John.* 2 Vols. Int. C. C. (1929).

Bert, G., *Das Evangelium des Johannes* (1922).

Blass, F., *Das Evangelium secundum Johannem* (1902).

Baehmer, *Das Johannesevangelium nach Aufbau und Grundgedanken* (1928).

Bornhauser, K., *Das Johannesevangelium eine Missionsschrift für Israel* (1928).

Brooke, A. E., *The Historical Value of the Fourth Gospel* (Cambridge Bibl. Essays, 1909).

Büchsel, F., *Johannes und der hellenistische Synkretismus* (1928).

Burch, V., *The Structure and Message of St. John's Gospel* (1928).

Burkitt, F. C., *The Gospel History and Its Transmission* (1906).

Burney, C. F., *The Aramaic Origin of the Fourth Gospel* (1922).

Calmes, Th., *L'Évangile selon Saint Jean* (1904).

Chapman, Dom John, *John the Presbyter and the Fourth Gospel* (1911).

Charnwood, Lord, *According to St. John* (1925).

Clemen, C., *Die Entstehung des Johannesevangeliums* (1912).

Colwell, E. C., *The Greek of the Fourth Gospel* (1931).

D'Alma, *La Controverse du quatrième évangile* (1908).

D'Alma, *Philo et le quatrième évangile* (1911).

Dausch, *Das Johannesevangelium* (1909).

Delff, H., *Das vierte Evangelium wiederhergestellt* (1890).

Delff, H., *Neue Beiträge zur Kritik und Erklärung des vierten Evangeliums* (1890).

Delafosse, H., *Le Quatrième Évangile* (1925).

Dibelius, M., *John 15:13. Eine Studie zum Traditionsproblem des Johannes-Evangeliums* (Festgabe für Adolf Deissmann, 1927).

Dods, M., *Expositor's Bible* (1891).

Dods, M., *Expositor's Greek Testament* (1897).

Drummond, James, *An Inquiry into the Character and Authorship of the Fourth Gospel* (1904).

Evans, H. H., *St. John the Author of the Fourth Gospel* (1888).

Gardner, P., *The Ephesian Gospel* (1915).

Garvie, A. E., *The Beloved Disciple: Studies in the Fourth Gospel* (1922).

Godet, F., *Comm. on the Gospel of St. John.* Tr. 2 Vols. (1886-90).

Goguel, M., *Les sources du récit Johannique de la passion* (1910).

Goguel, M., *Le quatrième Évangile* (1924).

Gore, C., *Exposition of the Gospel of John* (1920).

Gregory, C. R., *Wellhausen und Johannes.* 2 Aufl. (1910).

Grill, J., *Untersuchungen über die Entstehung des vierten Evangeliums* (1902, 1923).

Gumbel, *Das Johannesevangelium Eine Ergänzung des Lukasev* (1911).

Harris, J. Rendel, *The Origin of the Prologue to St. John's Gospel* (1917).

Hayes, D. A., *John and His Writings* (1917).

Heitmüller, W., *Das Johannes-Evangelium.* 3 Aufl. (1918).

Hoernle, E. S., *The Record of the Loved Disciple* (1931).

Holland, H. Scott, *The Philosophy of Faith and the Fourth Gospel* (1920).

Holland, H. Scott, *The Fourth Gospel* (1923).

Holtzmann, H. J., *Evangelium des Johannes.* 3 Aufl. (1908).

Holtzmann, O., *Das Johannesevangelium* (1887).

Howard, W. F., *The Fourth Gospel in Recent Criticism and Interpretation* (1931).

Jackson, H. L., *The Fourth Gospel and Some Recent German Criticism* (1906).

Jackson, H. L., *The Problem of the Fourth Gospel* (1918).

Johnston, J. S., *The Philosophy of the Fourth Gospel* (1909).

Keisker, *The Inner Witness of the Fourth Gospel* (1922).

Lagrange, M. J., *L'Évangile selon Saint Jean.* Ed. 2 (1928).

Lenski, *An Interpretation of St. John's Gospel* (1932).

Lepin, M., *L'Origine du quatrième Évangile* (1907).

Lepin, M., *La Valeur historique du quatrième Évangile* (1910).

Lewis, F. G., *The Irenaeus Testimony to the Fourth Gospel* (1908).

Lewis, F. W., *Disarrangements in the Fourth Gospel* (1910).

Lightfoot, J. B., *Essays on the Book Entitled Supernatural Religion* (1889).

Biblical Essays (1893)

Loisy, A., *Le Quatrième Évangile* (1903). 2 Ed. (1921).

Lyman, Mary Ely, *The Fourth Gospel and the Life of Today* (1931).

Luthardt, C. E., *St. John the Author of the Fourth Gospel* (1875).

Macgregor, G. H. C., *The Moffatt Comm.* (1928).

Manson, W., *The Incarnate Glory* (1923).

Maurice, F. D., *The Gospel of St. John* (1906).

Montgomery, J. A., *The Origin of the Gospel According to St. John* (1923).

Morgan, G. Campbell, *Studies in John's Gospel* (1933).

Muirhead, L. A., *The Message of the Fourth Gospel* (1925).

Nolloth, C. F., *The Fourth Evangelist* (1925).

Nunn, H. P. V., *The Son of Thunder and the Fourth Gospel* (1927).

Odeberg, H., *The Fourth Gospel Interpreted in Its Relation to Contemporaneous Religious Currents* (1929).

Orr, James, *The Authenticity of St. John's Gospel Deduced from Internal Evidence.*

Overbeck, *Das Johannesevangelium* (1911).

Plummer, A., *Cambridge Greek Testament* (1913).

Réville, Jean, *Le Quatrième Évangile, son origine, sa valeur historique* (1901).

Reynolds, H. R., *Pulpit Comm.* (2 Vols. 1887-8).

Richmond, W. J., *The Gospel of the Rejection* (1906).

Robertson, A. T., *The Divinity of Christ in the Gospel of John* (1916).

Robinson, B. W., *The Gospel of John* (1925).

Robinson, J. A., *The Historical Character of the Gospel of John* (2 ed., 1929).

Sanday, W., *The Authorship and Historical Character of the Fourth Gospel* (1872).

Sanday, W., *The Criticism of the Fourth Gospel* (1905).

Schlatter, A., *Die Sprache und Heimat des vierten Evangelisten* (1902).

Schlatter, A., *Der Evangelist Johannes wie er spricht denkt und glaubt* (1931).

Scott, E. F., *The Fourth Gospel: Its Purpose and Theology* (1906).

Scott, E. F., *The Historical and Religious Value of the Fourth Gospel* (1909).

Selbie, W. B., *Belief and Life: Studies in the Thought of the Fourth Gospel* (1916).

Smith, J. R., *The Teaching of the Fourth Gospel* (1903).

Smith, P. V., *The Fourth Gospel: Its Historical Importance* (1926).

Soltau, W., *Das vierte Evangelium in seiner Entstehungsgeschichte dargelegt* (1916).

Speer, R. E., *(John's Gospel) The Greatest Book in the World* (1915).

Spitta, F., *Das Johannesevangelium als Quelle der Geschichte Jesu* (1910).

Stanton, V. H., *The Fourth Gospel* (Part III of Gospels as Hist. Doc'ts, 1921).

Strachan, R. H., *The Fourth Gospel: Its Significance and Environment* (1917).

Strachan, R. H., *The Fourth Evangelist: Dramatist or Historian?* (1925).

Streeter, B. H., *The Four Gospels* (1924).

Tillmann, Fritz, *Das Johannesevangelium Uebersetzt und Erklärt* (1931).

Tayler, J. J., *An Attempt to Ascertain the Character of the Fourth Gospel* (1870).

Tholuck, A., *The Gospel of John.*

Warschauer, Jacob, *The Problem of the Fourth Gospel.*

Watkins, H. W., *Modern Criticism Considered in Its Relation to the Fourth Gospel* (1890).

Watson, H. A., *The Mysticism of St. John's Gospel* (1916).

Wearing, *The World View of the Fourth Gospel* (1918).

Weiss, B., *Meyer Komm*, 9 Aufl. (1902).

Weiss, B., *Das Johannesevangelium als Einheitliches Werk* (1911).

Wellhausen, J., *Erweiterungen und Aenderungen im vierten Evangelium* (1907).

Wellhausen, J., *Das Evangelium Johannis* (1908).

Wendt, H. H., *Das Johannesevangelium* (1900).

Wendt, H. H., *The Gospel According to St. John: An Inquiry into Its Genesis and Historical Value* (1911).

Wendt, H. H., *Die Schichten im vierten Evangelium* (1911).

Wescott, B. F., *Gospel According to St. John* (Speaker's Comm. 1880).

Westcott, B. F., *Greek Text and Notes* (1908).

Whitelaw, R., *The Gospel of John* (1888).

Windisch, H., *Johannes und die Synoptiker* (1926).

Wolsley, *The Fourth Gospel and the Synoptists* (1909).

Wrede, W., *Charakter und Tendenz des Johannesevangeliums* (1903).

Wright, C. J., *The Meaning and Message of the Fourth Gospel* (1933).

Zahn, Th., *Das Evangelium des Johannes* (1908). 6 Aufl. (1921).

Zahn, Th., *Das Evangelium unter den Händen Seiner Neuesten Kritiker* (1911).

The Epistles

Alexander, Wm., *Epistles of John* (Speaker's Comm., Expositor's Bible, 1889).

Barrett, G. S., *Devot. Comm. on I John* (1910).

Baumgarten, O., *Die Schriften des N. T.* 3 Aufl. (1918).

Belser, *Kommentar* (1906).

Bennett, W. H., *The Century Bible.*

Bresky, *Das Verhältnis des zweiten Johannesbriefes zum dritten* (1906).

Brooke, A. E., *Int. Crit.* (1912).

Büchsel, F., *Die Johannesbriefe* (1933).

Candlish, T. S., *Epistles of John.*

Cox, S., *Private Letters of St. Paul and St. John.*

Ebrard, J. H. A., *Die Briefe Johannis* (1859).

Fancher, H. W., *Fellowship with God* (1929).

Findlay, G. G., *Fellowship in the Life Eternal* (1909).

Gibbon, *Eternal Life* (1890).

Gore, Charles, *Epistles of John* (1921).

Häring, Th., *Die Johannesbriefe* (1927).

Haupt, E., *The First Epistle of John* (Tr., 1893).

Hilgenfeld, A., *Das Evangelium und die Briefe Johannis nach ihrem Lehrbegriff dargestellt* (1849).

Holtzmann (H. J.)—Baur (W.), *Hand-Comm.* 3 Aufl. (1908).

BIRDVILLE
BAPTIST CHURCH
LIBRARY

Holtzmann, H. J., *Das Problem des I Johannesbr. in seinem Verhältniss zum Evang.* (Jarhbuch für Prot. Theol. 1881, 1882).

Huther, J. E., *Komm.* (1882).

Jeremias, Johannes, *Das Evangelium nach Johannes* (1931).

Karl, W., *Der 1er Johannesbrief* (1898).

Law, R., *The Tests of Life* (2 ed. 1909).

Lias, J. J., *Epistles of John* (1887).

Loisy, A., *Les épîtres dites de Jean* (in *Le quatrième évangile*, 1921).

Luthardt, C. E., *Strack-Zoeckler Komm.* (1895).

Maurice, F. D., *The Epistles of John* (1857).

Plummer, A., *Cambr. Gk. Test.* (1886).

Poggel, II, III John (1896).

Ramsay, A., *Westminster N. T.* (1910).

Ritter, K. B., *Die Gemeinschaft der Heiligen* (1929).

Roberston, J. A., *The Johannine Epistles* (1920).

Rothe, R., *Der Erste Brief Johannis* (1878).

Smith, D., *Expos. Grk. Test.* (1910).

Watson, Charles, *First Epistle of John* (1910).

Weiss, B., *Meyer Komm.* 6 Aufl. (1900).

Wendt, H. H., *Die Johannesbriefe und das Johanneische Christentum* (1925).

Westcott, B. F., *The Epistles of St. John.* 3rd Ed. (1892).

Windisch, *Handbuch zum N. T.* 2 Aufl. (1930).

Wrede, W., *Die Schriften des N. T.* 2 Aufl. (1924).

Wurm, Alois, *Die Irrlehrer im 1ten Johannesbriefe* (1903).

The Apocalypse

Allo, E. B., *L'apocalypse et l'epoque de la parousia* (1915).

Allo, E. B., *Saint Jean. L'apocalypse* (1921).

Baldensperger, W., *Mess. Apok. Hoffnungen.* 3 Aufl. (1903).

Baljon, J. M. S., *Openbaring van Johannes* (1908).

Beckwith, J. T., *The Apocalypse of John* (1910).

Benson, E. W., *The Apocalypse* (1900).

Berg, H., *The Drama of the Apocalypse* (1894).

Bisping, A., *Erklärung der Apocalypse* (1876).

Bleek, F., *Vorlesungen über die Apocalypse. Tr.* (1875).

Boll, Fr., *Aus der Offenbarung Johannis* (1914).

Bousset, W., *Die Offenbarung Johannis.* 2 Aufl. (1906).

Bousset, W., *Zur Textkritik der Apokalypse* (1894).

Brown, Charles, *Heavenly Visions* (1911).

Brown, D., *The Structure of the Apocalypse* (1891).

Bullinger, *Die Apokalypse* (1904).

Bungeroth, *Schlüssel zur Offenbarung Johannis* (1907).

Burger, C. H. A., *Offenbarung Johannis* (1877).

Cadwell, *The Revelation of Jesus Christ* (1920).

Calmes, Th., *L'Apocalypse devant la Critique* (1907).

Campbell, *The Patmos Letters Applied to Modern Criticism* (1908).

Carrington, P., *The Meaning of the Revelation* (1931).

Case, S. J., *The Millennial Hope* (1918).

Case, S. J., *The Revelation of John* (1920).

Charles, R. H., *Studies in the Apocalypse* (1913).

Charles, R. H., *The Revelation of St. John.* Int. Crit. 2 Vols. (1921).

Chevalin, *L'apocalypse et les temps presents* (1904).

Crampon, *L'apocalypse de S. Jean* (1904).

Davidson, S., *Outlines of Comm. on the Revelation* (1894).

Dean, J. T., *The Book of Revelation* (1915).

Delaport, *Fragments sahidiques du N. T. Apocalypse* (1906).

Douglas, C. E., *New Light on the Revelation of St. John the Divine* (1923).

Düsterdieck, F., *Offenbarung Johannis.* 4 Aufl. (1887).

Eckman, G. P., *When Christ Comes Again* (1917).

Elliott, E. B., *Horæ Apocalypticæ.* Four Vols. 4 Ed. (1851).

Erbes, *Offenbarung John. Kritischuntersucht* (1891).

Forbes, H. P., *Int. Handbook on the Apocalypse* (1907).

Gebhardt, H., *Doctrine of the Apocalypse* (1878).

Geil, W. E., *The Isle That Is Called Patmos* (1905).

Gibson, E. C. S., *The Revelation of St. John* (1910).

Gigot, *The Apocalypse of St. John* (1915).

Glazebrook, *The Apocalypse of St. John* (1924).

Glasgow, J., *Comm. on the Apocalypse* (1872).

Guinness, H. G., *The Approaching End of the Age* (5 ed. 1880).

Gunkel, H., *Schöpfung und Chaos* (1895).

Gwynn, *The Apocalypse of St. John* (1897).

Hadorn, W., *Die Offenbarung des Johannes* (1928).

Hill, E., *Apocalyptic Problems* (1916).

Hill, E., *Mystic Studies in the Apocalypse* (1931).

Hirscht, *Die Apokalypse und ihre neueste Kritik* (1895).

Holtzmann, H. J., *Die Offenbarung Johannis* (3 Aufl. von W. Bauer (1908).

Horne, *The Meaning of the Apocalypse* (1916).

Hort, F. J. A., *The Apocalypse of St. John.* Chs. 1-3 (1908).

James, M. R., *The Apocalypse in Art* (1931).

Jowett, G. T., *The Apocalypse of St. John* (1910).

Kraemer, R., *Die Offenbarung des Johannis im überzeitlichen Deutung* (1932).

Kübel, R., *Offenbarung Johannis* (1893).

Laughlin, T. C., *The Solecisms of the Apocalypse* (1902).

Lee, W., *Revelation.* Speaker's Comm. (1881).

Linder, *Die Offenbarung des Johannis aufgeschlossen* (1905).

Lohmeyer, E., *Die Offenbarung des Johannis, Handbuch zum N. T.* (1926).

Loisy, W., L'Apocalypse de Jean (1923).

Matheson, George, *Sidelights upon Patmos* (1900).

Milligan, W., *The Revelation of St. John* (1885).

Milligan, W., *The Book of Revelation.* Exp. Bible (1889).

Milligan, W., *Lectures on the Apocalypse* (1892).

Milligan, W., *Discussions on the Apocalypse* (1911).

Moffatt, James, *Revelation.* Expos. Gk. T. (1910).

Moule, H. C., *Some Thoughts on the Seven Epistles* (1915).

Mozley, J. B., *The Christian's Hope in the Apocalypse* (1915).

Oman, John, *The Book of Revelation* (1923).

Oman, John, *The Text of Revelation* (1928).

Osborn, *The Lion and the Lamb* (1922).

Palmer, F., *The Drama of the Apocalypse* (1922).

Paul, *Latter Day Light on the Apocalypse* (1898).

Peake, A. S., *The Revelation of John* (1921).

Porter, F. C., *The Messages of the Apocalyptic Writers* (1905).

Pounder, *Historical Notes on the Book of Revelation* (1912).

Prager, L., *Die Offenbarung Johannis* (1901).

Ramsay, A., *Revelation.* Westminster N. T. (1910).

Ramsay, W. M., *The Letters to the Seven Churches of Asia* (1904).

Rauch, *Offenbarung des Johannis* (1894).

Reymond, *L'apocalypse* (1908).

Ross, J. J., *Pearls from Patmos* (1923).

Sabatier, *Les Origines Littéraires et la Comp. de l'Apoc.* (1888).

Schneider, K., *Die Erlebnisechtheit der Apok. des Johannes* (1930).

Scott, C. Anderson, *Revelation*. New Century Bible (1902).

Scott, C. Anderson, *Revelation*. Devot. Comm. (1906).

Scott, J. J., *The Apocalypse*.

Selwyn, E. C., *The Christian Prophets and the Prophetic Apocalypse* (1901).

Shepherd, W. J. L., *The Revelation of St. John the Divine*. 2 Vols. (1923).

Simcox, W. H., *Revelation*. Cambridge Gk. Test. (1893).

Smith, J. A., *Revelation*. Amer. Comm. (1888).

Smith, C. E., *The World Lighted* (1890).

Spitta, F., *Die Offenbarung des Johannis* (1889).

Strange, C., *Instructions on the Revelation of St. John the Divine* (1900).

Swete, H. B., *The Apocalypse of St. John*. 2 ed. (1907).

Trench, R. C., *Comm. on the Epistles to the Seven Churches* (1897).

Vaughan, C. J., *Lectures on the Revelation of St. John*.

Vischer, E., *Die Offenb. Johan, eine jüdische Apokalypse* (1886).

Voelter, D., *Entstehung der Apokalypse* (1885).

Voelter, D., *Offenbarung Johannis*. 2Aufl. (1911).

Voelter, D., *Das Problem der Apokalypse* (1893).

Weiss, B., *Die Johannes-Apokalypse*. Text. Krit. 2 Aufl. (1902).

Weiss, J., *Offenbarung Johannis* (1904).

Wellhausen, J., *Analyse der Offenbarung* (1907).

Weyland, *Omwerkings en Compilatie-Hupothesen Toegepast op de Apok.* (1888).

Whiting, *The Revelation of John* (1918).

Zahn, Th., *Die Offenbarung des Johannes* (1926).

Printed in the United States of America